LAST TSAR

S. S. OLDENBURG

LAST TSAR

Nicholas II, His Reign & His Russia

❧

Volume I

THE AUTOCRACY, 1894-1900

Translated by Leonid I. Mihalap and Patrick J. Rollins
Edited by Patrick J. Rollins

❧

With

Searching for the Last Tsar

by

Patrick J. Rollins

Cop. a

ACADEMIC INTERNATIONAL PRESS

1975

THE RUSSIAN SERIES / Volume 25-1

Sergei S. Oldenburg **Last Tsar! Nicholas II, His Reign and His Russia. Volume 1: The Autocracy, 1894-1900.** Translation of *Tsarstvovanie Imperatora Nikolaia II,* Volume 1 (Belgrade, 1939), Part I, Chapters I-VI.

With **Searching for the Last Tsar** by Patrick J. Rollins.

ISBN: 0-87569-063-7

Maps by Richard D. Kelly, Jr.
Typography by Susan D. Long
Title page by King & Queen Press

Illustrations from S.S. Oldenburg, *Tsarstvovanie Imperatora Nikolaia II.* Volume 1; *Finland: The Country, Its People and Institutions.* Helsinki, 1926; E. Flourens, *Alexander III. Sa vie, son oeuvre.* Paris, 1894; Thomas Michell, *Russian Pictures.* London, New York, 1889; Count Paul Vassili [pseud. Juliette Adam?], *Behind the Veil at the Russian Court.* London, 1914.

Printed in the United States of America

ACADEMIC INTERNATIONAL PRESS
Box 555 Gulf Breeze Florida 32561

CONTENTS

☙❧

ૹ

THE   EMPIRE

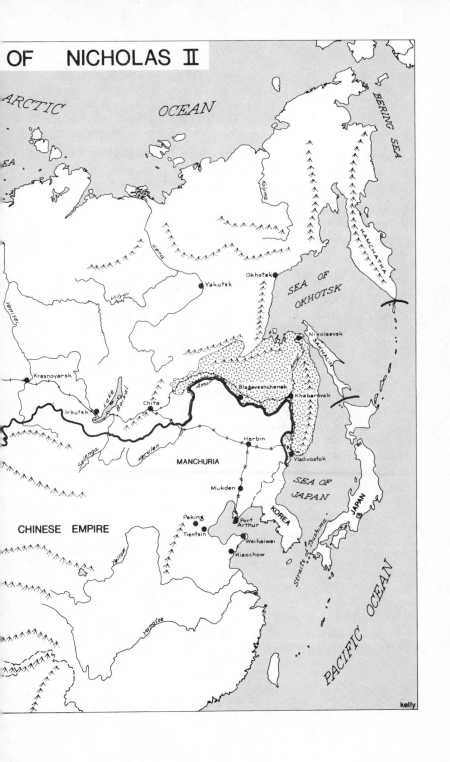

LIST OF ILLUSTRATIONS

❧

PREFACE

Sergei S. Oldenburg's *Tsarstvovanie Imperatora Nikolaia II* [The Reign of Emperor Nicholas II] is a major document in modern Russian historiography. The final contribution of a Russian nationalist historian, it provides uniquely sensitive insights into the character, personality, and policies of Russia's last tsar. It has no rival as a political biography of Nicholas II and is without peer as a comprehensive history of his reign.

Soon after the Russian Revolution, the author wrote a brief sketch of the life and reign of the last tsar—*Gosudar Imperator Nikolaia II Alexandrovich* [The Sovereign Emperor Nicholas II Alexandrovich], published in Berlin in 1922. In 1934 he returned to that subject. He conceived and completed a full-scale investigation in two volumes of two parts each—published here as four separate volumes. Oldenburg's first volume, covering the years 1894-1907, was published in Belgrade in August 1939. World War II and the author's death delayed the appearance of the second volume until 1949. At that time the publisher, the Society for the Propagation of Russian National and Patriotic Literature, relocated in Munich and completed the project. Originally issued in a limited edition by a little-known emigre organization, this important work attracted scant notice outside a fairly narrow circle of scholars and expatriates. It is hoped that this English-language edition will bring Oldenburg and his achievement the wider recognition that both deserve.

The present edition is a complete translation without deletions or abridgements. In a few places the editor has reordered the text slightly for cohesion, and these rare alterations are indicated by footnotes. Oldenburg's chapters are untitled, but for the reader's convenience the editor has introduced subheadings throughout the text.

Only one significant rearrangement of material appears in the translation. Parts I and II of the original edition consist of eight and four chapters respectively. In the translation Volume I has been reduced to six chapters, and Chapters VII and VIII, originally in Oldenburg's Part I, have been shifted to Volume II. This transposition serves to stress the author's basic reinterpretation of the early years of Nicholas's reign. Oldenburg concluded that the tsar reached a turning point after the first six years of his reign. By 1900 several developments had convinced Nicholas to reappraise his domestic policy, and thus he began to seek and to follow a new course.

Oldenburg seldom committed references or substantive information to footnotes, but the editor has provided extensive annotations to guide and assist readers unfamiliar with modern Russian history, institutions, and figures. A biographical sketch of persons mentioned by the author appears in a directory at the end of Volume IV, where also the entire work is indexed. In some instances imprecise references or simply obscurity made it impossible to identify some persons. These problems and omissions are indicated in footnotes. The editor frequently has inserted information on prominent figures at appropriate places in the text but not necessarily at the first mention. The general biographic entries in Volume IV list all notes containing further personal information.

The transliteration of Russian names and terms follows the Library of Congress system with some modification. Most Russian names have been anglicized—Konstantin is given as Constantine, Aleksei as Alexis, and so on—but Russian names have been retained when no convenient or clear English equivalent exists—thus Vasily rather than Basil, Ivan in preference to John, Feodor, Yemelyan, and the like. Christian names and the initial of patronymics have been inserted into the text without editorial brackets. The "ii" suffix common in Russian names is rendered as a "y" as in Dostoevsky, Meshchersky, or Dmitry. The soft sign" is dropped with no indication by an apostrophe.

In dating events Oldenburg followed the Julian or Old Style calendar. In the nineteenth century the Russian calendar lagged twelve days behind the Gregorian calendar used throughout the West. In the twentieth century, beginning 1 March 1900, the discrepancy increased to thirteen days and continued until January 1918, when the Soviet government adopted the Gregorian calendar. Oldenburg, however, commonly gave two dates when referring to international events. In those cases the first or earliest is the Russian date.

It is a pleasure for us to acknowledge the editorial and technical advice and assistance of Hope Mihalap and Martha

Rollins through every stage of the translation and preparation of the manuscript; the research assistance of George F. Fuderer, a gifted student of history and languages; the admirable craftsmanship of Richard D. Kelly, Jr., who prepared the maps that accompany the text; and the services, released time, and grant for research travel that Old Dominion University generously provided.

In addition I extend personal thanks to Warren B. Walsh of Syracuse University and Ronald R. Rader of the University of Georgia for their durable friendship and particular interest in this project. I wish, too, to thank my friend Heinz K. Meier, historian and Dean of the School of Arts and Letters of Old Dominion University, for his customary interest in the endeavors of his colleagues and his effective help in smoothing the way. I am particularly grateful to Peter von Wahlde, the general editor and publisher of this series, and a constant and welcome source of encouragement and good advice. Finally, I wish to thank my congenial collaborator, Larry Mihalap, for his persistence and dedication to accuracy.

Patrick J. Rollins

Old Dominion University
April 1975

SEARCHING FOR THE LAST TSAR

by *Patrick J. Rollins*

In the ancient Russian city of Pskov just before midnight on
2 March 1917 in the forty-eighth year of his life and the
twenty-third of his reign Nicholas II, Emperor and Autocrat
of All the Russias, surrendered the crown that his forebears
had held since 1613. Nicholas's varnished signature on the act
of abdication seemed finally to have resolved the bewilder-
ment and dread that he had expressed in 1894 on the death of
his father: "What am I going to do? What is going to happen
to me . . . to all of Russia? I am not prepared to be a Tsar.
I have never wanted to become one. I know nothing of the
business of ruling."[1] Ironically, he never seemed more fit for
the crown than in the final hours of losing it. Then his
nobility, composure, and resolve amazed every witness. He
accepted every blow without visible emotion; his extraordinary self-possession and affability were singular amid the
confusion and embarrassment of his entourage. Nicolas de
Basily, who drafted the tsar's act of abdication, was one of
the contemporary witnesses who recorded "admiration for
his dignity, for his stoicism in the face of adversity. He had
been virtually deposed without anyone's lifting a hand to
defend him. He accepted fate without the least revolt, without the least show of anger or ill-humor, without the least
reproach to anyone. This man, who on so many occasions
had seemed to us to lack will, had made his decision with
great courage and dignity, without hesitation. Now that his
destiny demanded the sacrifice, he accepted it with all his
heart, with real grandeur."[2] The tsar's formidable bearing
during the last days of the monarchy touches on one of two
questions central to the interpretation of Nicholas II, his
reign and his Russia. That question is whether Nicholas really
was the blind, spineless, ineffective monarch perceived by
his contemporaries and subsequently by historians. The second, related question concerns the course of Russia's development and the viability of Imperial Russia on the eve of the
first world war.

On the question of Nicholas's fitness for the crown the
historical interpretation, held almost without exception, ac-
cepts at face value Nicholas's statement of 1894 that he was
unprepared to rule. Moreover it generally asserts that he never
learned much about the job through more than twenty years'
experience. The last Romanov typically is depicted as a wood-
en figure who, overwhelmed by events and his own deficiencies, mechanically attempted to perpetuate the outmoded
principles and formulas of his predecessors. The conventional
view holds that the death of Alexander III placed the ship of
state in the hands of an immature twenty-six-year-old admiral.
The new helmsman set the throttle at full speed and attempted to negotiate treacherous shoals in the face of a
rising gale. With crew and passengers shouting all kinds of
warning and advice, he locked himself in the wheelhouse.
From there he watched the stern and steered by the wake, all
the while poring over medieval charts in search of the proper
course.

This harsh judgment allows that Nicholas II was a man of
modest intelligence and essentially noble instincts—considerate, generous, and unpretentious. But it also insists that he
was poorly equipped temperamentally for the role of monarch in that he was weak-willed, indecisive, and capricious.
At best, it grants, he was a pitiable character. All of his
nineteenth-century predecessors had borne without difficulty
the mantle of Emperor and Autocrat. In addition they had
acquired ennobling epithets—Alexander I the Blessed, Alexander II the Emancipator, Alexander III the Peacegiver. Only
his great-grandfather and namesake had failed to achieve such
distinction: Nicholas I was known simply as the Colonel. To
his people, however, Nicholas II was the Unlucky or Ill-fated
Tsar. Though he worked tirelessly at his job, his efforts all
seemed unproductive, his life and reign repeatedly marred by
tragedy, and he himself only a caricature of his autocratic
ancestors.

The basic question of Nicholas's character hinges on his
decisiveness and will, and the commentaries are almost unan-
imous in portraying him as fatally deficient in firmness and
purpose. His stalwart bearing in the crisis of 1917 is attributed
generally to fatalistic resignation. Basily's observation suggests, however, the slight possibility that the last tsar, who

was very jealous of his privacy, may have been misjudged. S.S. Oldenburg, the author of the present work, is almost alone[3] in affirming that possibility and in asserting the forceful and dynamic character of Nicholas II and his reign.

Considering the momentous events of his reign, the accessible personal documentation from the life and monarchy of the last tsar is slender and quite unsatisfactory. Reconstruction of Nicholas's character depends principally on half a dozen documentary collections published before World War II. The material includes about a thousand letters and telegrams exchanged between Nicholas and Empress Alexandra Feodorovna, his wife, in 1914-17 and a portion of some five-hundred letters between the tsar and Dowager Empress Maria Feodorovna, his mother, from 1897 to 1917. The original correspondence is preserved in the state archives in Leningrad. The Soviet archives also contain fifty-one leather notebooks in which for thirty-five years Nicholas kept a daily journal. Selected entries spanning the years 1890-1906 have been published, with complete entries only for 1904; another published collection covers the years 1917-18. Finally there are three collections of Nicholas's official and semi-official correspondence: with several grand dukes, mainly his uncles; with Kaiser William II in the years before the war; and with various ministers in 1906-11 and 1914-17.[4]

This material is sufficient to establish that Nicholas was indeed a troubled ruler beset with complex problems, but it leaves open to question his personal considerations and role in the formulation of a number of critical policies. It only rarely reflects the character of the tsar and the deep emotions that his imperturbable public facade undoubtedly concealed. Modern historians, lacking access to new material, have been inclined therefore to ignore or dismiss Nicholas. He has become an extraneous digit, rounded off and lost in the summation of forces and movements that destroyed the old regime. Yet Robert K. Massie's popular biography, *Nicholas and Alexandra*,[5] indicates that Nicholas still can be viewed from fresh perspectives. Despite its narrow theme, Massie's work is a salutary reminder that history is inseparable from life and that all the digits matter.

Russia's emergence from agrarian backwardness and illiteracy directed historians naturally and appropriately to the economic, social, and political conditions that attended the transformation of Imperial Russia. But meanwhile Nicholas II, who presided over that transition, became lost as though some impersonal arbiter ruled that he was a cipher in a "parallelogram of forces." Seen retrospectively, he became an inevitable casualty of 1917, Soviet historiography, and a line of sociological inquiry that ran amok in the "behavioral revolution" of the 1950s and 1960s.[6]

Behaviorists allege that "facts" are distinct from values and that the distinctively human issues that constitute the basis of civilized existence can be analyzed much like microbes. They dismiss "normative" phenomena—values, morals, ethics, myths, and the like—as insubstantial, meaningless abstractions that mask deeper hidden motives. Thus, recognizing man as "human, all too human," they are compelled to accept him as their incomplete technology abstracts him—morally neutral, devoid of ennobling aspirations, an insensate victim of environmental forces.

Behaviorist delusions have not led history, including the "new history," as far astray as the social sciences. But in order to become more "relevant," Clio has been under pressure to do less musing and more tinkering along utilitarian lines. Historians beguiled by scientism consequently tend to over-emphasize the "objective environment" to the neglect of the personal and subjective factors that form the underpinnings of all human relations and social activity. Such an attitude has helped to make Nicholas II one of history's orphans.

PLOTTING THE DESTINY OF IMPERIAL RUSSIA

The character of Nicholas II is only part of the puzzle that stands at the core of modern Russian historiography. The fundamental questions center on the fall of the monarchy and the Russian Revolution. The events of 1917 involved the clash of three major ideologies: conservative monarchism, liberalism, and radicalism. The subsequent interpretation of that upheaval generally followed the lines drawn in 1917, although monarchism, thoroughly discredited at the time, found few spokesmen. Early polemics yielded eventually to more temperate and sophisticated inquiries. Nevertheless, the writing of Russian history retained and largely still retains a fundamentally ideological character.

At present two schools or traditions dominate the interpretation of the reign of Nicholas II. Historians of the Soviet or communist school propound a formula based on Marxist-Leninist theory and doctrine. In the West historians of liberal persuasion approach Russian history from a perspective that assumes the virtue of classical political liberalism and the validity of the western democratic experience.

Since 1917 Soviet historians unswervingly have portrayed the fall of the monarchy as the manifestation of laws of history discovered by Marx and elaborated by Lenin. They maintain that Russia was plunged into revolution by an irreversible process of material and social development that expressed itself in irreconcilable class conflict. In that process the old degenerate social system of feudalism was destined to be swept away by capitalism and that to be succeeded in turn by socialism, the most progressive of all forms of social development before the advent of the communist millenium. And so it came to pass. The crisis of the old order erupted with the Revolution of 1905. The revolution ebbed before the tsarist repression of 1907-11, surged forward again in 1912-14, yielded temporarily to the patriotic fervor of the early war years, and finally re-emerged triumphant in 1917. In February of that year the Russian bourgeoisie, powerfully assisted by workers and peasants, destroyed Russian feudalism. Eight months later Russia's masses, led by its Leninist proletarian vanguard, overthrew the weak bourgeois dictatorship and established the world's first socialist state.[7]

In interpreting modern Russian history Soviet historians build on one insuperable advantage, that the history of tsarist Russia ended in revolution and the triumph of Bolshevism. Their task, therefore, has been to explain the inevitability of an indisputable fact. But questions of evitability or inevitability cannot be resolved empirically—on the basis of verifiable evidence. Such questions are metaphysical, and usually they are preceded by the adverb "why." Indeed, Soviet historians ask, "Why did Bolshevism succeed?" or less frequently "Why did the Russian monarchy fall?" To either question the ultimate Marxian answer is that it was written in the stars.

Non-communist western historians naturally found the Soviet interpretation to be philosophically and politically unpalatable. To accept the inevitability of communism in Russia meant to acquiesce in its eventual victory everywhere. Moreover, the Marxist analysis appeared to over-simplify a very complex problem and to pose a truth to be demonstrated rather than a hypothesis to be tested.[8] These defects enabled western historians to deny the inevitable outcome of Russian history as it was cast in the mold of Soviet historiography. That raised the problem of demonstrating positively that the triumph of Bolshevism was an aberration, an accident of Russian history, and therefore not the manifestation of some universal law or process. Liberal historians ultimately settled on an empirical impossibility—the quest for an explanation that disregarded the facts of 1917.

They began with the proposition that the Russian collapse was not the result of some implacable Marxian law but of the excessive burden of World War I. That altogether reasonable hypothesis offered the possibility of moving western historiography from the metaphysical "why" to the more substantive problem of how the process of war-making undermined or hastened the disintegration of autocratic Russia. Although the development of Russian historiography resists strict chronological categorization, the impact of the war was a major question for historians in the inter-war period.[9] The effect of war on society is obviously an empirical problem of major importance in the twentieth century. However, it could not demonstrate the inevitability of progress as manifest in the triumph of liberal democratic values, a task that western liberal historians tacitly accepted as their moral obligation after World War II.

With the magnification of Soviet power and the inauguration or intensification of the Cold War after 1945, liberal historians seemed intent primarily to assert or "prove" their own version of the truth. They virtually abandoned the genuine question concerning the impact of the war, and they gravitated to a fictional question that now appears in various guises—what would have become of Russia if it had avoided World War I?—was Bolshevism inevitable?—or, as stated in a series noted for trading in false dichotomies, *Russia in Transition, 1905-14: Evolution or Revolution?*[10]

Since that question is not really an open-ended interrogatory but essentially the vehicle for an ideological statement, it is no surprise that the response of western liberal historians has been fairly uniform: Since the later nineteenth century, Russia had been advancing across a broad front—industrial, agricultural, educational, civic, and cultural. Progress in all areas of social endeavor was channeling Russians inexorably into broad constructive political activity. Fundamental changes taking place in other areas of life had to produce some corresponding change in Russia's autocratic political structure. Given time enough, therefore, Russia was destined to evolve some form of full-fledged constitutional, democratic polity. World War I, however, cut short that promise. The liberal consensus is that the stress of war accentuated deep-seated institutional deficiencies in the Russian state, ruptured the feeble tissue of social and political cohesion, and plunged the empire into revolution and chaos before it could be reorganized on more solid foundations.[11]

The liberal interpretation can be restated as a syllogism: basic structural change was inevitable (because it occurred); prerevolutionary Russia's incipient democracy was a form of change; therefore (under normal conditions) Russia would have produced a democratic constitution. Seen in that perspective, the Bolshevik coup of October 1917 was a monstrous crime which destroyed Russian democracy or its potential—an appealing conclusion but not proven, and indeed incapable of proof. Tsarism's immediate successor in 1917 was anarchy not democracy. If the Bolsheviks destroyed a potential democracy, they probably also destroyed a potential fascism, averted the dissolution of the Russian Empire, and frustrated a variety of other unforeseen potentials. We will never know.

Contemporary western historiography identifies as "pessimists" those historians who maintain that prewar Russia was headed for disintegration. That label includes all Soviet historians and a few non-communist westerners—Leopold Haimson, Geoffrey Hosking, George F. Kennan (a recent convert to pessimism), and Theodore H. Von Laue—none of whom argue from Marxist premises.[12] The "optimists" are those who find one reason or another to contend that except for the war Russia would have survived in some form or other short of a revolutionary upheaval. That view is held by a

substantial majority of western historians, most of whom see
the salvation of Russia in its peaceful transition to constitutionalism. Soviet historians, constrained by sectarian dogma
and perspective, have no alternative but to pronounce a
sentence of death upon the regime of Nicholas II, and with
few exceptions western historians also hold that the Russian
monarchy was doomed. A handful of westerners, however,
dissents from that view. Oldenburg and George L. Yaney stress
the viability of the old regime and its basic potential for
survival. Others assert that tsarist Russia would have remained
intact and survived the war except for the extraordinary
circumstances surrounding the imperial family, circumstances
that produced their irregular and highly improbable behavior.
Still others, Hans Rogger, for example, and Arthur Mendel
(recently and tentatively), take the position that the question
is still open.[13]

The fictitious fate of Russia is not, of course, the central
theme for every western historian, and significant monograph-
ic studies are produced in spite of it. But all seem to feel constrained to defer to it. One of the more skeptical historians,
Arthur Mendel, inadvertently demonstrates how difficult it
has become for westerners to discuss the fall of the monarchy
on any other basis.[14] Had war been an unusual experience for
Imperial Russia, the question might have some value, because
a fictional question, like a metaphor or analogy, sometimes
can suggest useful ideas or lead to productive inferences.
Nevertheless, these indirect approaches never can prove anything. This particular fictional question, however, is probably
a dead end, because Russia regularly went to war—in 1854,
1877, and again in 1904—each time with significant domestic
repercussions. The consequences of the Russo-Japanese War
had been staggering. Military recovery was incomplete, and
several statesmen and industrialists were aware that Russia
was ill-prepared even for the limited war against Austria that
briefly seemed possible in July 1914. Although prewar diplomacy has been examined thoroughly, historians have yet to
examine thoroughly the interplay of Russian domestic and
foreign policy after the Balkan Wars of 1912-13. Stupidity
and miscalculation never can be ruled out of human affairs.
Still, if there is a valid question of viability in 1914, it
probably has less to do with constitutionalism than with the

viability of the Franco-Russian Alliance and the possibility of a Russo-German rapprochement or Russian neutrality in a Franco-German war.

It is difficult to retrace the route that western historians followed into the morass that currently describes much of the work in the West on the fall of the Russian monarchy. Some of the false turns are fairly evident, however. One occurred when western historians committed themselves to an ideological contest against Bolshevism, or failed to recognize that they had done so. A second, apparently stemming from that, was their departure from the basic methodological requirement that admonishes historians to pose precise, open-ended questions that can be analyzed and verified. A third error grew out of the general western tendency to perceive and judge Russia by western standards. In particular, the liberal assessment of prerevolutionary Russia rests on the questionable assumption that constitutionalism and the limitation of monarchical power signaled and measured Imperial Russia's political maturity and viability. In that connection George L. Yaney has provided a troublesome but nevertheless important caveat for anyone seeking to understand or interpret Russian history: "Almost all of the sources for Russian history since the seventeenth century—primary and secondary, Russian and Western alike—have been written by men who judged what was going on . . . by Western standards. For some it was Western ethical ideals, for others it was Western social and governmental organization, Western pipe dreams, or Western economic achievements . . . . In their eyes the [Russian] institutions and practices that already existed were obstacles to be swept aside, not social relationships to be understood or coped with. They are not reliable witnesses to their own deeds nor to the nature of the society of which they were a part."[15]

Westerners' reluctance to accept Russia on its own terms is the source of durable illusions. The western case for liberal constitutionalism in Imperial Russia rests to a great extent on the same unproven assumption that also inspired the naively optimistic theory of convergence with regard to Soviet Russia.[16] The common assumption in both cases is that the outcome of industrialization is basically the same everywhere. In the interpretation of Russian history assumptions rooted in western liberalism are reflected specifically in the hoary cliché about Nicholas II's suitability for the role of constitutional monarch and generally in the treatment of liberal constitutionalism in the reign of the last tsar.

INTO THE ROSE GARDEN

Liberals and liberal historians since the early years of the century repeatedly have contended that Nicholas II would have made an excellent constitutional monarch.[17] It is equally valid to observe that ruthless efficiency admirably equipped Joseph Stalin to head General Motors Corporation. Nicholas would have made an admirable autocrat in traditional Russia. If he had possessed the slightest capacity or inclination for another role, he might have found it possible to cooperate effectively with the conservative Third and Fourth State Dumas. But he was an autocrat to the marrow, just as he was Orthodox and Russian to the depths of his soul.

The tsar's personal and political philosophy rested on a simple and straightforward faith in autocracy based on a sacred union between himself and his people. He believed that "only that authority which stood outside and above the interests of the country's separate groups and strata could carry out basic reforms . . . . Legislative institutions could serve the government not so much as the foundation but as an occasional *brake* and also as an instrument to measure the 'temperature' or the 'barometric pressure' of the nation . . . . He did not perceive in the Duma or in Russian society in general those elements to which his imperial authority *would have the right to delegate the destiny of Russia.*"[18] Nicholas could not reconcile himself to the limitations imposed by the October Manifesto of 1905 and the Fundamental Laws of 1906. He repeatedly insisted that the manifesto and constitution had been extorted. They represented a blemish on his honor, an indignity to be reversed, a betrayal of his sacred trust to be avenged.

To what purpose, then, is the contention that he might have made an excellent constitutional monarch, when the record boldly proclaims that he could not and would not? Writers undoubtedly intend it as a compliment, as a chivalrous gesture that lends "balance" to an otherwise negative portrait. The tsar himself undoubtedly would have regarded it as an insult. The characterization is a misleading and un-necessary obstruction that seems to reflect an incapacity to understand and, more importantly, to accept Nicholas for what he was. It seems to betray an assumption, perhaps typi-cally western but definitely anachronistic and ill-founded, that an autocrat was inherently inhuman and evil. Nothing in the union rules, however, required an autocrat to be domi-neering, vicious, or even mildly misanthropic.

Western liberal assumptions and values are most evident in the general treatment of the constitutional struggle in the reign of Nicholas II. The general interpretation, already noted, revolves around and responds to a fictitious and unanswerable question. The result is an inversion of modern Russian history. In the first place, the vital stirrings of liberal constitutionalism in Russia loom large only as a short-term condition—for a decade or two before 1917. But considering Russian history in its larger perspective, in the continuity of political absolut-ism from 1470 to 1970, the stillborn constitutional move-ment represents a divertissement of some interest but of no apparent consequence in the long run. In that sense any case for Russian democracy is (to paraphrase T.S. Eliot) a fanciful trip, down a path never taken, through a door never opened, into the rose garden.[19]

In the second place, western historiography tends to convey the impression that after 1905 democracy was the destined or established order which deposed monarchists plotted against and attempted to overthrow. The monarchy, however, was prerevolutionary Russia's going concern. The central fact of modern Russian history is its disintegration and collapse. The central problem, therefore, is not the prospect of a potential democracy but the viability of the established autocratic order. The valid historical questions are those that seek to analyze the disintegrative process that ultimately consumed the old order. The constitutional struggle must be viewed from that perspective, as one of several critical factors in the isolation and exhaustion of Russian absolutism.

The standard western periodization of the reign of Nicholas II affords still another reason for some skepticism toward the conventional liberal interpretation. Western historiography typically concludes Russia's "constitutional experiment" in 1914, an eminently reasonable date for periodizing almost anything but the constitutional issue. For, curiously, then the struggle between the duma and crown in 1915 and 1916 becomes mere "politics," even though their conflict, ostensibly over the prosecution of the war, involved many of the same issues at the core of the "constitutional" struggle of 1907-14. The author of the work here presented first raised the point, and more recently George Katkov and Arthur Mendel have suggested that the western explanation of politics during the war years may be inadequate and in need of reconsideration.[20]

The conventional interpretation follows, perhaps too facilely, the descriptions, explanations, and rationalizations of spokesmen of the liberal and moderate opposition. In sum their interpretation lays the burden of responsibility for the loss of the war and the crown on Nicholas himself. It is more than possible, however, that those champions of the *vox populi* and a ministry of confidence have minimized their own responsibility for Russia's collapse. With the nation's existence at stake what was the proper role of a responsible opposition? Did the constitutional struggle really end in 1914, or did the Progressive Bloc of the Duma, formed in 1915, confuse patriotism with its own quest for power? Was the cooperation of the progressives contingent on concessions, real or implied, and thus did they force Nicholas into obstinacy and isolation in defense of his own illusions and what remained of his historic prerogatives? Amid the rubble of their own illusions and against the backdrop of their own dismal performance in 1917, Russian liberals reduced their original charge against the government from treason to criminal incompetence and misfeasance. Their record as witnesses and judges is well established; their complicity, willful or otherwise, has been all but ignored.

RETURN TO THE ROYAL ROAD

Readers of Oldenburg's history will encounter a characterization of the tsar and an evaluation of his reign that often contrast sharply with the conventional western interpretation. In print in a Russian-language edition for over a quarter of a century, Oldenburg's *Tsarstvovanie Imperatora Nikolaia II* was the first and remains the only comprehensive scholarly history of Nicholas's reign. Historians of Russia in the West, though basically in disagreement with its conclusions, generally recognize its richness and invariably acknowledge it as the best political biography of the last tsar. Readers whose perspective and views were formed in mid-century America may find Oldenburg's views somewhat unfamiliar, for he was not only a conservative historian but also a *Russian* historian who retained his traditional native values even as an exile.

Born into a cultured family that was part of Imperial Russia's intellectual elite, the author received a typically cosmopolitan education.[21] But he remained first of all a Russian, and westernism only rarely clouded his perception of Russian institutions and values. He lived a good part of his life in Western Europe and appreciated the validity of western institutions for the West. Likewise, he was convinced that Russia was best served by institutions and solutions rooted in its own historic traditions. His history of the reign of Nicholas II reflects that conviction. He believed that Russia's westernized reformers and renovators understood Europe as superficially as they understood Russia. He perceived that the West offered Russia not deliverance but destruction. Although not one of them, he respected some Slavophiles whom he believed understood and accepted the real Russia. A staunch patriot with a tinge of chauvinism, he held Panslavism in contempt but believed that Russia was destined to dominate Asia.

Oldenburg's history of the reign of Nicholas II is unique in modern Russian historiography in that it is the only comprehensive defense of the autocracy. Except for this imposing work, one must look for a defense of the tsar and the old regime to the memoirs and apologetics of former tsarist statesmen, civil servants, and courtiers. With rare exceptions those highly personal accounts lack perspective and depth and, typical of that genre, they tend to substitute passion for perceptivity and critical judgment. Oldenburg, too, wrote with a frankly apologetic intent and occasionally with passion. But, in addition, his study reflects the professional training of an historian, which he was, and (although he omitted both references and a bibliography) extensive research into original and secondary sources. Though decidedly complimentary to Nicholas, autocracy, and old Russia, he was not blind to the deficiencies of certain policies and figures of the imperial regime. On the question of Nicholas's character, however, or his fitness for the crown, Oldenburg's advocacy is almost relentless. Nowhere in the professional historical literature has the last tsar found a champion so able or unremitting.

Instead of the feeble, irresolute nonentity obvious to most historians, Oldenburg found in Nicholas II a resolute and imaginative autocrat. The emperor's weakness, he writes, existed only in the warped imagination and allegations of the hostile Russian intelligentsia. They distorted Nicholas's unfailing generosity into weakness, and they twisted his gentle manner into indecision. The real emperor, according to Oldenburg, was a strong-willed, independent-minded monarch who personally directed Russia's foreign and domestic policies and who took counsel only with himself. He dominated his ministers far more than that supreme autocrat, his father Alexander III. Time and again his personal intervention resolved ministerial deadlocks on critical issues and moved government policy off dead center. The last tsar, concludes the author, epitomized "the iron hand in the velvet glove."

Oldenburg characterizes the last tsar as a conservative, not a reactionary. Nicholas tried to follow the basic course charted by his two immediate predecessors. His grandfather Alexander II had abolished serfdom and set Russia on the road to modernization, but he failed to control political radicalism, and that failure cost him his life. Revolutionary terrorism compelled Alexander III to temporize and retrench somewhat on social and political questions. Nevertheless, he had accelerated the process of industrialization in order to guarantee Russia's continuation as a great power and to enhance the material well-being of its citizens. Although Nicholas II came to the throne without preconceived policies, he accepted the developmental goals of both of his predecessors. At the same time he was determined in the spirit of his father to avoid the errors of his grandfather and to preserve intact the principle of unlimited autocratic power. Consequently only those changes and reforms that did not jeopardize the sovereign power of the emperor could be encouraged or tolerated.

Despite great difficulties on that account, Russia by 1914 had made great strides in escaping from its backwardness. Change was evident in nearly every aspect of Russian life.

The autocratic principle, though compromised, remained essentially intact. Oldenburg insists that there was every reason for optimism. Russia was building a more viable political foundation as it advanced in other areas. But this progress was not leading to a limited monarchy! On the horizon was an enlightened autocrat, Nicholas II, indissolubly linked with and supported by an equally enlightened bureaucracy and citizenry that had become immune to the false blandishments of liberalism and revolution. Oldenburg resists the idea that change was making the autocracy obsolete. Nor does he agree, as western liberal historians assert, that change in other aspects of Russian life required a corresponding transformation of Russia's constitutional structure. He points instead to the inconsistency of that argument: apostles of progress, both before and after the revolution, hailed Russia's spectacular material and cultural development; yet at the same time they slandered and declared anachronistic and inept the very institution and the autocrat whose wise, forceful, and far-sighted guidance had achieved that progress.

Given Oldenburg's enthusiastic portrayal of the determined and creative leadership of Nicholas II and Russia's progress under his direction, the obvious question is how everything came to be lost. The author's explanation basically follows Nicholas's complaint in March 1917, that he found himself surrounded by "treason, cowardice, and deception." The hostility of the Russian intelligentsia was the Achilles heel of the old regime. The egoistic demands and uncompromising antagonism of the intelligentsia, their incessant criticism and short-sighted negativism, their irreconcilable insistence on both pluralism and domination—all these created a menace that tsarism could neither placate nor destroy. No polity can survive without the support of its educated elite. The Russian monarchy was deserted, first by the radical intelligentsia, and then successively by the moderate and conservative publics who formed the vital foundation of the monarchical order. The progressive disaffection of educated society insidiously undermined, isolated, and ultimately paralyzed and toppled the Russian monarchy.

The alienation of Russia's educated elite forms the major theme and one of three distinguishing characteristics of Oldenburg's history. The author's analysis reflects a sophisticated historical conception of the nature of political power. That conception regards power as the expression of a social-political consensus which upholds the authority of a regime, willingly obeys its commands, and generally prefers it to all other alternatives. That concept of power differs from the traditional political theory which identifies or equates power with coercion. In the traditional equation obedience stems from fear; the power of a regime is expressed by its monopoly over the instruments of violence, by its ability to coerce its "subjects."[22]

Power understood in terms of a consensus dispels the notion that revolutions are "made." When power—or the consensus behind it—disintegrates, a revolution becomes possible, but it is no longer necessary. The coercive superiority of a government over its citizens exists as long as the armed forces or police are willing to use their weapons in behalf of the regime. The general refusal of soldiers and police to defend the government indicates that the power structure has collapsed. Their defection confirms the fact that nothing exists to be overthrown.[23] At that point revolutionary elements come to the fore and, using any means including violence, they attempt to forge a new consensus and to create power anew.

The fall of the Russian monarchy followed that scenario rather precisely. The most striking aspect of the collapse of the old order was the apparent spontaneity of its debacle. During the Petrograd riots that preceded the tsar's abdication, his power visibly dissolved to everyone's amazement. For decades the government readily had crushed similar demonstrations. But in February 1917 a relatively modest test of strength revealed clearly that the autocrat's decrees no longer commanded obedience. The abdication of Nicholas II confirmed an erosion of power that obviously had been underway for some time. Initially, no one protested the decision, not even monarchists.

Although Oldenburg meticulously chronicles the disaffection of society, his account fails to explain how the policies and actions of the monarchy withered the confidence and support of its citizens and thus eroded its power. His approach, nevertheless, focuses attention on the tsarist administration and imperial society. The effect is to relegate the revolutionary movement to the background where it naturally existed as a peripheral factor in the constituent relation between imperial society and the government. His approach runs counter to the excessive concentration on "revolutionary Russia" by historians, east and west. Even Soviet historians have recognized over-emphasis on the revolutionary movements as a deficiency in Russian historiography, and they recently called for greater efforts to analyze the broader antecedents of the Russian collapse.[24] Oldenburg's approach maintains the proper historical perspective on the crisis of the old order. The old regime fell victim to failures largely of its own making, or it succumbed to some process understandable only in retrospect and therefore beyond its capacity to comprehend or respond. In either case an investigation of the fate of Imperial Russia never can stray far from the monarchy itself.

A second distinguishing characteristic of Oldenburg's study is its skillful portrayal of the subjective character of the tsar amid the changing environment of Imperial Russia. Readers must judge for themselves how Oldenburg's portrait is enriched by its attention to such factors as Nicholas's faith in the myth of tsar and people, his belief in his mystical transformation into a demi-god through the ritual of the coronation, or his confidence in the possibility of divine intervention. The reasonableness or absurdity of the tsar's faith is beside the point. His belief in the spiritual qualities conferred by his office affected his social and political views and colored his decisions. His faith was a vital reality which cannot be dismissed merely as a rationalization for the defense of dynastic prerogatives or class interests. Russian history itself is not wholly comprehensible without reference to the myths and other illusions shared by broad sections of the nation.[25]

Oldenburg's history, finally, is distinguished by its skepticism and distrust of westernism. He maintains that the antagonism of the Russian elite sprang from their adherence to alien western social and political theories. Those ideas never could take root in the soil of Russia, but they could and did inspire the irrepressible defection of Russian society from its traditional adherence to conservative and monarchical principles. Seeking the source of Russia's collapse in its social and political fabric, Oldenburg misjudged the virulent effect that industrialization, the epitomy of westernism, had on the structure of traditional Russia. Like most of his contemporaries, the author took great pride in Russia's industrial progress, and industrialization partly inspired his optimistic appraisal of Imperial Russia. Theodore H. Von Laue, however, stresses the negative consequences of industrialization in Russia and elsewhere. The process, he writes, is inevitably one of "subversion of unprepared societies by alien influences and necessities."[26] Whatever its origins or his impression of its roots, it was that "subversion" of traditional Russian values and institutions that Oldenburg, a Russian traditionalist, details with unrivaled perception. Because of that, Oldenburg's history is far more than a chronicle or pageant of old Russia. It is the authentic expression of the nobler, progressive outlook and aspirations of the old regime.

The generation of Russians of whom Oldenburg was a literate, humane, and loyal representative has all but passed. It was a generation destined to leave few monuments. Oldenburg's history of the reign and Russia of Nicholas II is one of its more substantial legacies. Its place is assured whatever the course of the debate on the fate of Imperial Russia, because it is history on a human scale. It narrates a compelling drama which produced many victims and scarcely any heroes. Russia's collapse merged into a larger tragedy that formed the threshold of our own historical era, an age which has continued to produce an excess of victims. Thus we are linked inseparably with the fate of Imperial Russia, even though our bond with the past offers but few clouded guideposts for the future. The old regime could not save itself, nor in retrospect has anyone discovered a fool-proof plan for its salvation. History, posing open-ended questions, unfortunately yields no more certainty than life itself affords.

❦

LAST TSAR

Volume I
THE AUTOCRACY, 1894-1900

CHAPTER ONE

MANIFESTO ON THE ACCESSION OF NICHOLAS II

Almighty God in His mysterious wisdom has been pleased to take the precious life of Our Beloved Father, the Sovereign Emperor Alexander Alexandrovich. His grave illness would yield neither to treatment nor the beneficial climate of the Crimea, and at Livadia on October 20th, surrounded by His August Family, he died in the arms of Her Imperial Highness the Empress and Ourself.

Words cannot express Our sorrow, but every Russian heart will understand it. We know that throughout Our vast Empire anguished tears will mark the passing of Our Sovereign from the native land which He loved with the full strength of His Russian soul and for whose prosperity He devoted all His energies, sparing neither health nor life. Not only in Russia but far beyond her frontiers men will never cease to honor the memory of this Tsar who personified justice and the peace that remained unbroken throughout His Reign.

Thus began the manifesto announcing to Russia the accession of Emperor Nicholas II Alexandrovich to the ancestral throne of the Romanovs.

Although few international complications marked the reign of Alexander III, his foreign policy profoundly affected Russia and the world and earned him the title of Tsar-Peacegiver. The foreign and domestic policies of his thirteen-year reign produced several knotty problems that his son and successor Nicholas II had to unravel or cut. Both friends and enemies of Imperial Russia recognized that Alexander III had enhanced considerably the influence of Russia in international affairs. They were cognizant as well of his success in extending and augmenting the autocratic power of the monarchy within the empire.

Alexander III had set the Russian ship of state on a course different from that of his father, Alexander II [1855-81]. The great reforms of the sixties and seventies were not to his mind an indisputable good. He strived therefore to modify them to fit his conception of the internal equilibrium essential to Russia. Besides the reforms, the Russo-Turkish War of 1877-78, fought in behalf of the Balkan Slavs, had strained the resources of the empire.[1] He believed it necessary to consolidate and digest the many changes that had taken place.

CONTEMPORARY APPRAISALS OF THE REIGN OF ALEXANDER III

The renowned Russian historian Vasily O. Kliuchevsky[2] memorialized Alexander III a week after his death in an address at Moscow University to the Imperial Society of Russian History and Antiquities:

> During the reign of Alexander II, in the space of only one generation, we peacefully carried out a series of far-reaching reforms of our state system, reforms that were guided by the spirit of Christianity and rooted therefore in the very spirit of Europe. Age-long and frequently violent efforts were required to achieve this in Western Europe—the same Europe that traditionally regarded Russia as an example of Mongolian backwardness, and Russians as step-children of the civilized world . . . .
>
> Emperor Alexander III reigned for thirteen years before the swift hand of death rushed to close his eyes and to open wide the eyes of Europe to the universal significance of his brief reign. But finally even the stones cried out, and the voices of public opinion in Europe began to tell the truth and to discuss Russia with unaccustomed candor. They had to admit that the peaceful development of European civilization was neither so firmly nor securely guaranteed as once was thought. Instead they discovered that Europe, seeking security, had taken refuge in a powder magazine, that a burning fuse had approached this dangerous arsenal more than once and from different quarters, but that each time the solicitous and patient hand of the Russian tsar quietly and carefully had turned it aside . . . .
>
> Now Europe has recognized that the tsar of the Russian people was also the sovereign of international peace. In acknowledging this Europe has confirmed Russia's historic mission, for in the Russian system the tsar's will expresses the thought of his people, and the people's will becomes the thought of the tsar. Europe has recognized that our country, which it once regarded as a threat to its civilization, stood and stands guard over that civilization—understands, values, and defends its foundations no less than its creators do. Europe has recognized that Russia is an organically essential component of its cultural framework and a vital natural member of its family of nations . . . .
>
> Science will accord Alexander III a special place not only in the history of Russia and of Europe in general but also in Russian historiography. It will record that he was victorious in a field where victories are

the most difficult to achieve: he triumphed over the prejudice of nations and thus helped bring them together; he won the conscience of society to the side of peace and truth; he ignited a moral revolution among mankind; he encouraged and elevated Russian historical thought and Russian self-consciousness. History will record that he accomplished all of this so quietly and tacitly that only when he was gone did Europe understand what he had meant to it.

Kliuchevsky, an *intelligents* and, more, a "westerner,"[3] concentrated on the foreign policy of Alexander III, apparently with the rapprochement with France in mind. Constantine P. Pobedonostsev,[4] one of the closest collaborators of the late monarch, concisely and expressively described another aspect of the reign: "Everyone knew that he would never sacrifice historic Russian interests for the sake of the Poles or any other peripheral foreign minority. He held deep within his soul the same faith and love as his people for the Orthodox Church. Together with his people he believed in the enduring necessity of autocratic power in Russia, and he regarded the disastrous confusion of languages and opinion as an intolerable illusion of freedom."

The president of the French senate told the upper chamber that the Russian people "mourned the loss of their sovereign who was so boundlessly devoted to their future, their greatness, and their security; under the just and tranquil reign of its emperor, the Russian nation attained security, which is the highest blessing and the instrument of true greatness." The French press echoed the tone of those remarks. "He left Russia greater than he received it," observed the *Journal des Débats*. The *Revue des deux Mondes*, seconding Kliuchevsky, recorded that "Russia's sorrow was also our sorrow; it became part of our national character, and other nations experienced almost the same emotions.... Europe felt it had lost an arbitrator who had always pursued the idea of justice."

EUROPE IN 1894

The year 1894 formed part of the long "calm before the storm" that characterized the last two decades of the nineteenth century. This era of tranquility, the longest period in medieval and modern history to experience no major war, left a deep impression on its generation. By the end of the nineteenth century material well-being and education were growing

Empress Maria Feodorovna

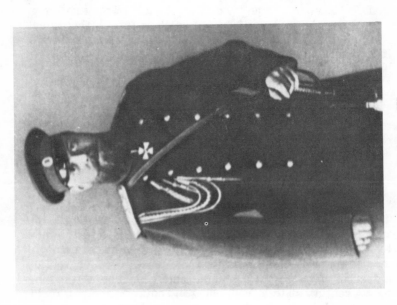

Emperor Alexander III

and spreading apace. Technology leaped from one invention to another, and science from one discovery to another. Railroads and steamships had made it possible to travel "around the world in eighty days." Telephone lines followed the telegraph in spreading a network over the earth. Electric lighting rapidly was replacing gas. The automobiles of 1894, however, were clumsy vehicles unable to compete with the elegant horse-drawn carriages and coaches of the day. Motion pictures were still in the experimental stage. Piloted balloons were only a dream, while heavier-than-air machines were still unheard of. The radio awaited its inventor, radium its discoverer.

An identical political process could be observed in almost every country: the increasing influence of parliaments, the expansion of suffrage, and the shift of power to the left. In fact no one in the West mobilized resistance against this trend, which appeared at the time to reflect the spontaneous course of "historical progress." Conservatives, whose traditional policies were slipping gradually toward the left, were content occasionally to arrest the pace of this development. The year 1894 witnessed such a deceleration in most countries.

In France a slight turn to the right occurred with the assassination of President Sadi Carnot [by an Italian anarchist in June 1894]. This act was the culmination of a series of senseless anarchist attempts which included the explosion of a bomb in the chamber of deputies [December 1893]. These events shook a republic already weakened by the notorious Panama scandal. The new president, Jean Casimir-Perier, was a republican conservative inclined toward the expansion of presidential power. Charles Dupuy, supported by a substantial bloc of moderates, led the new government. But the moderates of 1894 were the same politicians who formed the extreme left in the national assemblies of the 1870s. Moreover a considerable number of French Catholics had joined the republican ranks in response to Pope Leo XIII's encyclical [Rerum novarum of 1891].[5]

Prince Otto von Bismarck's retirement [1890] enabled the German Reichstag to expand its influence. The social democratic movement, gradually winning control of the major cities, was becoming Germany's largest political party. The

conservatives, based on the Prussian Landtag, were conducting a stubborn struggle against the economic policy of Kaiser
William II. Chancellor Leo Caprivi was unable to mount an
effective campaign against the socialists. He was replaced in
1894 but his successor, the aged Prince Ludwig von Hohenlohe, produced no significant change in domestic policy.

In England the Liberals, defeated in 1894 on the Irish
question, gave way to the "interim" ministry of Lord Rose-
bery [Archibald Primrose]. He soon yielded to Lord Salisbury
[Robert Cecil] who enjoyed the support of Conservatives and
Liberal-Unionists (opponents of Irish home-rule). Led by
Joseph Chamberlain, the Unionists commanded such a dominant position in the ruling majority that they soon dropped
that label and for the next twenty years were known simply
as Conservatives. The British labor movement, unlike the
German, had not yet adopted a political program. The powerful trade unions, successful in a number of impressive strikes,
were relatively satisfied with their economic and organizational gains. In their struggle the unions had received greater
support from conservatives than liberals—an alignment caus-
ing a prominent English statesman to quip that "we are all
socialists now."

Parliamentary government had emerged even more vigorously in Austria-Hungary than in Germany. Cabinets lacking
parliamentary majorities had to resign, but the parliament
itself opposed any extension of suffrage because the ruling
parties feared the loss of power. At the time of Alexander
III's death the ministry of Prince Alfred Windischgrätz, lean-
ing on a heterogeneous coalition of German liberals, Poles,
and clerics, temporarily exercised power in Vienna. Meanwhile in Italy Francesco Crispi, one of the authors of the
Triple Alliance, returned to power in 1894 [December 1893].
His recovery followed a period of leftist rule under Giovanni
Giolitti, whose government collapsed in the scandalous Tanlongo affair.[6] In the peculiar setting of Italian politics Crispi
played the role of a conservative.

The Second International was founded in 1889, and socialist ideas were spreading throughout Europe. Even so, by 1894
socialists were a serious political force only in Germany
(where in 1893 they elected forty-four deputies). Parliamen-
tarianism had advanced further among the smaller states—
Belgium and the Scandinavian and Balkan countries—than

among the great powers. Turkey and Montenegro were the only European countries besides Russia to lack representative institutions.

The era of tranquility was at the same time an era of armed peace. All the great powers, with the small states close behind, expanded and improved their armaments. As Kliuchevsky said, Europe's search for security led to a powder keg. All the major countries of Europe except insular England had introduced compulsory military service. The technology of war was not falling behind the art of peace.

Mutual distrust was rampant among nations. The Triple Alliance of Germany, Austria-Hungary, and Italy appeared to be the most powerful combination. But even these partners did not trust one another fully. Until 1890 Germany still found it necessary to "reinsure" herself through a secret agreement with Russia, and Bismarck regarded the kaiser's failure to renew this treaty a fatal mistake. France had tried repeatedly through negotiation to draw Italy away from the Triple Alliance. Still nursing the unhealed wound of their defeat in 1870-71, the French were prepared to join forces with any enemy of Germany. The British meanwhile lingered in "splendid isolation."

The partition of Africa was all but completed by 1890. Only parts of the unexplored interior remained unsecured, and enterprising colonizers were plunging forward to be first to raise the flag and claim these "no-man's lands" for their countries. Only at the middle reaches of the upper Nile did the Mahdists, a nation of Muslim fanatics, block the progress of the British; in 1885 they managed to seize Khartoum and kill the British commander, General Charles Gordon. Mountainous Abyssinia meanwhile was preparing an unexpected and forceful rebuff for the Italians who were beginning to encroach on it. But these were only small outposts of resistance. Africa, like Australia and America earlier, was becoming the property of the white race. Indeed, until the very end of the nineteenth century the conviction prevailed that Asia too would meet the same fate. England and Russia eyed one another over a thin barrier of still independent but weak countries—Persia, Afghanistan, and semi-independent Tibet. War nearly erupted in 1885 when the Russians routed the Afghanis at Kushk [Penjdeh], fanning British vigilance over "the gateway to India." An agreement reached in 1887 averted a serious conflict.[7] On the Pacific the slumbering nations of the Far East were beginning to stir. In the 1850s Russia had seized the Ussuri region from China without a fight. But even as Alexander III lay dying, cannons were thundering on the shores of the Yellow Sea where tiny Japan, having mastered European technology, was winning its first victories over the still listless hulk of China.

THE RUSSIAN EMPIRE IN 1894

With an area of twenty million square versts [8,791,400 square miles] and a population of 125 million, the Russian Empire occupied a prominent position in the world. Since the Seven Years War [1755-63] and especially since 1812, Western Europe had stood in awe of Russian military power. The Crimean War revealed the limitations of that power but at the same time affirmed its stability. The era of reform, which included military reorganization, created new conditions for the development of Russian power. At the same time Russia was becoming an object of serious study in Europe. In France Anatole Leroy-Beaulieu and in England Donald MacKenzie Wallace published major survey studies of Russia.[8] The formation of the Russian Empire had taken place under conditions quite different from those in Western Europe, and foreigners were beginning to comprehend that the contrast was a matter of dissimilarity not "backwardness."

THE AUTOCRACY

According to the Fundamental State Laws, "the Russian Empire is ruled strictly in accordance with the Fundamental Laws emanating from the authority of His Imperial Highness. The Emperor is an autocratic and unlimited monarch."[9] Legislative and executive power were reserved exclusively to the emperor. Yet this was not tyranny, for the law provided precise guidance in all essential matters, and any law not repealed was to be enforced. In the area of civil law the tsarist government generally avoided sharp departures and recognized the legal precedents and acquired rights of the population. Thus there remained in force within the empire the Napoleonic Code (in the Kingdom of Poland), the Lithuanian Statutes (in the provinces of Poltava and Chernigov), Magdeburg Law (in the Baltic region), the customary laws of the peasantry, and the diverse local laws and customs of the Caucasus, Siberia, and Central Asia.

The right to enact legislation belonged exclusively to the tsar. The State Council, appointed by the sovereign from among his highest officials, considered prospective legislation. The tsar, however, was free to accept the view of the majority or the minority or to reject both, at his own discretion. Special commissions or boards usually considered particularly important legislation, but their competence too was only advisory.

The executive power of the tsar was similarly unlimited and absolute. Louis XIV, after the death of Cardinal Mazarin, declared that henceforth he would be his own prime minister. All Russian sovereigns enjoyed that position, for the office of prime minister was unknown to Russia. Rulers occasionally bestowed the title of chancellor upon their foreign ministers (the last chancellor being Alexander M. Gorchakov, who died in 1882). The chancellorship was the highest rank in the Table of Ranks,[10] but it did not imply superiority over the other ministers. The Committee of Ministers had a permanent chairman (who in 1894 was the former finance minister, Nicholas Kh. Bunge), but the committee was actually only an inter-departmental panel. All ministers and heads of autonomous departments reported personally to the emperor, as did the governors and the governors-general of both capitals.[11] This did not mean that the sovereign concerned himself with the detailed operations of the various agencies (although Alexander III was his own foreign minister to whom everyone "entering" [receiving information or returning from abroad] and "originating" reported; Nicholas K. Giers was, so to speak, the "deputy minister"). Individual ministers sometimes wielded great power and initiative but only as long as the emperor retained confidence in them.

THE ADMINISTRATION

Implementation of the government's directives required a staff of numerous officials. Nicholas I [1825-1855] once joked that thirty-thousand department heads governed Russia. The "bureaucracy" and the "obstacles" that it created formed targets for general reproach and complaint in Russian society. Foreigners gained the impression that nearly all Russian officials engaged in bribery, a judgment derived from the satires of Nicholas V. Gogol and Michael E. Saltykov-Shchedrin. But caricatures, regardless of how cleverly drawn, are not portraits. In fact low pay scales did encourage widespread graft in certain departments such as the police. Other agencies, however, like the ministry of finance or the judiciary, after the reform of 1864, enjoyed reputations for the highest integrity. Admittedly one of the characteristics in which Russia was similar to oriental countries was its lenient attitude toward many acts of questionable honesty. Psychologically this phenomenon was difficult to combat. Some professions, engineers for example, acquired even worse reputations than bureaucrats— reputations that frequently were undeserved. The senior levels of government were not infected with corruption, and therefore instances of high-level abuse produced sensations because they were so exceptional.

Regardless of the situation and notwithstanding its tainted officials, the Russian administration carried out its responsibilities even under the most trying conditions. The tsarist government was served by an obedient, well-organized apparatus attuned to the diverse requirements of the Russian Empire. This organization had evolved from the old Muscovite bureaus, and in many respects it had achieved the summit of perfection.

THE RUSSIAN ORTHODOX CHURCH

The Russian tsar was not only head of state, he was also head of the Russian Orthodox Church, a pre-eminent institution throughout the country. His position implied no right to interfere with religious dogma, for the synodal constitution of the church excluded such an interpretation. But upon recommendations of the holy synod, the supreme college of the church,[13] the tsar appointed all bishops and likewise named the members of the synod itself. The director-general of the holy synod linked church and state, and for more than a quarter of a century Pobedonostsev filled this position. A man of exceptional intellect and determination, he was the tutor of two emperors, Alexander III and Nicholas II.

THE RULING CIRCLE: "DEMOPHILES" AND "ARISTOCRATS"

Two fundamental positions on the role of authority developed among officials and courtiers of Alexander III. One grew from and expressed a skeptical (or at least judiciously negative) attitude toward the "progressive" approach [of Alexander II]. The other tendency reflected an urge to reinforce the inner unity of Russia by enlarging the privileged status of the empire's Russian subjects. These two attitudes produced within the government two lines of policy which contended with and yet also complemented one another.

One policy was predicated on the need to protect the weak from the strong. It expressed an affinity for the broad masses as against the upper classes, which had become detached from the people. This policy displayed an inclination toward equality, what in contemporary terms might be called "demophilism" or Christian socialism. Among the proponents of this view were the Minister of Justice, Nicholas A. Manasein (who retired in 1894), and Pobedonostsev, who felt that "the nobility like the people must also be bridled." The "demophiles" ardently defended the peasant commune as the distinctively Russian solution to the basic social problem. They also endorsed the policy of russification.

The other policy sought to strengthen the ruling classes and establish a recognized hierarchy within the state. Its leading advocate was Count Dmitry A. Tolstoy, the Minister of Interior [1882-89]. Constantine N. Leontiev,[14] a staunch champion of this aristocratic policy, published a pamphlet in 1888 on "National Policy as an Instrument of World Revolution" (in subsequent editions the word "tribal" replaced "national"). He asserted that "the contemporary trend toward political nationalism is nothing more than cosmopolitical democratization propagated by different means." Among the eminent conservative journalists, Michael N. Katkov endorsed the "demophile" line, while Prince Vladimir P. Meshchersky subscribed to the aristocratic view.[15]

Alexander III, despite his utterly Russian mentality, did not condone unrestrained russification. In a letter to Pobedonostsev in 1886 he wrote: "There are some gentlemen who think that they alone are Russian and no one else. Do they imagine by any chance that I am a German or Finlander

A Peasant Collecting Donations for the Church

[*chukonets*]? They have it easy, with their farcical patriotism, when they are not responsible for anything. I will stick up for Russia."

FOREIGN POLICY IN THE REIGN OF ALEXANDER III

Major changes in Russian foreign policy marked the reign of Alexander III. A noticeable coolness replaced the traditionally close ties with Germany, or more accurately with Prussia. Friendship with Berlin, a cardinal feature of Russian foreign policy since the reign of Catherine the Great [1762-96], ran uninterrupted through the reigns of Alexander I [1801-25], Nicholas I, and especially Alexander II. The reversal has been attributed at times, and erroneously, to the anti-German sentiments of Empress Maria Feodorovna,[16] a Danish princess who wed the Russian heir shortly after the Danish-Prussian war of 1864. Unlike the preceding reigns, perhaps at this time cordial personal relations and familial ties between the two dynasties were not available to smooth over political complications. But the causes were primarily political.

Bismarck believed that he could combine the Triple Alliance and friendly relations with Russia. But the Austro-German-Italian alliance lay at the root of the separation of the two old friends. The Congress of Berlin [1878] left a residue of bitterness in Russian feelings. Anti-German notes echoed through the ruling circle, especially General Michael D. Skobelev's strident speech[17] and Katkov's campaign in *Moskovskie vedomosti* [The Moscow Gazette]. By the middle eighties tension had increased. Germany's seven-year military budget (the *Septennat*) provoked a further deterioration in relations until finally the German government closed the Berlin exchange to Russian securities.

These aggravations seriously alarmed both Alexander III and Bismarck, and in 1887 they concluded for a period of three years the so-called Reinsurance Treaty. This secret agreement committed each side to benevolent neutrality in the event of an attack upon one of them by a third country. The agreement constituted an important modification of the treaty governing the Triple Alliance, because it signified that Germany would not support Austrian aggression against Russia. The two treaties were juridically compatible, since the

Triple Alliance called for assistance only if the partners became victims of aggression. (This provision enabled Italy to declare its neutrality in 1914 without violating the treaty.)

The Reinsurance Treaty lapsed in 1890. Negotiations for its renewal were in progress when Bismarck retired. With military bluntness his successor, General Caprivi, informed William II that the treaty was disloyal to Austria. For his part Alexander III, who sympathized with Bismarck, did not attempt to contact the new rulers of Germany. Relations then deteriorated into a tariff war between Russia and Germany. The personal efforts of Sergei Yu. Witte,[18] the Minister of Finance, finally ended this conflict. The new trade agreement of 20 March 1884 provided Russia substantial advantages over a ten-year span.

Nothing occurred to worsen Russia's relations with Austria-Hungary. Although Nicholas I had rescued Austria from the Hungarian revolution in 1848, Austria had "surprised the world with her ingratitude" during the Crimean War.[19] Subsequently Russia and Austria clashed everywhere in the Balkans, just as Russia and England confronted one another throughout Asia. England continued to regard the Russian Empire as its chief enemy and rival, "a huge iceberg hanging over India," as Benjamin Disraeli [Lord Beaconsfield] told the British Parliament.

The Balkan Peninsula was the scene of Russia's weightiest disappointment in the eighties. The war of 1877-78, so expensive to Russia in blood and treasure, yielded no immediate benefits. Austria gained virtual control over Bosnia and Herzegovina, and Russia had to acquiesce or face a new war. In Serbia the Obrenovich dynasty came to power in the person of King Milan, who was clearly a client of Austria. As for Bulgaria, even Bismarck observed scornfully in his memoirs that "liberated peoples are not grateful, but pretentious." The Bulgarians went so far as to suppress persons friendly to Russia. The replacement of Prince Alexander of Battenberg, the leader of the anti-Russian factions, by Prince Ferdinand of Coburg did not improve Russo-Bulgarian relations. That became possible only in 1894 with the retirement of Stefan Stambulov, who was the main inspiration of Bulgaria's russophobic policy.

Offended by Russia's re-annexation of a small section of Bessarabia lost in the Crimean War,[20] Rumania formed alliances with Austria and Germany. Even though Rumania received as compensation the entire Dobrudja with the port of Constanza, it preferred the close friendship of Russia's Balkan opponents. When Alexander III proposed his famous toast "to the only faithful friend of Russia, Prince Nicholas of Montenegro," he was speaking all too truthfully. Russian power was great enough that St. Petersburg did not feel threatened by diplomatic isolation. Nevertheless, with the expiration of the Reinsurance Treaty and the sharp deterioration of Russo-German economic relations, Alexander took definite steps toward a rapprochement with France.

THE FRANCO-RUSSIAN ALLIANCE

France, saddled with republicanism, political instability, and scandal, scarcely commended itself to the tsar of Russia who cherished conservative and religious principles. Therefore a Franco-Russian agreement seemed out of the question. But the grand reception of the French squadron at Kronstadt [July 1891], when the tsar stood bare-headed for the playing of the *Marseillaise*, demonstrated that neither sympathy nor antipathy for the internal structure of France was decisive in the mind of Alexander III. Few people in 1892 could have thought that Russia and France already had concluded a secret defensive alliance. The supplementary military convention stipulated the forces that each side would mobilize in a war against Germany.[21] Such secrecy prevailed that only two or three ranking officials of the ministries of foreign affairs and war knew of it. Even the heir to the throne was not informed. The French were eager to publish the alliance, but the tsar insisted on complete secrecy. He feared that the certainty of Russian support would inspire the French to belligerence and revive their appetite for revenge. He had no faith in the ability of a democratic government to resist public opinion.

THE ARMY AND NAVY

The Russian Empire maintained the largest peacetime army in the world. Twenty-two corps, excluding cossacks and irregular formations, numbered about 900,000 men. The annual levy of recruits for four-year terms produced twice the required manpower. Consequently the army inducted only the fittest and granted deferments in hardship cases. Only sons, elder brothers responsible for younger members of a family, teachers, doctors, and others were exempted from active duty. They enrolled directly in the inactive reserve which would be mobilized only as a last resort. Only 31 percent of all conscripts were summoned to active duty in Russia in comparison to 76 percent in France.

State factories produced most of the army's arms and ammunition. Those "merchants of death," who earned such unflattering reputations in the West, did not exist in Russia. Some fourteen to fifteen thousand officer candidates prepared for service in thirty-seven middle and fifteen higher military institutes. All lower ranks received some additional education while on active duty. The army taught illiterates to read and write, and every soldier received some basic educational instruction.

Alexander III revived and rebuilt the Russian navy which had fallen into disrepair after the Crimean War. Seventeen battleships and ten armored cruisers were among the 114 new ships launched. The fleet's total displacement of about 300,000 tons ranked Russia third in the world behind England and France. Russia's naval weakness stemmed from the international agreements that confined the Black Sea Fleet to its home waters. Consequently one-third of the navy was unavailable for service in other seas.[22]

LOCAL GOVERNMENT

Russia had no institution representative of the empire as a whole. According to Pobedonostsev, Alexander III believed in "the unshakeable importance of autocratic power for Russia," and he would not tolerate "the disastrous confusion of languages and opinions under the illusion of freedom." But the legacy of his predecessors included certain organs of local self-government—the zemstvos, municipalities, and (from the reign of Catherine II) the provincial and district assemblies of the nobility. The reform of 1864 had introduced the zemstvos into thirty-four of the fifty provinces of European Russia,[23] that is, to more than half of the population of the empire. Peasants, landowners, and townsmen elected the members of the zemstvos. The amount of taxes paid by each group determined its local representation, but a law of 1890 strengthened the influence of the nobility in the zemstvos.[24] Since it was the better educated rural constituency, the gentry class generally dominated provincial affairs. In a few parts of the country (the provinces of Viatka and Perm) peasants controlled the zemstvos. Russian zemstvos enjoyed a wider sphere of activity than comparable institutions of local government in France. Medical and veterinary services, public education, road maintenance, statistics, insurance, a-gronomy, cooperatives, and other activities fell within the competence of the zemstvos.

In the cities property owners elected a municipal *duma* [assembly] which in turn elected a municipal executive board over which presided the mayor of the city.[25] The municipal dumas exercised basically the same functions as the zemstvos.

The government in the rural areas was the village com-munity (mir). All adult male peasants were eligible to partici-pate, and wives could appear in the absence of their husbands. The mir decided local questions and elected representatives to the *volost* assembly. A village elder served as chairman. [Government-appointed] officials (or secretaries) guided these primary units of peasant government.[26]

By the end of the reign of Alexander III elected organiza-tions expended about 200,000,000 rubles of the total state expenditure of 1,200,000,000 rubles. Zemstvos and cities ac-counted for approximately 60,000,000 rubles of the total. The zemstvos spent about one-third of their annual budgets on medical services and about one-sixth on education.

THE ASSEMBLIES OF THE NOBILITY

All the gentry of every province and district formed local assemblies of the nobility, corporations created in the reign of Catherine the Great. Membership was restricted to those who actually owned property in that jurisdiction.[27] The pro-vincial assemblies of the nobility were the only public insti-tutions legally empowered by the fundamental laws to discuss matters of general policy from time to time. Assemblies of the nobility frequently presented political resolutions to the emperor. Other than that their scope was quite limited. If the nobility played any role at all, it was in the zemstvos where the local marshal of the nobility, by virtue of that position, served as chairman of the provincial or district zemstvo assembly. The importance of the nobility was declining markedly. In the early nineties, contrary to western conceptions, the nobility owned only 55,000,000 [about 14 percent] of the 381,000,000 desiatins of arable land in European Russia and practically none of the land in Siberia, Central Asia, or the Caucasus. They did, however, own 44 percent of the land in Russian Poland.

Wherever the electoral process existed, there were factions of the left and right, and thus also liberal and conservative zemstvos. But these groups had not yet crystallized into political parties. Moreover, after the collapse of "the People's Will," no significant illegal organizations remained active in Russia. Some revolutionary literature was published abroad. A London-based organization of revolutionary emigres[28] reported that in 1893 it distributed 20,407 copies of illegal books and pamphlets, of which 2,360 reached Russia—an unimpressive figure for a country of 125,000,000 inhabitants.

A special situation obtained in the Grand Duchy of Finland which was governed by a constitution conferred by Alexander I. The Finnish diet consisting of representatives of four classes (nobility, clergy, townsmen, and peasantry) convened every five years. In 1885 Alexander III granted the Finns the right to initiate legislation. A senate appointed by the emperor conducted local affairs; a minister and state secretary for Finnish affairs handled relations with the imperial administration.

CENSORSHIP AND THE PRESS

The absence of representative institutions left Russia without organized political activity, and the police quickly stifled attempts to form political organizations. The authorities kept the press under close supervision. Some of the large newspapers, in order to speed printing, went to press without preliminary censorship and thus accepted the risk of subsequent disciplinary action. Newspapers usually received two warnings; the third meant they had to cease publication. Nevertheless the newspapers remained independent. Operating within recognized bounds and exercising a prudent degree of restraint, they could and often did express views quite antagonistic to the government. Most of the large newspapers and journals were notoriously oppositionist. The government prohibited only blatant expressions of hostility. It made no effort to influence the substance of what was published.

The Russian government lacked both the inclination and the aptitude for self-advertisement. Its achievements and successes often remained unheralded, while its mistakes and shortcomings were detailed assiduously with alleged objectivity on the pages of the contemporary Russian press. Russian political emigres spread these distortions which often created a false impression of Russia among foreigners.

The censorship exercised by the church was absolutely inflexible with respect to books. Although less severe than the *Index* of the Vatican, the Russian Church compiled its register of forbidden books and had the power to prevent their circulation. Among the books proscribed were Count Leo N. Tolstoy's writings against the church and Ernest Renan's *Life of Jesus.* Censors also deleted sections mocking religion from the translations of Heinrich Heine. The strictness of the censors varied from one period to another, and a book once circulated was seldom withdrawn. Consequently the number of books prohibited to the "legal" reader in Russia comprised an insignificant portion of the world's literature. Alexander I. Herzen was the only important Russian writer whose works were banned in Russia.[29]

PUNISHMENT AND THE COURTS

In the land that foreigners knew as "the kingdom of the knout, chains, and Siberian exile," the laws in fact were extremely lenient and humane. Russia was the only country to have abolished the death penalty for civil crimes (in the reign of Elizabeth Petrovna [1740-62]). The death penalty was retained only for courts-martial and for the highest crimes against the state. Throughout the entire nineteenth century—except for executions during the Polish revolt [1863-64] and violations of military discipline—fewer than one hundred persons were executed in one hundred years. Omitting the regicides of 1 March [1881], the reign of Alexander III witnessed the execution of only the handful of persons who conspired to assassinate the emperor [1887] (one of whom was a certain Alexander I. Ulyanov—Lenin's brother).

The Fundamental Law on State Security[30] instituted administrative exile for broad application against all types of anti-government agitation. There were various degrees of exile: to Siberia, to the northern provinces (or "not so distant places"), and sometimes merely to provincial cities. Exiles without means received a state subsidy for living expenses. In places of exile special colonies formed among those who shared a common fate. Often these exile colonies produced subcultures which bred future revolutionaries, permitting them to establish connections, develop acquaintances, and reinforce their hatred for the system. The Schlüsselburg fortress on an island in the upper Neva River [near St. Petersburg] was the place of confinement for those considered most dangerous.

Russian courts, reorganized under the judicial statutes of 1864, operated on the highest plane. The "Gogolesque characters" receded into the realm of legend. Respectful consideration for the accused, the broadest protection of the rights of defendants, and a distinguished corps of jurists won the justifiable pride of the Russian people and reflected the mood of society. The judicial regulations were among the few laws that the public not only respected but was ready to defend against authorities determined to amend and vitiate the liberal code in an effort to bolster their fight against crime.

EDUCATION

The cultural level of the Russian people was difficult to assess. Based on the ratio of educational institutions and students to the general population, most European countries clearly surpassed Russia. In 1894 the nine Russian universities enrolled 14,327 students. All higher education including technical, military, and art academies and institutes, numbered 25-30,000 students. Approximately 900 secondary schools counted 224,000 students, with 75,500 of them enrolled in schools for women. Some 3,360,000 children attended 72,000 primary schools of all types. Students altogether accounted for slightly less than 3 percent of the empire's population.[31] This percentage was comparatively large for an Asian country, but students formed about 10 percent of the population of western countries with systems of compulsory public education.

About 850 periodicals and one hundred daily newspapers (exclusive of official provincial bulletins) were available to Russians in 1894. The leading opposition papers were St. Petersburg's *Novosti* [The News] and Moscow's *Russkiia vedomosti* [Russian Gazette]. Alexis S. Suvorin's moderate *Novoe vremia* [New Times] enjoyed the widest circulation. On the right were Prince Meshchersky's *Grazhdanin* [The Citizen] and Katkov's *Moskovskie vedomosti* [Moscow Gazette], the influence of which declined after Katkov's death [in 1887]. Among the "thick magazines" [monthlies] only *Russkii vestnik* [The Russian Herald] maintained a conservative orientation. *Vestnik evropy* [The Herald of Europe] and *Russkaia mysl* [Russian Thought] expressed liberal views, while *Russkoe bogatstvo* [Russian Wealth] and *Mir bozhii* [The World of God] were beginning to acquire a socialist tinge. *Severnyi vestnik* [The Northern Messenger] stood alone, scorning the hackneyed materialism of the sixties but holding politically aloof from the government. The provincial press was more barren and dull than the journals of the capitals. Even so, a restrained oppositional tone permeated provincial journalism except for the *Kievlianin* [Kiev Citizen] of Professor Dmitry I. Pikhno. The Bolsheviks remember the provinces as the nursery of the Marxist press. Russia's 1,315 publishing houses issued 16,541 editions of books and other non-periodic literature in 1894. St. Petersburg produced about 6,000 and Moscow about 2,500 titles. Several tens of millions of copies went into circulation.

With the entry of the zemstvos into the field, public libraries increased rapidly to approach four thousand. The leading institution was the Imperial Public Library with its collection of one-and-a-half million books and readers numbering fifteen thousand annually. Major collections also existed in the Academy of Sciences, the Rumiantsev Museum in Moscow, and at all universities. The law required publishers to deposit one copy of each book with the Academy of Sciences and the Imperial Library.

Foreign observers repeatedly noted the high level of culture among Russia's educated circles, a fact expressed in the international pre-eminence of nineteenth-century Russian literature. Foreigners also noted that Russian women enjoyed greater access to education and were closer to achieving civil and social equality with men than women in Western Europe and especially in the Roman Catholic countries. In reminiscing about a visit to Russia in 1892 Professor Jules Legras[32] remarked that "Russia is literally swarming with lycées (gymnasia) for women.... The serious development of women's education in Russia also has its advantages.... One feels that their minds have passed through a school different from the fashionable convents of our pupils.... Russian young ladies are less reserved, and more natural than the girls in our boarding schools." This was an interesting observation for a man who generally discussed Imperial Russia without sympathy.

LITERATURE

The early nineties formed a colorless interlude in Russian literature. Feodor M. Dostoevsky and Ivan S. Turgenev were dead. Tolstoy had set aside belles-lettres and was engaged in preaching his doctrines. Afanasy A. Fet, who had devoted the last years of his life to his magnificent *Evening of Lights*, died in 1892. Of the lesser writers Vsevolod M. Garshin, Gleb I. Uspensky, and Alexis F. Pisemsky were dead, as were the poets Alexis N. Apukhtin and Semyon Ya. Nadson, so widely acclaimed in their time. Others were living out their last years: Apollon N. Maikov, Jacob P. Polonsky, and Nicholas S. Leskov. Among the newer writers Anton P. Chekov, still not generally recognized, waited in the shadow of Vladimir G. Korolenko. Dmitry S. Merezhkovsky, Vladimir V. Hippius, and Nicholas M. Minsky, leaders of the so-called "decadents" centered on *Severnyi vestnik*, were beginning to cause a few ripples. Constantine D. Balmont published his first book in 1894. The talented but alcoholic poet Constantine M. Fofanov stood off by himself. A political bias dominated literary criticism over which Nicholas K. Mikhailovsky exerted considerable influence. Critics judged literature for its social value, and that was understood to be rather limited. Nearly the entire literary world heaped abuse on *Severnyi vestnik* for daring to defend art for its own sake.

THE ARTS

Russian architecture shared the doleful universal decline of the art. The utilitarian spirit of the century seemed to have overwhelmed all creativity in this field. Enormous quantities of ugly four and five-story apartment houses were thrown up to shelter the rapidly growing urban population. There was no time for churches or palaces.

A school of realist painters concerned with "social utility" enjoyed great popularity. Known as *peredvizhniki* (wanderers), they moved their exhibits from city to city and attracted uncommon numbers of viewers—25-44,000 in St. Petersburg and up to 27,000 in Moscow.[33] Exhibits at the Academy of Arts meanwhile never drew more than 18-20,000. Valentin A. Serov was not yet the equal of the contemporary masters, Ivan N. Kramskoy, Ilya Ye. Repin, Vasily I. Surikov, and Vasily V. Vereshchagin. Ivan K. Aivazovsky's seascapes were fashionable, but the religious spirit of the works of Victor M. Vasnetsov and Michael V. Nesterov won them a devoted admirer in Alexander III. The sculptor Mark M. Antokolsky had no rival.

AGRICULTURE

Seven-eighths of the population of the Russian Empire lived in rural villages and only one-eighth in cities. The overriding importance of agriculture was obvious, and yet it was the most stagnant sector of the national economy.

The abolition of serfdom seriously undermined private landownership without significantly improving the economic lot of the peasantry. Communal landownership prevented the poor from becoming landless, but at the same time it inhibited the strong energetic peasants. The worst possible situation resulted. Nevertheless prosperous individuals gradually began to emerge out of the peasantry and they began to buy up the land of the gentry. By the early nineties the gentry had sold more than a quarter of its holdings of 1861. This process together with some improvement of agricultural technique barely managed to offset the rapid growth of population.

A Village in Northern Russia

Enough bread was available to feed the growing number of mouths, but the allotment per person barely increased. Crop failures therefore affected the entire economy. The famine of 1891, exceptional in magnitude, cost the government about half a billion rubles in relief to suffering peasants, loss of tax revenues, suspended grain exports, and delay of the pending monetary reform.

The birth rate in European Russia declined from its 1891 average of 4.9 percent to 4.5 percent in 1892, while the death rate rose from 3.4 percent to 4 percent. The natural growth of population in 1892 was 600,000, about a third of the norm. Deaths directly attributable to starvation were few, but weakened resistance to disease caused the death rate to accelerate.

European Russia annually produced about two billion puds of grain. Although Russia exported only one-fifth of its harvest, the empire was Europe's chief source of grain. Russian flax has been famous since ancient times, and Russian fields raised more than half of the world's production. In the western provinces blue fields of flax alternated with golden fields of wheat. Sugar-beet cultivation, rapidly expanding, covered about 300,000 desiatins in 1894. Russia ranked first in horses with twenty-six million at the beginning of the nineties, and land cultivation depended almost entirely on horse power. Russia also had about thirty-three million head of cattle and sixty-four million sheep. In the distant regions of the north reindeer, and in Central Asia camels, served practical purposes and there were a half million of each. Swine-breeding—Russia had about eleven million pigs—was rather poorly distributed. Russians annually consumed about 175,000,000 puds of meat. The fishing industry, according to incomplete statistics, annually yielded about 70,000,000 puds.[34]

INDUSTRY

The pace of industrial development was quickening. By 1894 industry employed more than a million and a half workers, and the value of manufactured goods approached two billion rubles. Textiles, the largest industrial sector, employed more than a third of the industrial work force. The domestic market originally supplied most of industry's raw materials, but by

Batum around 1890.

1894 the textile makers were consuming imported cotton, wool, and silk. Cotton production had expanded rapidly, [35] but Russian producers could meet only 30 percent of the industrial requirement.

Just under a third of the labor force worked in mining and metallurgy. The old mining and metallurgical centers of the Urals, once an abundant source of diverse natural resources, were falling behind the Donets Basin in coal production, Krivoy Rog in iron ore, Baku in oil, and even behind the Lena gold fields of eastern Siberia. Only platinum production, a natural monopoly of Russia, remained supreme in the Urals.

Labor legislation already on the books included prohibitions against night work for women and children, restrictions on the workday for juveniles, regulations on hiring practices and safety measures, and the establishment of a system of factory inspectors to monitor compliance with the protective labor laws. Workers were an indistinguishable minority in the population until the 1880s. Most workers traditionally retained their ties with the villages, and factories provided only seasonal work. But then a "hereditary proletariat" began to form around some of the biggest factories. By 1894 industrial expansion had made labor a vital factor in the national economy.

The state itself was a major factor in the economy. It owned more than half the land of the empire, although it was mostly wasteland—tundra, desert, marshes, and Siberian taiga. Although state lands practically disappeared from European Russia after the emancipation of the state peasants, they continued to produce a modest annual income of 14,000,000 rubles. The richest source of state revenue was the northern and Siberian forests which, even lightly exploited, yielded several million rubles a year. State factories, primarily for the production of armaments, were not operated for profits.

RAILROADS: THE GREAT SIBERIAN RAILWAY

The unusual variety of climatic, soil, and animal breeding conditions required an unceasing struggle to hold the empire together. Consequently enormous effort went into the development of communications. By the end of 1894 the empire contained 32,500 versts [21,450 miles] of railroad, 150,000 versts [99,000 miles] of telegraph lines, 45,000 versts [29,700 miles] of navigable rivers (and two thousand river steamers), and 23,000 versts [15,180 miles] of paved road.

In 1891 the government began construction of the world's longest railway, the Great Siberian. In May 1891, at the end of his tour across Asia, Tsarevich Nicholas Alexandrovich laid the first track at the eastern terminus in Vladivostok. Economic factors provided less justification for the construction of the Siberian railway than Russia's determination to "secure a firm footing" on the Pacific and play an active role in the destiny of Asia, and particularly the Far East. The heir-apparent chaired the construction committee and took an active interest in its enterprise.

THE STATE BUDGET

After fifteen years of peace, Russian finances had recovered from the shock of the war of 1877-78. For several years after the war the paper ruble traded at two-thirds its nominal value. The policy of the government was to raise foreign loans with gold while using paper rubles at home. In this way it would accumulate a gold reserve sufficient to stabilize the ruble. Tax revenues increased substantially without an increase in the tax rate. Under the direction of Witte, who became minister in 1892, the ministry of finance managed not only the budget but in effect the entire national economy. It negotiated trade agreements, directed industry, commerce, and shipping, and even operated its own training institutes. The state budget surpassed one billion rubles around 1890. In 1894 direct taxes contributed less than 10 percent of estimated revenues. Indirect taxes added about 50 percent (half of that from taverns). State properties, mainly railroads and forests, produced about 15 percent, while redemption payments from peasants (for land received at the time of emancipation) made up about 8 percent. The rest came from stamp, mail, and telegraph revenues and from the redemption of government loans. Governmental expenditure per person was about 10 rubles, far less than the other great powers. Even so, it was an appreciable sum for a nation with such a low standard of living. Contemporary socialist "economists" nevertheless grossly exaggerated and fantastically distorted the facts.

Nicholas F. Danielson ("Nikolay-on") for example asserted
that the treasury took 90 percent of the peasants' income and
gradually forced them into bankruptcy and the sale of their
equipment and livestock.

FOREIGN TRADE

After nearly two centuries of international economic activity
Russia had established a secure place for itself in the world
market. For the past decade the annual value of exports
had exceeded a billion rubles, although in 1892 the embargo
on wheat reduced the total to 880,000,000 rubles. This gave
Russia an annual trade surplus of 150-200,000,000 rubles.
England was Russia's best customer, but Germany was a close
second, and together they accounted for half of Russia's
foreign trade. France held third place with only 7 percent.
Russia enjoyed a favorable balance of trade with all countries
except the United States, Egypt (a source of cotton), and
China (tea). Wheat, accounting for more than half, was the
leading export followed by flax and timber; petroleum ranked
sixth. The chief imports were cotton, metals and machinery,
tea, and wool. Nearly ten million tons of shipping turned
around in Russian ports.

About a third of the 313,000 subjects who emigrated in
1894 were Russian nationals, while less than one-third of
the 300,000 immigrants were Russian. On balance Russia lost
about 40,000 persons a year to emigration, mainly to the
United States. A sizable number of the emigrants were Jews
departing for America from the Pale of Settlement, a belt
extending through the Kingdom of Poland and the fifteen
western provinces of Belorussia, Malorussia, and Novorossiia.[36]

THE ANTAGONISTIC ATTITUDE OF THE INTELLIGENTSIA

Some of the Russian intelligentsia wanted to prove that the
peasantry were impoverished and headed for ruin. Others,
venting the same animosity toward the established order,
attempted to prove the inevitability of an economic renaissance according to a western model. Some even welcomed
such a development as a step forward. "All of today's spiritual
and material culture is closely tied to capitalism," wrote

the young economist Peter B. Struve in 1894 in his first legally published book. "They grew together in the same soil." "But," he continued, "blinded by excessive vanity, we think we can substitute the moods of our own 'critical thought' for generations of difficult cultural achievement and the hard struggle of economic forces and interests. . . . No, let us admit our lack of culture and go to capitalism for schooling." The Russian economy had many deficiencies, of course. The western nations, with their limited areas and concentrated populations, had far outdistanced Russia in technological development.

But the principal threat to the Russian state was neither economic inadequacy nor technological backwardness! The root of the evil was the abysmal antagonism between the crown and a considerable part of educated society. The intelligentsia regarded the emperor with fixed hostility, which it sometimes expressed openly. Sometimes these antagonists suppressed their animosity, but if so it was certain to erupt with redoubled intensity. In the first half of the nineteenth century Russian authors still appreciated the necessity of the tsar's authority. Alexander S. Pushkin, Gogol, and Vasily A. Zhukovsky, not to mention Nicholas M. Karamzin, all left many pages clearly attesting to that. Even then their contemporaries among the intelligentsia followed a different course. Vissarion G. Belinsky's scathing denunciation of Gogol's *Correspondence with Friends* was far more characteristic of the intelligentsia than of Belinsky himself.[37] The intelligentsia ignored the mature Pushkin's appraisal of Nicholas I and instead copied and circulated his youthful attacks against the emperor.

The Decembrist revolt first created this schism among the educated elite by undermining the tsar's confidence in his military aristocracy.[38] He was compelled then to favor and rely increasingly on courtiers and civil servitors formerly dependent on the crown. The era of the great reforms initially improved relations by creating new careers for the educated in agronomy and rural administration and development. Once again, however, extremists poisoned the cooperation between the crown and intelligentsia. Reform generated demands for yet more reform, and dissidents used the new freedoms to defame the government. Only five years after emancipation, a terrorist made the first attempt on the life of the Tsar-Liberator, Alexander II.

Still, the best writers of the day sided with the government rather than the intelligentsia. Leo Tolstoy's work appeared in Katkov's *Russkii vestnik* until the late seventies. As a youth Dostoevsky joined a socialist circle and had suffered cruelly for it.[39] Then in *The Possessed* he brilliantly exposed the nature of the Russian revolutionaries, while in *The Diary of a Writer* he defended Russia's imperative need for unlimited monarchial authority. Also arrayed in the conservative camp were Fet, Feodor I. Tiutchev, Maikov, and basically even Count Alexis K. Tolstoy—"not a fighter in either camp, but an occasional guest."[40] Pisemsky's *Aroused Sea* presented an unattractive sketch of the "men of the sixties," and even Turgenev, a westerner, portrayed the "nihilists" in an unappealing light in *Fathers and Sons*, *Smoke*, and *Virgin Soil*.[41]

REVOLUTIONARY MOVEMENTS OF THE 1870s AND 1880s

Unfortunately, these writers did not set the tone! The most pervasive influence came from the radical critics, those preachers of materialism, irreconcilable prosecutors of the existing order. They demanded not only political but also basic social change, as if the abolition of serfdom was not in itself a tremendous social reform. The intelligentsia adopted the most extreme teachings of the west. The "going to the people" movement [*V narod*] began with the aim of spreading these doctrines among the peasantry in order to incite revolutions like those of Yemalyan I. Pugachev and Stenka Razin, or "ataman Stepan" as he appeared in the popular novel *The Cliff*.[42] But the peasants were not tricked by these exhortations and promises. The people mistrusted these strange ideas, and "going to the people" was a complete fiasco. Then, under the leadership of the infamous "party of The People's Will" [*Narodnaia volia*], an armed guerrilla campaign burst out against the crown.[43]

Compensating for lack of numbers with daring and imagination, the revolutionaries succeeded in creating the impression of a powerful anti-monarchic movement. They confounded the government and impressed foreigners. The People's

The English Quay, St. Petersburg

Will posed a constant threat to the life of the tsar-liberator, blowing up the rails in front of his train and even a section of the Winter Palace. Educated Russians maliciously stood aside while the struggle raged between the emperor and the nihilists. Alexander II decided to win this vacillating element to the side of the crown, but he failed to devise a workable plan. Inevitably, on the first day of March 1881 the tsar was murdered.

The horrible report stunned the nation, sobered many, and isolated the leaders of The People's Will. Fully aware of the extreme danger, Alexander III courageously decided, nevertheless, to meet his enemies head on. Confronted with such resoluteness, the nihilist onslaught disintegrated like a phantom.

PASSIVE RESISTANCE AND REPRESSION

Was there really any change in the attitude of the intelligentsia during the reign of Alexander III? They settled down and grew silent; their hostility receded from the surface, but it did not vanish. Every constructive effort by the government encountered their muted, politely restrained, but uncompromising opposition. The fever only appeared to have broken. There was another ominous character to these years. Writers of the new generation no longer dissented from the intelligentsia's attitude toward the existing order. The few who felt suffocated in the barracks of radicalism simply moved into pure art and remained aloof from public affairs. Among Tolstoy's radically revised teachings, the doctrines of "non-resistance to evil" and Christian rationalism gained far fewer adherents than his renunciation of all political systems.

The passive resistance of the intelligentsia placed a great strain on the government, especially in the field of education. Despite, or partly because of a series of strict new regulations on student life (uniforms, compulsory attendance, and the like), sedition seethed within the universities. The authorities naturally harbored distrust for institutions of higher learning. They simply closed some, like the Medical College for Women, and they suspended admission to others. The Women's University at St. Petersburg accepted no applications for three years.[44] But the government had to tack between the Scylla of stifling education and the Charybdis of nurturing its own enemies. A typical incident demonstrated the extent of the intolerance confronting the government: Professor Kliuchevsky, the famous historian, was very popular with the students, but his speech honoring Alexander III evoked such a hostile reaction that it was some time before he regained his former prestige. Under the circumstances the authorities found it difficult to expand local education for fear of transforming the villages into centers of anti-government agitation.

To continue to develop and improve the world's largest state in the face of substantial opposition from educated Russians was a task of extraordinary difficulty. Efforts to expand the role of the nobility in the state—through the creation of the Nobles' Bank and establishment of the post of superintendent of peasantry [*zemskii nachalnik*][45]—seemed essential to Russia's rulers in order to augment the ranks of the power structure.

"Our youth, I say it with bitterness, are skeptical," Leontiev had written two decades earlier. "We have lived a long time, yet our spirit has created little, and we are standing at the dreadful brink . . . .   In the West storms and outbursts generally were louder, more majestic. The West possesses a more platonic character. But the unique, more peaceful and profound vitality that permeates the soil and structure of our Russia is worth the turmoil and convulsions of the West.

"In the West the spirit of self-preservation was stronger among the upper classes, and the eruptions consequently were more violent. Our sense of self-preservation is weak. Our society is more inclined to follow the course of others. . . . Who knows? Faster than others? God grant that I am wrong!"

⟡

Attempted assassination

CHAPTER TWO

NICHOLAS AS TSAREVICH

Russia knew very little about its new emperor at the time of his accession. The dominating personality of Alexander III shielded him from outsiders, so the public had acquired only the scantiest information about the tsarevich. He was twenty-six years old and in build and appearance resembled his mother, Empress Maria Feodorovna. He held the rank of colonel in the Russian army. In Japan during a world tour, which itself was unusual for his time, an Asiatic fanatic had attempted to assassinate him.[1] The tsarevich served as chairman of the commission for the construction of the Great Siberian Railway, and in 1891-92 he headed the famine committee. His tenure on the state military council brought no special notice. He was engaged to Princess Alice of Hesse, the granddaughter of Queen Victoria, and his fiancée had joined him in Livadia just before the death of his father. That was about the extent of the public's knowledge about the new monarch.

"Rarely does a nation have such a vague idea of the personality and attributes of its new sovereign as the Russian nation today," reported the German charge d'affaires. "The basis for estimating his virtues and attitudes is extremely meager. From my own personal impressions and the opinions of highly placed persons of the Russian court I gather that the emperor is a spiritually gifted person, noble in thought, discrete, and tactful. His manner is quite unpretentious, and he appears so passive that one easily could conclude that he lacks determination. His associates assure me, however, that he is strong-willed but that his utterly mild manner disguises his firmness."

His Majesty the Emperor Nicholas II was born on 6 May 1868, the feast of St. Job the Long-Suffering, as he himself often recalled. As eldest son of the heir to the throne, he too

Tsarevich Nicholas Alexandrovich

was "raised to the purple," and his entire upbringing bore the
mark of his destined role. He received a rather thorough
education. From childhood he studied several foreign languages [English, French, and German], which he learned to
perfection. Following a course of general studies directed by
General Gregory G. Danilovich, the tsarevich moved on to
advanced legal and military studies. His tutors were all distinguished professors: C.P. Pobedonostsev, N. Kh. Bunge,
Michael N. Kapustin, Yegor Ye. Zamyslovsky, and Generals
Genrikh A. Leer and Michael I. Dragomirov. On completion
of his formal studies, the heir was introduced to the practical
side of military affairs. He served with the household troops
of the Preobrazhensky regiment and the Horse Artillery and
spent two summers with the Life Guards Hussar regiment. He
also began to attend the sessions of the State Council and the
Committee of Ministers and thus to become familiar with
state policy. The premature death of Alexander III interrupted
the heir's thorough, meticulous preparation for the throne,
and this side of Nicholas's education was never completed.
Alexander, confident of a long life, had failed to initiate the
heir into the higher affairs of state. Nicholas had to absorb
most of those matters after his accession from the reports of
his ministers.[2]

THE EMPEROR'S CHARACTER

By the time he came to the throne the emperor's character
and philosophy were fully developed, of course. Scarcely anyone, however, appreciated their dimensions. His entire conception of his role rested on his faith in God and in the tsar's
obligations as God's agent. He believed that he alone was
responsible for the destiny of Russia and that he would
answer for this trust before the throne of the Almighty. Some
might assist and others might obstruct him, but God would
judge him alone for his custodianship of Russia. As the
responsibility was solely his, so too was the power. Responsibility could not be delegated to those not chosen to rule. The
ministers, in his opinion, already exerted too much influence.
"They will mess things up, but I will have to answer for it"—
that comment summed up how the emperor saw things.

Nicholas possessed a lively mind. He quickly grasped the
essence of a report, as anyone who had official contact with

him attested without exception. He had an extraordinary memory, especially for recalling faces. He completed his programs with persistent, unflagging determination, continuously returning to projects set aside and in the end bringing them to fruition.

His velvet glove concealed an iron fist, but his will did not reveal itself like a peal of thunder that erupts in a crescendo or a rumbling cadence. It was more like the even flow of a stream from a mountain through the plains and into the sea, circumventing obstacles, meandering, but persevering steadfastly to the end of its course. His detractors mistook this manner for weakness.

Ministers whom the emperor had to dismiss frequently complained that he was "undependable." But what did that mean? The testimony of these very same ministers revealed quite the opposite. Witte, for example, admitted that even under unfavorable conditions Nicholas displayed cool resolve in carrying out projects that he (Witte) had recommended. The ministers, in truth, could not depend on the sovereign to further their personal careers. He always put business ahead of personalities. When he disagreed with a minister's actions, he dismissed him without regard for past service. But he always tried to "sugar-coat the pill." Some formal sign of appreciation and the award of a generous pension invariably accompanied dismissal. He disliked face to face confrontations over anything disagreeable; perhaps to some extent this was a shortcoming. He particularly disliked confrontations with those with whom he had worked for a long time and to whom he was grateful for many past services. But that was a matter of form not substance. There was no "perfidy" in this, as his enemies alleged. Perfidy presupposes intent and calculation. But what was the advantage to the tsar if he cordially received a minister in the afternoon and dismissed him by letter in the evening? The cordial audience emphasized the absence of personal animosity while the dismissal testified to a conflict over matters of state.

Before his accession, Nicholas II had demonstrated his strength of will in only one important matter. In Russia tradition did not permit members of the tsar's family to express political differences. Nicholas could not applaud publicly a speech against his father's government, as the German *a courtship*

crown prince did in the Reichstag in 1911. The tsarevich showed his determination only in matters that concerned him personally. Early in his youth he fell in love with the little princess, Alice of Hesse, younger sister of the Grand Duchess Elizabeth Feodorovna, the wife of his uncle. For ten years he cherished her in his memory. Alexander III and the Empress Maria Feodorovna opposed his marriage—they wanted no union with a German princess.[3] Speculation centered on a marriage to Princess Helen of Orleans, daughter of the [Count of Paris], the pretender to the French throne. But the tsarevich yearned only for Alice, and with gentle persistence he rejected the French plan. Finally his parents gave in, and their engagement took place in the spring of 1894. In this struggle of several years the tsarevich proved the stronger.

Even his enemies acknowledged his exceptional personal charm. He despised ceremonies and demonstrative speeches, found protocol burdensome, and deplored artificiality, pomp, and publicity (a deficiency of our own time as well!). In intimate circles or personal conversation, whether speaking with lofty officials or lowly workmen during a factory inspection, he fascinated his interlocutors. His large radiant grey eyes peered directly into one's soul and lent power to his words. His thorough training reinforced these natural qualities. "Never in my life have I met a person of better breeding than the reigning sovereign, Nicholas II," wrote Count Witte after he had parted with the emperor.

POBEDONOSTSEV'S VIEWS AND INFLUENCE

Absolute monarchs seldom have time to expound their theories in lengthy tracts. Catherine II was an exception, but neither Louis XIV nor Maria Theresa paused to philosophize, and only a few winged phrases of Peter the Great have come down to us. Monarchs act out their convictions; their actions speak for themselves. It is for others to provide abstract justifications for the labors of monarchs.

Pobedonostsev published his *Moscow Collection* in 1896, at the very beginning of the new reign. The contention that the philosophy he expressed was identical to the native attitudes of the tsar was not far from the mark. A French newspaper correctly recommended a translation of this work to its readers for these reasons: "One must read this book, first because Mr. Pobedonostsev thinks profoundly, second because he thinks differently than we do, and third because Emperor Nicholas II and his people think as he does." Even now, after forty years, many of the thoughts in this remarkable book seem uniquely appropriate. One must pause over them, however briefly, to understand much about the reign of Nicholas II. Even then people were warning that Russia was *not ready* for democracy, *not ready* for socialism, *not ready* for this or that type of reform—all the shibboleths seemingly dictated by progress. Those who stood at the helm of the Russian Empire in 1894 did not regard western institutions as a step forward or even as evidence of great maturity. Instead, they critically examined the essence of those institutions.

Parliamentary government is "the greatest lie of our time," wrote Pobedonostsev. "History bears witness that the most essential, productive, and enduring measures emanate from the concentrated will of statesmen or the lofty ideas and deep thought of an enlightened minority. It also testifies that the debasement of political ideas and the vulgarization of popular opinion originated with the representative principle."[4]

Legislative and executive irresponsibility virtually dominated the democracies, he continued. "Mistakes, abuses, and arbitrary actions occur daily under ministerial rule, and yet how often we are reminded of what sober, responsible people these ministers are. Once in fifty years perhaps is a minister tried for misconduct, but the result is inconsequential compared with the fanfare attending the trial." (This observation, although probably inspired by the Panama scandal, is no less relevant to our own time.) The evil that Pobedonostsev perceived in the parliamentary system was that the electoral process selected not the best but "the most ambitious and impudent." He held that electoral campaigns were particularly dangerous to a multi-national state:

Autocracy manages to avoid or to reconcile demands and disruptions not simply by resorting to force but by equalizing all rights and relationships through its unifying power. But democracy cannot resolve this competition, and particularist impulses disrupt the state. The nationalities of each region elect delegates, but these delegates do not express the interests of the state and community. They represent tribal instincts, tribal aspirations, and tribal hatred for the dominant and other allied nationalities and for the political structure that unites them all. Austria

offers a vivid example of the cacophonous consequences of parliamentary government in a multi-national state . . . .

The absolute power of parliament supersedes the absolute power of
the monarchy, but with this difference: the person of the sovereign
embodies a unified will, whereas in a parliament everything is fortuitous, for the parliamentary will is nothing but the expression of a
majority. . . . Such a condition leads irresistibly to anarchy. Then, only
dictatorship can save society, that is, only the restoration of a single
will and a single power. . . .

After some time, faith in the parliamentary mechanism weakens.
Only the liberal intelligentsia exalt it; the people groan under its yoke
and comprehend the lie that it conceals. We may not see it, but our
children and grandchildren most assuredly will witness the destruction
of this idol before which self-deluded intellectuals now bow and scrape.

Pobedonostsev was even more incisive and caustic in his
criticism of the periodical press—

Who are the representatives of that dreadful power that calls itself
public opinion? Who confers on them the right and the authority to
rule in the name of society? Who nominates them to subvert the existing order and to proclaim new ideals of moral and positive law?

Any rogue off the streets, any windbag from the herd of unacknowl-
edged geniuses, any confidence man with funds of his own or money
filched from others can establish a newspaper, even a prominent one.
. . . Experience shows that money is always able to buy the talent it
needs and that those phrasemongers will produce whatever their editors
demand. The record proves that the most contemptible persons—retired usurers, Yid merchants, touts, card sharks—can found a paper,
hire gifted writers, and put out a sheet purporting to be an organ of
public opinion.

In journalism, as in parliaments, the same irresponsibility pre-
vails: "Have not a few superficial and unscrupulous journalists paved the way for revolutions? Have they not fanned
minor aggravations into class and national hatreds and produced devastating wars? Conduct like this would cost a monarch his throne; a minister would be disgraced, prosecuted,
and punished. But the journalist stands above the turmoil he
creates. Emerging triumphant from the ruin and general disaster that he has produced, the journalist cheerfully resumes
his work of destruction."

The idea of progress—the demand for unremitting change
—elicited this rebuke from Pobedonostsev:

There is among humanity a force of the utmost importance, the earthen
force of inertia. Like the ballast of a ship, inertia sustains mankind

Constantine P. Pobedonostsev

through the buffeting of history. Without it measured progress becomes unthinkable. This force, which the vapid thinkers of the new school confuse with ignorance and stupidity, is absolutely essential to the welfare of society. Destroy it, and you deprive society of the stability which is the basis of any further development. The principal fallacy of modern progressivism is its contempt for or ignorance of this force . . . .

Ambition or the craving for recognition is the ailment common to all so-called statesmen. In our day life surges by at an immeasurable pace, statesmen succeed statesmen, and everyone burns with impatience to achieve fame while there still is time, while he still holds the wheel . . . . Everyone wants to be the initiator of something, to put everything on some new basis. . . . Modern statesmen are enamored of that supreme act of creation—to make something out of nothing. Their excited imaginations answer every objection with the well-worn response that 'the establishment will support itself—it will produce its own men, and they will appear at the right moment . . . .'

The word *reform* is now so common that we have confused it with *improvement* . . . . The person posing as the representative of new ideas, the reformer who walks around with plans for the construction of new institutions in his hands—he is the one who wins credence right from the start. Politics is full of *architects.* Anyone who would be a laborer, landlord, or tenant must first be an architect . . . . Is it any wonder that the best people retire—or worse and even more common —that without leaving their posts they become indifferent to their duties, that they simply hang on and go through the motions for the sake of personal gain or preferment? Such are the fruits of the unrestrained passion for reform . . . . The ancient oracle advised: 'Do not exceed the limits of your destiny. Do not attempt more than your capacities allow.' What excellent advice! All wisdom lies in the concentration of strength and thought, all evil in its dispersion.

These words, which partly reflected Pobedonostsev's critical judgment of the era of Alexander II, were also meant as a warning to his contemporaries.

Pobedonostsev also reflected on the question of public education. He recognized that it was more complex than the simple notion which held that any accumulation of knowledge was a blessing.

It goes without saying that knowledge is light and ignorance is darkness. But those who apply this formula must recognize its limitations and employ common sense . . . . What great harm we have done by merging the concepts of knowledge and skill! Swept along by the illusion of general enlightenment, we have come to define education as a certain sum of knowledge . . . . We forget, or choose to ignore, that most of the children in our care must live by the daily bread that they must

earn. They do not survive on the possession of pure knowledge, they
live by their ability to perform certain tasks . . . .

The people's conception of education is valid. Unfortunately, thinkers of the modern school have distorted it. The popular idea holds that
the school is responsible for teaching reading, writing, and arithmetic
and, inseparable from these, the duty to know, love, and fear God, to
love the fatherland, and to honor one's parents.

Another Russian thinker expressed this idea even more forcefully: "To scatter schools everywhere and fill them with
embittered blockheads is like feeding people stones instead of
bread."

The new sovereign absorbed all these ideas in his youth,
and they formed the essential part of his philosophy. He also
held the firm conviction that a hundred million Russian
subjects revered the sacred power of the tsar. He always
distinguished between the goodness of the people and the
animosity of the intelligentsia. Nicholas II was a faithful
and devoted son of the Orthodox Church, dedicated to the
greatness of Russia, and convinced especially of its destiny
in Asia. Yet he was also aware of the complexity of his times
and knew that the evil welling up throughout the world could
not be overcome simply by ignoring it.

Nicholas was, of course, the student of Pobedonostsev,
but only two months into the reign the German diplomat,
Count [Rex] correctly observed that "the Pobedonostsev era
has passed even though he will probably retain his position."
A decade later Pobedonostsev recalled, "In the first months I
was consulted occasionally . . . but later I was never consulted.[5] The *Moscow Collection* in other words formed a point of
departure for Nicholas II, not "law and prophecy." Mere
speculation? No, the entire course of his reign confirmed
it. No other direct proof existed. As a youth, he preferred
seclusion and scarcely confided even a portion of his inner-
most thoughts to anyone. Perhaps only the Empress Alexandra Feodorovna came to know the real emperor.

TAKING ON THE NEW PILOT

For about ten days after the death of Alexander III, all
official activity ceased. His remains were returned from the
Crimea to St. Petersburg for the solemn funeral and interment
in the Cathedral of Saint Peter and Paul. The streets of

St. Petersburg were draped in black mourning and white flags. A huge throng followed the cortege to the tomb. Only in early November did the ministers report to the new monarch. Besides disposing of pending matters, the ministers had to initiate Nicholas into the general operation of the machinery of state. He proved to be well informed on all essential matters except the more secret aspects of foreign policy. His questions to Witte indicated that as tsarevich he had been an attentive observer.

Foreign minister Giers "was delighted with His Majesty," according to the diary of Vladimir N. Lamsdorf. It was Giers who informed Nicholas of the essential provisions of the secret treaty with France. Nicholas immediately perceived the advantages of the agreement but was aware also of its challenge for the future. If it reduced the danger of war with Germany, it simultaneously created possible new areas of conflict. He realized that only by transforming the Franco-Russian Alliance into a general agreement among the great powers could he truly guarantee the peace of Europe and ensure the superiority of Christian Europe. The first circular of the ministry of foreign affairs on 28 October 1894 declared that "Russia will remain unwaveringly faithful to its traditions. It will devote all efforts to the maintenance of friendly relations with all countries and, as before, will seek the true guaranty of its security in respect for international law and the legal order."

The tsar's attitude was no mere expression of felicitous sentiments. Two or three months later, in connection with the international convocation to mark the opening of the Kiel Canal, Nicholas told Lamsdorf, "It would be a pity if France refuses to participate. The French are wrong in withholding their response. Every country is invited, and French participation is essential."

"What does it actually matter to us?" asked Lamsdorf of his diary. But the emperor considered it a matter of great consequence in avoiding a new European war.

A FATEFUL MARRIAGE

The first major event of the reign was the marriage of the emperor and Princess Alice on 14 November 1894. The festivities were modest because of the period of mourning.

During the journey of the royal couple from the Winter Palace to the Anichkov Palace, the tsar ordered the removal of the soldiers who lined the route. As a result the well-wishers gathered in the streets crowded around the tsar's sleigh, and for the first time in many years Russians were able to see their sovereign at close hand. "It was a beautiful and daring gesture," wrote the *Journal des Débats*, noting that the new monarch was more accessible to the people than Alexander III, who had lived under the cloud of his father's tragic death.

Alice, who became the Empress [Alexandra Feodorovna] three weeks after Nicholas's accession, remained throughout her life his best friend and most faithful companion. Theirs was an exceptionally amicable and happy marriage. Only occasionally did the illness of the children darken the life of the imperial family. The empress, who fully shared her husband's views, had little to do with affairs of state until the last difficult years of his reign.

MINISTERIAL CHANGES

Out of deep respect for his father, Nicholas at first did not replace any of Alexander's associates. He parted with them gradually as differences arose over official policies. Two important changes did take place in the first weeks of the reign however. Nicholas dismissed General Joseph V. Gurko, the governor-general of Poland, and he removed [Apollon K.] Krivoshein from his post as minister of transportation.[6] If Witte is correct, Gurko's retirement resulted from a "ministerial request" that he submitted to the emperor: do as I ask or retire me. Such tactlessness is difficult to believe, but true or not the emperor hardly appreciated such bluntness. Ministers and other officials had no right in his opinion to present ultimatums. Krivoshein's removal became necessary because of allegations that he used his position for personal enrichment. Strictly speaking he did nothing illegal, but Nicholas regarded indiscretion in financial matters intolerable conduct for a minister of the crown.[7]

Gurko's dismissal coincided with the tsar's reception of a delegation of the Polish nobility and immediately gave rise to rumors of a de-emphasis of "russification" in Poland. This produced undisguised joy in Warsaw, but no fundamental change in policy was forthcoming.

THE ZEMSTVO PETITIONS

The accession of the new sovereign initially inspired a dim hope of change in Russian society. The press welcomed the new empress and hinted that she might introduce into Russian life the traditions in which she had been raised. To the intelligentsia the advantages of the western political tradition were all too obvious and irrefutable. They were convinced that anyone who lived under a parliamentary system naturally endorsed and treasured it.

The zemstvo and noble assemblies heard voices that had been silent during the reign of Alexander III. Calls for popular representation—"the crowning of the edifice" as it was known in the reign of Alexander II—rang forth again. These were not isolated speeches. The assemblies of the nobility heard and approved appeals of this kind from some of the most loyal subjects of the crown. In the zemstvos the more radical elements sided with moderates in order to achieve greater unanimity. The zemstvo assemblies pretended to intercede for the majority of the Russian public, but most of the intelligentsia naturally found the zemstvo resolutions too mild. Not even a western constitution would have pleased them—witness their characterization of western life in the opposition press and the "thick [monthly] journals." But the first step is the most difficult; they assumed that once past this initial hurdle, other changes would follow at a rapid pace.

"SENSELESS DREAMS"

Nicholas therefore found it necessary to state his position publicly. A vague general acknowledgment of the petitions of the zemstvos would have been interpreted instantly as consent to begin a discussion of state affairs. Then constitutional reform, which the sovereign opposed, would have become inevitable, lest the public have felt itself betrayed. It is always difficult to reject the requests of loyal subjects. If the superficiality alleged to him was the real indication of the emperor's character, he would have issued some equivocal statement and later reversed himself in private. If the inconsistency which so irritated his ministers was genuine, he would have issued some obscure reply to these petitions for constitutional change. But Nicholas had no desire to deceive the public. Whatever the interpretation placed on his blunt rejection, the monarch's forthright statement was an act of political honesty.

In his speech to the zemstvo delegations on 17 January 1895 the sovereign declared: "It has come to my attention that recently the zemstvo assemblies have heard voices of those carried away by senseless dreams concerning the participation of zemstvo representatives in domestic affairs. Let everyone know that I, having dedicated all my strength to the welfare of the people, will preserve the principle of autocracy as firmly and steadfastly as my late unforgettable Father."

The phrase "senseless dreams" perfectly expressed the tsar's mind, although his unfortunate wording proved embarrassing. (It did appear, as has been insisted, in the original draft.) What mattered to him was the substance and not the form of the remark. Russia learned immediately that the young monarch did not intend to deviate from the firm defense of autocracy expressed in his predecessor's manifesto of 29 April 1881.[8]

THE HOSTILE PRESS

In the contradictory chorus of the foreign press the editorial of the most influential English paper, *The Times*,[9] was particularly noteworthy:

Russian institutions are not to be judged from a Western standpoint, nor is it much better than an impertinence to condemn them for want of conformity with ideas springing from widely different circumstances and a wholly dissimilar history. Judged by all the ordinary tests of national prosperity, the absolute rule of the Tsar seems to suit Russia very well, and it is not for foreigners in any case to presume to affirm that something else would suit her better. The mode of government which the Tsar has just asserted his determination to maintain can at least show a history of achievement in the building up of States which its rivals cannot pretend to equal. In Russia, at any rate, it must for the present be accepted as an ultimate fact.

The majority of the educated Russian public received the tsar's speech as a challenge, but because of the censorship the Russian press could not openly express this reaction. The "domestic reviews" of the monthly journals were typical. *Severnyi vestnik* of 1 February 1895 listed the tsar's speech to the zemstvo delegations first in its table of contents, followed by a series of insignificant items. It published the speech without a word of comment and proceeded directly to the next piece of trivia. The editors clearly were telling their readers, "Nothing could be added that would not be censored." The moderate-to-liberal *Russkaia mysl* remained bitterly quiet, but the socialist *Russkoe bogatstvo* took malicious delight in commenting that "Our public awaited the year 1895 with uncertainty in its soul, with anxiety and hope. The very first month of the new year has resolved all uncertainties. Our sovereign's speech of 17 January . . . was the historic event that ended all uncertainty and doubt . . . . The reign of Emperor Nicholas Alexandrovich begins as a direct continuation of the preceding reign."[10]

The speech of 17 January immediately gave rise to a myth which alleged that the firm tone of the speech scarcely corresponded to the general views of the emperor. Obviously someone else had dictated the speech to him. People then began to seek to determine "who was behind it," and speculation centered on Pobedonostsev and interior minister Ivan N. Durnovo. The German ambassador, General Bernhard F.W. von Werder, gave this version however: "Early in his reign, the people took a liking to him, praising to the skies all his actions and speeches. Now how everything has changed! It all began with the unexpectedly sharp speech of the emperor to the delegations. The speech was not written, as first thought, by minister Durnovo who learned from the war minister that the emperor intended to speak. The emperor personally wrote the speech and slipped it into his cap. The speech is being sharply criticized throughout the whole of Russia." The speech of 17 January dispelled any hope of the intelligentsia for constitutional reform from above. Thus it marked the resurgence of revolutionary agitation which now found a new target.

Foreign minister Giers died in the fourth month of the new reign. The vacancy precipitated a behind-the-scene struggle, because the advocates of the French alliance feared a new orientation. The emperor finally selected Prince Alexis B. Lobanov-Rostovsky, a former ambassador to Vienna, recently appointed to Berlin. The new and aged foreign minister, a connoisseur of rare books, represented the old aristocratic culture. The more ardent supporters of the French alliance at the court regarded Lobanov's appointment without sympathy.

The far eastern situation had grown extremely complex. After suspending military operations for the winter, Japan had resumed its offensive, destroying the remnant of the Chinese fleet at Weihaiwei and occupying southern Manchuria and the Liaotung Peninsula with Port Arthur. By spring Peking was easily within its grasp, and at that point China sued for peace.

The rapid growth of Japanese power signalled the awakening of Asia to Russia and the other European states. "Slumbering China" and even weaker Korea obviously made more desirable neighbors than the regenerated militaristic Japanese Empire which successfully had absorbed western military technology. Russia therefore took the lead in forming a united European front to reverse the Japanese conquests. Little could be expected from England, and the British immediately rejected a proposal to participate in the Sino-Japanese negotiation. Germany and France, however, accepted. In the Treaty of Shimoneseki of 5/17 April 1895 China ceded Formosa, the Pescadores Islands, and the Liaotung Peninsula, including Port Arthur, to Japan. China also surrendered its rights to Korea and agreed to pay an indemnity. The occupation of the Liaotung Peninsula gave Japan a strong position on the continent and a commanding position over the Gulf of Pechili and the seaward approaches to the Chinese capital. The Europeans decided to demand that Tokyo yield its territorial conquests on the mainland in return for a larger indemnity.

On 23 April the ambassadors of Russia, France, and Germany presented their demands to the Japanese foreign minister. The German ambassador pointed out that "resistance

against three great powers would be useless." Prince Lobanov-
Rostovsky already had reached an understanding with the
other powers. If Japan rejected the demand, their combined
fleets would sever communications between Japan and its
troops on the mainland. London would not consent but neither did it object. After some delay, the Japanese gave in. Japan retained most of its conquests and to "save face" was permitted to declare the validity of the Treaty of Shimoneseki.
By protecting defenseless China against powerful Japan the
three powers in this instance safeguarded the general interests
of Europe. The absorption of massive China by technically
powerful Japan would have upset the balance of power not
only in Asia but throughout the world. But France participated only because of the alliance with Russia, and for this
the French government came under strong domestic pressure.

THE FRANCO-RUSSIAN ALLIANCE

At Nicholas's insistence France agreed to participate in the
opening of the Kiel Canal. By this time President Casimir-
Perier, embittered by the constraints on presidential power,
had departed. Felix Faure succeeded him, and Alexander
Ribot with Gabriel Hanotaux as foreign minister replaced
Charles Dupuy as prime minister. The radicals continued their
bitter campaign against the government and, as usual, never
missed an opportunity to hurl patriotic arguments against it.

Protests against the dispatch of a French naval squadron to
Germany resounded through parliament and the press. Led by
Paul Déroulède, the guardians of the spirit of revenge already
had raised the alarm against French cooperation with Germany against the Treaty of Shimoneseki. Another outburst
occurred when the possibility of a combined naval action became known. The prospect of reconciliation with Germany
met no sympathy in leading political circles. The French government, in deference to Russia's wishes, leaned slightly in
that direction but without enthusiasm.

The latest assault against the cabinet opened in the chamber
of deputies on 10 June. An opposition spokesman demanded
to know the state of French relations with Russia and what
Russian friendship meant to France. In their response Ribot
and Hanotaux decided to pronounce for the first time the

term *alliance.* "Our fleet at Kiel," replied Ribot, "will be taking its position side by side with the fleet of our ally." The statement had a dramatic effect, and a vast majority carried a vote of confidence in the government.

The distinguished French journal *Revue des deux Mondes* (15 June 1895) discussed the opposition speeches: "They ask —what is an alliance to us if it does not begin with the return of Alsace and Lorraine? . . . Whatever the good intentions of the government in St. Petersburg, it would break off relations at the first hint of a move in this direction." This in fact revealed the inner contradiction of the Franco-Russian Alliance. Whereas Russia saw it as a means to achieve peace in Europe, it interested the French mainly as a means to recover Alsace, an objective that was hardly possible without a new great war.

To make attendance at Kiel more palatable to the French, the Russian government proposed that both squadrons rendezvous in Dutch waters and proceed together to Kiel. The celebration went off without a hitch. The Germans provided a grand reception for their guests. Their consideration even extended to the removal of the warships *Weissenburg* and *Wört*, reminders of the French defeats of 1870.

The German government was convinced thoroughly of the impossibility of an alliance between autocratic Russia and republican France. The ambassador to France, Count George H. Münster, stressed this theme in his account of Ribot's speech to the chamber: "It does not matter whether they say 'agreement' or 'alliance;' it is still an illegal cohabitation lacking the sanction of the emperor . . . . The majority of Frenchmen are satisfied with the expression 'alliance' and the comedy of a Franco-Russian debut at Kiel." Three years later, after formal ratification of the alliance, Münster observed that diplomatic secrets had been well kept in those days!

The Germans began to grow concerned when General Michael I. Dragomirov arrived in France to witness the autumn maneuvers just as a great new demonstration of Franco-Russian friendship welcomed Prince Lobanov-Rostovsky to Paris. On his return from France Lobanov was a guest at the estate of Count Phillip Eulenburg, who missed no opportunity to complain about Russian friendship with "the republicans." In response the Russian minister stressed the peaceful mood of France and expressed the opinion that since a restoration of the monarchy was impossible, Russia did well to support a moderate government in France. This conversation took place at the beginning of October. At the end of the month Ribot's government was overthrown, and the radical ministry of Leon Bourgeois was installed.

RAPPROCHEMENT WITH BULGARIA

The arrival of a delegation from Bulgaria marked another major event in foreign relations. Russia considered the Bulgarian government unlawful and maintained no diplomatic relations with it. With the overthrow of Stambulov, however, the Bulgarians made every effort to re-establish relations with Russia. A delegation led by Metropolitan Kliment arrived in St. Petersburg during the summer, and the tsar received it cordially. The government immediately announced, however, that the tsar was receiving representatives of the Bulgarian people, whose attitudes Russia had never doubted, and not "a clique of individuals representing themselves as the Bulgarian government." Nevertheless the ice was broken, and recognition followed the next year.

DOMESTIC DEVELOPMENTS IN 1895

The domestic projects of the previous reign continued through 1895 without significant alteration. A new railway tariff, providing extremely favorable long-distance rates, and the Russo-German trade agreement took effect in January. The state monopoly of the production and sale of liquor was introduced into four provinces.[11] Construction of the Great Siberian Railway moved forward rapidly, and 1895 marked in general a record year in railway construction.[12]

Some new policies began to take shape. Nicholas took an interest in women's education, and when the report of the governor of Tula province mentioned the desirability of attracting more girls into public schools, the emperor concurred. "I fully agree," he noted. "This is a matter of extreme importance." He also approved the re-opening of the Women's Medical Institute, closed since early in Alexander III's reign when it fell under the influence of revolutionaries. The allocation of funds for parish schools nearly doubled. During the spring, the first All-Russian Exhibition of Printing opened in St. Petersburg, and every publisher of periodicals and books participated.

The appearance of the Moscow "decadents" [symbolists], headed by Valery Ya. Briussov, distinguished the year in literature. The press savagely ridiculed the entire school. Meanwhile, in the monthly journals a polemic erupted between the populists and the Marxists over the significance of capitalism in Russia. N.S. Leskov died on 21 February 1895, but the radical *Mir bozhi* considered it "best not to express our opinion, following the rule that one either says something good about the dead or nothing." Even *Russkaia mysl*, for which Leskov had written, said only that "this is not the time for a comprehensive and impartial appraisal." Such was the intelligentsia's power of ostracism in those days![13]

Witte remained in charge of economic policy, and he embarked on the first steps toward the currency reform. The government legalized [domestic] transactions in gold at the daily [international] rate of exchange. In other words, the government officially acknowledged the difference between the [old silver-backed] paper ruble and the [new] gold ruble. (The ten ruble [gold] coin brought fifteen paper rubles [or two-thirds the value of the old silver ruble].) The government also scheduled the first general census of the empire (for 1 January 1897).[14]

Interpreting Russian domestic policy for foreign readers, A.A. Bashmakov provided this explanation in the influential French journal *Revue politique et parlementaire* (1895): "Our state system contains an ideal . . . which, despite many contradictions and numerous shortcomings, focuses on the concept of a strong and absolute tsar who, like God, is accessible to everyone but belongs to no faction, and who thus restrains the appetites of the mighty. He is the ultimate source of power—judging, punishing, and correcting social injustice.

"Those most devoted to the country's welfare currently are full of doubt concerning the remedies [of liberalism], those universal panaceas which people everywhere think will enable them to cure all ills and solve all problems. Russia shows little interest in representative government and is even more distrustful of lofty expressions."

This statement, of course, reflected the official attitude of the government and not that of the majority of educated society. Nevertheless the animosity of some circles of the intelligentsia was beginning to wither. *Russkaia mysl* found it appropriate to comment favorably on the anniversary of the emperor's accession: "Emperor Nicholas II marked the first year of his reign by demonstrating special concern for the needs of education. In that first year an imperial decree re-established higher education for Russian women. Every monarch, especially a Russian monarch, contributes something new, something that corresponds to the spirit of the sovereign himself. The Russian public earnestly hopes that the reign of Emperor Nicholas II will revive our schools and our public initiative."

Sir Donald MacKenzie Wallace, author of a noted study of Russia, used these terms to describe the early years of the emperor's reign for the *Encyclopedia Britannica:*[15] "But a great alteration took place noiselessly in the manner of carrying out the laws and ministerial circulars. Though resembling his father in the main points of his character, the young tsar was of a more humane disposition, and he was much less of a doctrinaire. With his father's aspiration of making Holy Russia a homogeneous empire he thoroughly sympathized in principle, but he disliked the systematic persecution of Jews, heretics and schismatics to which it gave rise, and he let it be understood, without any formal order or proclamation, that the severe measures hitherto employed would not meet with his approval."

Emperor Nicholas II wished to maintain autocratic power undiminished in his own hands. At the same time, he deeply respected and honored the memory of his father. This did not mean, however, that his reign would be "a direct continuation of the preceding reign."

∽ख़∾

CHAPTER THREE

THE YEAR 1896

The coronation, the All-Russian Exposition of Trade and Industry at Nizhni Novgorod, and the sovereign's journey to Europe marked the second full year of the reign of Emperor Nicholas II. Late in 1895 Ivan L. Goremykin succeeded I.N. Durnovo as minister of interior. The change had no effect on policy even though Goremykin, who was also a member of the Novgorod provincial zemstvo, had a reputation as a liberal. Lacking any definite program of his own, he remained throughout his career an intensely loyal though somewhat passive executor of the emperor's will. Preparations for the coronation in Moscow and "the review of the Russian economy"—the great exposition at Nizhni Novgorod—filled the early months of the year. In other areas the work of the government proceeded routinely. The liquor monopoly, introduced in 1895 into four provinces, was extended into twelve more. The government established an annual fund of 50,000 rubles for needy authors. The press and the Imperial Free Economic Society began a discussion of the proposed monetary reform.[1]

RECOGNITION OF BULGARIA

The Russo-Bulgarian reconciliation, anticipated by the mission of Metropolitan Kliment in 1895, formally took effect on 3 February 1896 when the young crown prince, Boris, was baptized as an Orthodox Christian. The tsar himself was the boy's godfather. The Bulgarians prepared an enthusiastic welcome for Prince Alexander V. Golenishchev-Kutuzov who officially represented Russia and stood in for the tsar at the baptism. Prince Ferdinand hailed the tsar before a crowd: "Long live Emperor Nicholas II, patron of the Bulgars!" Formal recognition followed in April, and Ferdinand journeyed to St. Petersburg for the occasion.

In other parts of the world Japanese influence in Korea suffered a serious blow when the Korean king fled to the security
of the Russian legation in Seoul. In Africa the Abyssinians
(Ethiopians) routed the Italians at Adua. The French Senate
overturned the radical government of Leon Bourgeois. Felix
Méline formed a new moderate government in which--much
to the satisfaction of the Russian diplomatic corps—Gabriel
Hanotaux returned to the foreign ministry. The fact that the
Russians were "looking over their shoulders" played no small
part in the resolution of the French ministerial crisis.[2]

THE CORONATION

The coronation is a highlight of the life of a monarch, especially if he possesses a faith such as that of Nicholas II. The
coronation celebrates the heir's formal accession to the throne
after the period of mourning the dead monarch. For the first
time the new tsar appears before his people amid all the magnificent splendor of church and state.

Long before the appointed day, from all parts of the empire, guests began to arrive in Moscow, the ancient capital.
The whole city blossomed with flags and colored lanterns on
6 May 1896, the emperor's birthday and the date of his arrival in the city. On May 9th he made his solemn entrance into
the capital from the suburban Petrovsky Palace. Each day produced a new spectacle, the arrival of a foreign delegation or a
martial parade. The imperial couple moved into the Great
Palace of the Kremlin on May 13th. The newspapers daily
recorded the assembling royalty: the Queen of the Greeks
Olga Konstantinovna and her son Constantin, the Crown
Prince; Prince Henry of Prussia, brother of the kaiser; the
Duke of Connaught, son of Queen Victoria; Crown Prince of
Italy Victor Emmanuel; Prince Ferdinand of Bulgaria, Prince
Nicholas of Montenegro, Rumania's Crown Prince Ferdinand,
and scores of German dukes and princes. According to *Novoe
vremia's* final tally, the coronation was witnessed by one
queen, three grand dukes, two reigning princes, twelve crown
princes, and sixteen princes and princesses. Not least among
the notables was the head of the Chinese delegation, Li Hung-
chang.[3]

The Tsar Entering Moscow for His Coronation, 9 May 1896

Reception for the Tsar at the Troitsky-Sergeevsky Monastery
23 May 1896

GOD'S ANNOINTED ONE

On coronation day, 14 May 1896, the Preobrazhensky regiment mounted the guard. By 9:00 a.m. the dignitaries had
gathered in the Uspensky (Assumption) Cathedral, and foot-
men laid a carpet from the Great Kremlin Palace to the parvis
of the church. The clergy received the sovereign there, and the
metropolitan of Moscow greeted him: "Devout Sovereign!
Your resplendent procession signifies a rare occasion. You are
about to enter this ancient sanctuary to place upon your brow
the Tsar's crown and to receive the holy oil.[4] Your ancestral
crown belongs to you alone, as Absolute Tsar, but all Orthodox Christians are worthy of the unction which is given but
once. And should you be blessed through this sacrament to
perceive a new life, the reason is this—that as there is no
power higher, so there is no power on earth more arduous
than the power of Tsar, no burden so wearisome as the duty
of Tsar. Through this visible annointment, may the invisible
might of heaven descend upon you, to augment your prowess
as Tsar and light the way for your autocratic pursuit of the
welfare and happiness of your devoted subjects."

Within the cathedral the two sovereigns sat on canopied
thrones opposite the altar. On a separate throne at the side sat
the Dowager Empress Maria Feodorovna. Palladius, the metropolitan of St. Petersburg, ascended the dais to invite the emperor to recite the Creed, which he did in a loud distinct
voice. Next, vested in purple and wearing the crown, Nicholas
accepted the orb and sceptre and began to read the coronation
prayer beginning, "God of Our Fathers and Lord of Mercy,
You have chosen me to be Tsar and Judge over Your
people . . . ."

Palladius then prayed in behalf of all the people: "Enlighten
him, and thus render great his service to You; grant him reason and wisdom so that he might judge Your people according
to the Law and so that he might preserve Your kingdom in
peace and secure it from sorrow. Reveal him victorious to
enemies, dreadful to villains, merciful and trusting to the
good. Soften his heart to be charitable to the destitute, a
friend to strangers, and a champion to the defenseless. Direct
the government subordinate to him along the path of truth
and justice, shield it from partiality and corruption, and

sustain the true loyalty all those whom You assign to his service. Make him a father who takes joy in his children, and surprise him with Your mercy . . . .   Do not turn Your face from us, do not shame us for our hopes . . . ."   Then the choir burst into "Praise You, O Lord."

The emperor removed the crown and stood for the liturgy. When that ended, the metropolitans annointed him with the holy oil. At that instant the pealing of the bells and the thunder of a one-hundred-and-one-gun salute announced to the city that the tsar had received the holy sacrament. Palladius then led the emperor to the altar where he received holy communion in full regalia—man *and* tsar! From that dramatic and intensely solemn moment Nicholas truly felt that he was the Lord's Annointed. The coronation ceremony, so wondrous and yet so incomprehensible to most of Russia's intelligentsia, was a profoundly meaningful experience for him. He had been infused with the spirit of Russia since childhood, and this day was like being wed to her.

DISASTER AT KHODYNKA

On May 18th, near the end of the second week of celebration, the tragedy at Khodynka cast a pall over the coronation. Over half a million people gathered through the night on the vast parade ground and drill fields to await the distribution of gifts—rings bearing the imperial crest and sweets—scheduled for the morrow. The night passed quietly, but the crowd continued to swell. Suddenly, around 6:00 a.m. according to one eyewitness, "the mass leaped up in one body and began to surge forward as if panicked by fire . . . . Those in the rear pressed against the people in front of them. Ignoring the struggling bodies under their feet, they trampled over the fallen as though they were walking across stones or logs. The horror lasted only ten or fifteen minutes. When calm returned, it was already too late." The dead, including those who succumbed later, numbered 1,282, and several hundred more were injured.

The French ambassador had arranged a ball for that evening. To avoid a diplomatic incident, Nicholas (on the advice of his foreign minister, Lobanov-Rostovsky) decided not to cancel his appearance. But the next morning the emperor and empress attended a funeral service for the dead and then spent the day visiting the injured in several hospitals. The tsar donated one thousand rubles to each family of the dead and injured, and he established special orphanages for the children of the victims. The state bore the cost of the funerals. No effort was made to conceal or minimize the tragedy. The Chinese ambassador, Li Hung-chang, surprised by reports of the catastrophe in the newspapers, told Witte that such unfortunate news should not have been broadcast, and further, that the tsar never should have been told of it. The press began a lively search into the causes of the tragedy and the culprits behind it. The leftist papers stressed the "general state of affairs" and observed that the people would not have clamored so greedily for "sweets" if their lives possessed even a modicum of pleasures. An official investigation discovered no evidence of wrong-doing. Nevertheless an ukaz of 15 July dismissed the police official responsible for maintaining order on that day and disciplined several of his subordinates. The decree attributed the disaster to dereliction of duty and failure to coordinate security arrangements.

Mourning for the victims could not postpone the official schedule of events indefinitely. On May 21st the formal review of the troops took place on the same parade ground at Khodynka, and the celebration of the coronation formally ended on the 26th. By tradition one of the last coronation acts was the promulgation of a manifesto granting a variety of boons—the reduction of taxes and redemption payments, as well as the cancellation of 100,000,000 rubles of payments in arrear; amnesties, various gifts (including 300,000 rubles for a student dormitory), and numerous letters of appreciation to distinguished elder statesmen among the clergy and government—to all three metropolitans, to Field Marshall I.V. Gurko, General Peter S. Vannovsky, and others.

To emphasize its ties with Russia the Méline-Hanotaux government declared the tsar's coronation a holiday for all French school children. President Felix Faure and members of the government attended Mass at the Russian Church on Darieu Street. Russian and French flags billowed all over Paris. The troops received an extra ration of wine, and many punishments were cancelled. The German ambassador wrote

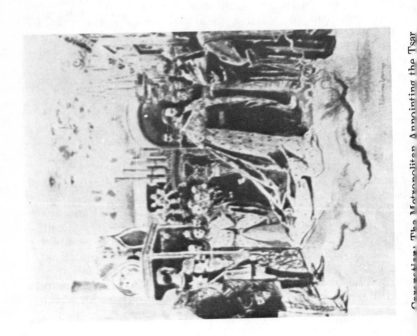

The Tsar Crowning the Tsarina

Coronation: The Metropolitan Appointing the Tsar

with displeasure of the "Russian cult" that the French government is "planting from the top."

On May 26th the tsar issued a manifesto to express his pleasure with the reception accorded him by the first capital. "The citizens of Moscow expressed their sentiments with special warmth on the day of the people's celebration. This provided heart-felt consolation for the misfortune that befell many of the well-wishers and saddened Us amid days of great joy."

THE NATIONAL EXPOSITION AT NIZHNI NOVGOROD

Two days after the conclusion of the coronation, on 28 May 1896, the All-Russian Exposition of Trade and Industry opened in Nizhni Novgorod [now Gorky]. The finance minister had proposed and planned the exposition during the reign of Alexander III. Its purpose was to demonstrate Russian economic achievements during the past fourteen years. The exhibition grounds occupied about 60 desiatins [162 acres] on the left bank of the river Oka, near the grounds of the annual fair. Work on some of the pavilions was still incomplete. Most of the ministers and a few coronation guests (including Li Hung-chang) attended the ribbon-cutting ceremonies. Witte in his opening address explained the choice of Nizhni—"the focal point of our domestic commerce, not far from Moscow, the first capital, on the most important river in Russia and on the historic route into the lands of Asia."

"Our goal here," continued Witte, "is to give Russia and the world a clear view of the results of the spiritual and material growth that our fatherland has achieved since the Moscow exhibit of 1882 .... Our country has made extraordinary advances in the last few years. Confronted by the evidence of this progress concentrated on this little speck of sand in the midst of the vast Russian land, we cannot help being overwhelmed with patriotic joy."[5] In conclusion the finance minister praised "the deep wisdom of the government" reflected in its system of industrial protectionism.

Attendance was light at first, despite the extensive preparations of some exhibitors such as "Northern Russia," the art division under the direction of the painter Alexander N. Benois. The admission fee was thirty kopecks, but factory workers and students were admitted free. Moreover they could obtain free round-trip railway tickets to Nizhni [from anywhere in Russia]. During the first five weeks, daily attendance averaged only 5,000 persons, and given the size of the exhibition, it seemed empty. Ill-disposed critics in the monthly journals wrote that "visitors come by the hundreds, but the government tallies them in the thousands and millions."

On the other hand, the exposition was very impressive: "Completing a tour of the various exhibits," said Savva T. Morozov, chairman of the Nizhni Novgorod fair committee, "one becomes convinced without being aware of it that Russia is marching forward with long strides, that whole industrial sectors can replace foreigners. Unconsciously one feels a surge of strength and energy, and realizes that the time has been well spent and not wasted...."

The newspapers, however—and not only those on the left —invariably commented on the lack of amusements. Dmitry I. Mendeleyev, however, the world-reknowned scientist who was also a proponent of industrial development, contrasted the Nizhni exhibits to the contemporary Indian Exhibition in London, which he characterized as "a farce." "At Nizhni everything is presented on the serious side, perhaps too seriously. The lack of consideration for average tastes and habits may explain the meager number of visitors. To visit our exhibit means to explore, to learn, to study, to think, and not simply to 'have a look around.' "[6] Mendeleyev also detailed Russia's growth between 1882 and 1896—in railways, from 22,500 verst to 40,000; coal production, from 230,000,000 puds to 500,000,000; oil production, from 50,000,000 puds to 350,000,000; pig iron, from 28,000,000 to 75,000,000 puds, and so forth.

Sergei Witte spoke with equal vehemence on 16 July 1896 as he opened the annual Nizhni fair (which ran simultaneously with the exposition). "It has been suggested that I enliven the exhibit with attractions for the visitor who has a penchant for amusements, restaurants, and cafe singers. But I say that ten people who learn something are more important than twenty thousand promenaders. In most matters of substance it is useless to count the votes 'for' or 'against,' because real accomplishments are the work of individuals not masses." A little later, however, the government opened some theaters, a ballet, and other popular amusements.

Nicholas and Alexandra visited Nizhni Novgorod on 17-20 July. A tremendous hailstorm erupted just as they reached the exposition. It shattered windows in several pavilions in a violent display which the superstitious took as a bad omen. The emperor was pleased nevertheless with the exhibit's comprehensive depiction of the country's productive strength. In July daily attendance reached 8,000 and it rose to 15,000 at the peak of the season in August.

AN ATTACK ON THE WITTE SYSTEM

The Third All-Russian Congress of Trade and Industry convened in Nizhni from August fourth to the seventeenth. The convention produced heated debates between the commercial and industrial interests on the one hand and the intelligentsia and agrarian interests on the other. Earlier, on 6 July 1896, the Nizhni Novgorod paper *Volgar* (Volgarian) had published a bold editorial declaring that "the merchant class stands in closest communion with the genuine spirit of Russia and constitutes its strongest component. In no other class does national consciousness appear so forcefully, so confidently or broadly. Of all the elements in Russia it alone is strong and prosperous. . . . There is nothing it cannot accomplish," proclaimed *Volgar*, directly contrasting this class to the nobility. "Because of changing social conditions, many estates no longer possess the vitality that was theirs in former times." The capital papers of both left and right reacted sharply to this editorial.

Most delegates to the congress were members of technical societies or simply "individuals known for their efforts in behalf of industry and commerce." They formed a majority in opposition to the industrialists' program of increased government support but even more importantly against Witte's entire protectionist system.[7] The section considering tariff policy adopted a resolution calling for the reduction of the tariff on agricultural equipment and submitted this demand to the plenum of the congress. There Mendeleyev defended the duties but endorsed the resolution's call for a comprehensive system of credit to finance the purchase of agricultural equipment and machinery. The convention by a majority of 140 to 63, however, approved Professor Leonid V. Khodsky's original resolution demanding a tariff reduction.

In his closing speech the chairman of the congress, Senator Dmitry F. Kobeko, endorsed the resolution of the agricultural interests. "A wave of foreign colonizers is already approaching the Ukraine, Volynia, and the Baltic," he warned. "It is proper for the land to be ploughed by a Russian plough, but it is even more important that the man who works the land be a Russian." Responding to the argument that the dispossessed could migrate to the cities, Kobeko continued: "A farmer—whether *pomeshchik* [gentry] or peasant is of no consequence—parts from the land with a heavy heart, for his soil contains the bones of his fathers; the land was his cradle, and the richest moments of his life are bound up with his possession of it . . . . The spiritual bond with the land is the great strength of the Russian nation. It must be respected, protected, and supported."

The representatives of industry and commerce were extremely dissatisfied with these proceedings and wanted the Nizhni fair committee to counter the anti-protectionist resolution. Witte, however, cooled them off. At a banquet to mark the end of the fair Morozov addressed Witte, the guest of honor, to say that the vote of the Third Congress carried no special weight: "We industrialists are accustomed to think twice before we grant credit to anyone."

Witte reasserted his own unflinching position: "What kind of government turns to a convention for advice? Ten people can say something intelligent, but thousands babble nonsense. Listen to the former, not the latter. Pardon the expression, but as long as they [foreigners] are stripping off our skin, a reduction of tariffs is unthinkable. One might think that these people were foreign agents." A tariff reduction, he declared firmly, would become possible only with a general international reduction of rates, "when people everywhere ask, why are we strangling each other."

The national exposition closed on 1 October 1896. September attendance fell off to 5-6,000 a day. Overall the exhibit attracted some 991,000 visitors, including 282,000 workers and students who received free admittance. The latter number was rather clear proof that the Nizhni Novgorod exposition had contributed significantly to the education of Russia.

AN IMPERIAL VISIT TO WESTERN EUROPE

Soon after his visit to Nizhni, Nicholas embarked on his first trip abroad as tsar. This journey, however, was unlike any other imperial tour in that it required a basic decision as to whether to visit republican France. Since the world exposition of 1867 in the reign of Napoleon III, Paris had not entertained a royal guest. The establishment of the Republic in the debacle of the Franco-Prussian War had isolated France from monarchial Europe. The French government, therefore, attributed special importance to the visit of the Russian emperor. Nicholas, however, could scarcely call on the enemies of France and ignore an ally of four years, even if the alliance remained an official secret. To refrain from an appearance in France would have had the effect of breaking with the foreign policy of Alexander III.

From the beginning of his reign Nicholas strived to convert the Franco-Russian Alliance from a weapon of revenge into an instrument of European reconciliation. Therefore he decided to soften the political impact of his visit by imposing certain conditions. He demanded, in particular, absolute abstention from any remarks hostile to Germany and also personal preliminary review of all speeches to be given in his presence. The French government agreed to these conditions.

The first visit (15-17 August 1896) to the oldest neighboring sovereign, Emperor Franz Joseph of Austria-Hungary, was brief and without political content. The foreign minister, Prince Lobanov-Rostovsky, died suddenly on the train from Vienna to Kiev, and a successor was not named for four months. The deputy minister, Nicholas P. Shishkin, accompanied the emperor on the remainder of the journey.

DEDICATION OF THE CATHEDRAL OF ST. VLADIMIR IN KIEV

Nicholas returned to Kiev for the consecration of the Cathedral of St. Vladimir, which was the most remarkable example of Russian religious art of the later nineteenth century. The masters Vasnetsov and Nesterov helped to create the murals. The tsar was present also for the unveiling of the monument to Emperor Nicholas I.

"The Cathedral of St. Vladimir represents a whole new era in the history of Russian religious painting," it was said in the journal *Mir i Iskusstvo* (The World and Art). "Our most highly trained painters usually ignore our ancient iconography . . . but Vasnetsov and Nesterov have changed everything. These artists understand our national religious spirit. Indeed, they are imbued with it, and for that reason they have created works that are close to the people . . . . Both artists have responded to the needs of the religious experience, and their contributions never will be forgotten. Vasnetsov represents the splendid and austere Byzantine character of Orthodoxy, while Nesterov captures its blissful, unaffected qualities."

A VISIT WITH THE KAISER

From "the mother of Russian cities" the imperial entourage proceeded to Breslau and Goerlitz where the German army was holding maneuvers. The newly crowned monarch's first meeting with William II took place in a congenial atmosphere, but he had to conduct himself with care. He wanted to allay German suspicions concerning his journey to France, but at the same time he had to be certain to make no gesture that might offend the French. The emperor handled the situation with characteristic skill. He allowed William to do all the talking and limited himself to a toast to the traditional sentiments of friendship that also had inspired his father.

The kaiser attempted to win Nicholas to the idea of a customs union of Europe against America, while the chancellor, Prince Hohenlohe, probed his attitude toward England and predicted that the British would lose India. "The emperor laughed at this," wrote Hohenlohe, "and asked how England might lose India. Who would take it away? We certainly are not so stupid as to embark on such a venture." At the same time the emperor stressed the importance of the Siberian railway to his far eastern policy and intimated that when it was completed Russia might have to deal with the Japanese. He was already quite concerned with Tokyo's intense armament program.

PREPARATIONS IN FRANCE

Next came ten days in Denmark and then two weeks in Scotland at Balmoral with Queen Victoria, the empress's grandmother. These were both family affairs, outside of politics.

Meanwhile the French were preparing feverishly for the arrival of the tsar. Raymond Poincaré, the brilliant young politician (in the estimate of *Le Temps*), told an audience in Commercy that "the forthcoming visit of a powerful monarch, the peace-loving ally of France, will be the visible coronation of our wisdom and determination. It will convince Europe that France has emerged from isolation and that we are worthy of friendship and respect." *Le Temps* itself observed that "French society has been preoccupied for two months with this first visit, so paradoxical in its novelty and yet so natural in its intent, this visit of the most powerful, most absolute monarch on earth to the youngest of republics."

French preparations were extensive. Rail fares to Paris were reduced by 75 per cent for the duration of the tsar's stay. The opening of the school year was moved back one week. Every available display window had been rented along the entire route from the Passy station, where the tsar's train would arrive, to the Russian embassy on the rue de Grenelle. Windows leased for as much as 5,000 francs.

"RUSSIAN WEEK" IN FRANCE

The imperial couple and their daughter, the Grand Duchess Olga,[8] arrived in Cherbourg on 23 September/5 October 1896. President Felix Faure welcomed them, and thus began the "Russian week" which ended at Chalons on 27 September.

Paris overflowed. Joining its two million residents were 930,000 visitors. Parties went on continuously in the streets. Everything became Russian or pseudo-Russian: a soap bore the label "Le Tsar;" there were candies decorated with the Russian flag and coat of arms, toy Russian bears, tableware bearing the portrait of the tsar, the tsar and tsarina, and even Olga. The tsar's visage appeared on jumping beans, and the popular toy, "the peasant and bear," became the tsar and Felix Faure. Advertisers exploited the Russian fad. "Pink pills" were recommended to ensure good health during the tsar's visit; shoemakers and glovers distributed their ads on the backs of free pictures of the tsar. Proprietors of ready-made clothes advertised their sale items as "presents of the tsar." One entrepreneur even sold a "Franco-Russian" Dutch cheese. While a certain lack of taste was evident in all this, the enthusiasm was undeniably sincere.

This same exuberance inundated the Russian embassy with letters and postcards. The newspapers seemed to compete in devising projects. Even the sensible *Journal des Débats* suggested that all girls born during October 1896 be named Olga in honor of the tsar's daughter. Another proposed a fund to purchase all houses opposite the Russian Church, demolish them, and construct a square with gardens in front of the church. Still another recommended the purchase of an estate for Baron Mohrenheim, the Russian ambassador, who had worked so strenuously to bring off the imperial visit. It was too much to keep up with.

The genuine enthusiasm of the people of Paris was abundantly clear. It reflected the combination of many things—the Parisians' natural love of spectaculars, the monarchist sentiments retained by the masses, the sense of increased security, the hope for revenge. Few Frenchmen, however, failed to succumb to a genuine fascination with the emperor and Russia. Nicholas's conditions, nevertheless, were fulfilled. No hint of anti-Germanism materialized, except for the silent protest of the League of Patriots in placing wreaths at the Strasbourg monument.[9] Cartoons in the foreign press used every device to evoke the unspoken word, *revanche*, short of actually using it.

The sovereign rode into Paris between ranks of soldiers who lined the streets from the station to the embassy. Behind the rows of troops stood a crowd a million strong shouting "Vive le Tsar! Vive le Tsar!" No monarch was ever acclaimed so enthusiastically in a foreign land. ("It reminds one of Moscow," wrote a disgruntled radical reviewer for one of the Russian monthlies. "French soldiers sang our anthem in the streets. Even the organist played it in Notre Dame.")

From the embassy, known then as the Imperial Palace, Nicholas went first to the Russian Church and then to the Elysée Palace to call upon the president. The French press took special note of the emperor's call on the presidents of both chambers, Emile Loubet and Eugene Brisson—an act which disarmed the latter, an old radical who was the jealous watchdog of republican traditions. After receiving the diplomatic corps, the tsar attended a banquet given by President Faure. Although Nicholas mentioned "valuable ties," he particularly stressed the importance of Paris as "the source of taste, talent, and enlightenment." Politics barely crept into his speech.

Indeed, most of the emperor's time in Paris was spent not on politics but on touring the capital. On their first evening in Paris the sovereigns attended the opera. The next morning, accompanied by the president, they visited the Cathedral of Notre Dame where they met Cardinal Richard, the Archbishop of Paris; then to Sainte Chapelle, where they were shown the ancient Slavic gospel of Anna Yaroslavna;[10] and finally to the Pantheon to view the tomb of Napoleon in the church of the Invalides. Returning for lunch at the embassy, the emperor hosted members of the French aristocracy. Among the notables were the Bourbon representatives, Duke Henry of Aumale and Robert of Chartres, Princess Mathilda Bonaparte (cousin of Napoleon III) and the flower of the French aristocracy.

Later, to choruses of "God Save the Tsar," Nicholas witnessed the laying of the cornerstone of the Emperor Alexander III Bridge (commemorated to this day on a marble plaque on the right bank of the Seine). To mark the occasion Claude Monet read poetry by the noted poet José-Maria de Hérédia which included the lines, "Let the future forever preserve within you the glorious name of your ancestor Peter." At the mint the tsar received a medal struck in honor of his visit, after which the imperial couple attended a session of the French Academy of Sciences. Ernest W. Legouvé, the presiding academician, greeted them with a reminder of the arrival of Peter the Great in Paris on 5 May 1717. (The arrival of other Russian monarchs was connected with less "pleasant memories:" Alexander I at the head of the Russian army in March 1814, and Alexander II in May 1867 when the Pole, Anton Berezowsky, attempted to murder him.) Legouvé begged "to celebrate in advance the two-hundredth anniversary of Franco-Russian friendship." Francois Coppée then read a poem dedicated to "the glorious son of the magnanimous Tsar, Alexander III the Just."

Every movement of the tsar was announced in advance, and huge crowds surrounded him wherever he went. "These are living rooms, not streets," he remarked to his companions. From the Academy the guests proceeded to a reception by the Paris municipal council. A mass of people completely

Entry of the Emperor and Empress into Paris, October 1896

covered the square in front of the Hôtel de Ville, where the city of Paris honored the Russian tsar. The second day ended with a variety performance at the *Comédie-Francaise*. A poem by Jules Claretie created a stir in the audience: "And now a hope comes to us from the North . . . ."

The imperial couple spent the morning of the third day touring the Louvre. At their expressed wish, they were conducted through the gallery of Italian primitivists. Fra Angelico's "Coronation of Our Lady" appealed particularly to the empress, and as she left she said, "This is my first visit here, but not the last." Unfortunately, that was not to be so. In the afternoon Nicholas and Alexandra drove to Versailles, past the Sévres porcelain factory and through the great park of Saint-Cloud where the fountains were playing. "When the sovereign entered the Hall of Mirrors," wrote *Le Temps*, "a remarkable scene opened before him: all the fountains from the upper terrace of the Grand Canal glistened in the sun, and every square, every walk, and every space between the trees was filled with the colorful crowd of people."

The third day concluded with a performance at the Salon Hercules. Sarah Bernhardt read a poem by René Sully-Prudhomme that described the conversation of a Versailles nymph with the ghost of Louis XIV. The nymph concluded by saying: "I cannot teach him the proper course; he has only to follow his father's example." These continuous complimentary allusions to Alexander III from the lips of French republicans were especially gratifying to the emperor, all the more because of the animosity toward that reign by Russians who were only moderately liberal and by no means republicans. The contrasting attitudes clearly indicated the relative nature of self-interest in political perception.

AT CHALONS—"AN INSEPARABLE BOND"

Only the final day of the emperor's visit to France bore "political" overtones. Nicholas knew that he could not accept his ally's hospitality without returning some sign of their affinity. But he reserved his comment for the last in order to avoid some demonstration with unforseeable results. He set out from Paris in the morning in order to review the French army at Chalons. He spoke at a lunch with officers of the garrison, declaring that "France can be proud of its army . . . . Our countries are united by an inseparable bond. A deep sense of brotherhood in arms exists between our armies."

That was all he said, but it was enough. His words spread instantly through the army. Newspapers reported that tears came to the eyes of many officers, and all agreed that "We are living at a historic moment." The emperor and empress meanwhile had departed for Germany where they spent three weeks in Darmstadt with Alexandra's relatives.

The emperor's visit had broken the ice and produced general satisfaction in France. "France has recovered its status among the powers," wrote the *Neueste Nachrichten* (Latest Bulletins). The French had shaken off the depression of defeat which had weighed so heavily for twenty-five years. They now felt they had achieved equality among the great powers. The tsar's visit, a landmark in the history of the Third Republic, was not without effect on French domestic politics. It enhanced the prestige and stability of the moderate government of Méline and Hanotaux,[11] which held power for a comparatively long twenty-six months, finally collapsing under the turbulent impact of the Dreyfus affair in 1898. The French even showed a slight inclination to accept political instruction from the tsar. The press noticed that the tsar frequently asked an official, "How long have you been a minister . . . a chairman?" When Jean Constans admitted to three years, the tsar remarked that that was "a long time." *Le Temps* questioned whether "we might have been stronger had we possessed more stability and consistency."

Extreme leftist circles in Russia were outraged at the reception accorded a "despot" by a "free country." Their irritation surfaced in their sarcastic accounts of the festivities. *Severnyi vestnik,* for example, briefly noted that "the heart of France began to beat on October 5th . . . the French squandered eight million francs and swilled ten million liters of wine." Liberal and moderate factions seemed well pleased, but some conservatives lost their equanimity.

THE "*GRAZHDANIN*" INCIDENT

The French press took particular delight in an incident involving the conservative *Grazhdanin.* On 7/19 October 1896 the minister of interior suspended Prince Meshchersky's journal for one month for its violation of regulations on "proprieties with regard to governments friendly to Russia." *Le Temps* observed that Prince Meshchersky opposed the Franco-Russian Alliance which, in his opinion, promised Russia war and ruin for the sake of Alsace-Lorraine and which, moreover, strengthened the liberal and constitutional tendencies in Russian life. Hence, *Le Temps* attributed great significance to its suspension.

In fact the suspension was not nearly so sensational. The censors closed *Grazhdanin* not for criticizing the alliance but for slurring French President Faure. Prince Meshchersky, who was in Paris at the time, provided a full explanation of the incident. The paper had exceeded the interior ministry's advice that "restraint should be exercised in making unfriendly remarks or evaluations of those heads of government who will host the sovereign." *Grazhdanin* resumed publication within three weeks, and as a mark of special favor its fine was cancelled.[12]

In Russia the chief effect of the emperor's visit was undeniably, as a leftist commentator put it, "the nation-wide announcement of the existence of the Franco-Russian Alliance." All official efforts to soften its impact or conceal its details were unavailing. Before the emperor's confirmation, "some had not dared to hope, and others were afraid to believe." "Although the word 'alliance' was scrupulously avoided, it exists nevertheless, and we must take it into account," wrote the German ambassador Münster after the review at Chalons. The German military attaché agreed: "There is no immediate danger . . . . But as long as France and Russia maintain the cordiality demonstrated during the tsar's visit, we can in no way count on either of these countries adopting a friendly attitude toward us."

A PLAN TO SEIZE THE BOSPHORUS

A major decision confronted Nicholas when he returned to Russia after two months abroad. The agony of "the sick man of Europe," the Ottoman Empire, appeared to be drawing to a close. Crete was in turmoil and preparing to break away from Turkey. The Turks were slaughtering Armenians in Asia

Minor and, indeed, even in Constantinople itself under the noses of the foreign delegations. The major new factor in the situation, however, was the British attitude. Long the staunch defenders of the integrity of the Ottoman Empire, London was now full of despair, and British diplomats were raising openly the possibility of a partition of Turkey.

Constantinople and the Straits formed a long-standing Russian objective. Since the War of 1877-78 and especially since the rupture with Bulgaria, the Russians appeared to have "left the Balkans." In fact Russia's ambition remained unchanged. In 1896, with the restoration of Russo-Bulgarian relations and the British assumption of an imminent Turkish collapse, Russia had the opportunity to determine the timing of events. Alexander I. Nelidov, the Russian ambassador in Constantinople, considered the moment opportune and rushed to St. Petersburg. A Crown Council on 23 November 1896 considered the problem. The Chief of Staff, General Nicholas N. Obruchev, earnestly supported Nelidov, and the acting foreign minister, Shishkin, raised no objections. Nelidov's plan was to send the Russian fleet to the Bosphorus. At the first outbreak of fresh violence, expected at any moment, Russian troops would seize the northern end of the Straits. The sultan would be given the choice of recognizing Russian suzerainty or being deposed. Then the Russian government would discuss "compensations" with the other powers. Only Witte resisted this scheme. The emperor listened to all the arguments and reserved the final decision to himself.

As a preliminary measure in anticipation of a major shift in its Turkish policy, Russia withdrew from the international commission on the Turkish debt. A concerned Hanotaux questioned the Russian ambassador about this decision. "Have you considered all the problems?" he urged—did St. Petersburg realize that if Russia seized Constantinople and the Bosphorus, England and Italy would occupy the Dardanelles? Paris remained unconvinced of the opportunity despite the extremely favorable circumstances. As a result the tsar did not order the seizure of the Bosphorus. The French could see no suitable compensation for themselves, since their traditional interest in the Near East was as a creditor to the Turkish government. The Triple Alliance surely would have objected, and the tsar had no desire to provoke a major

European crisis. He was reluctant, moreover, "to have too many irons in the fire" because he could foresee an almost certain clash in Asia. If Constantinople did not fall immediately, like a ripened fruit, if the project threatened to make excessive demands on Russian resources, then he would rather forego it.

THE RUSSIAN MARXISTS

Inside Russia, meanwhile, powerful revolutionary forces were beginning to take shape. The socialist [Marxist] "Union of Struggle for the Emancipation of the Working Class," organized late in 1895, was emerging as the principal source of propaganda among the industrial workers. This organization was uncompromising in its hostility toward the existing order, and its members were willing to employ any means to achieve their ends. They were agents of revolution not reform. The Union's founders were Vladimir I. Ulyanov (Lenin), recently returned from abroad where he had established connections with the revolutionary emigration; Julius O. Tsederbaum (Martov), Yury M. Nakhamkes (Steklov), Nadezhda K. Krupskaya, Mark T. Elizarov (Ulyanov's brother-in-law), and other subsequently well-known figures.

In 1896 Ulyanov-Lenin was in jail awaiting trial. He had been arrested the previous December for issuing a proclamation (printed, incidentally, on the backs of circulars announcing the birth of the Grand Duchess Olga Nikolaevna). "Our comrade was doing fine," wrote Elizarov, and Lenin indeed used this "involuntary leisure" to write a book entitled *The Development of Capitalism in Russia* [published in 1899 under the pseudonym "Ilyin"]. His associates remained active, however, abandoning their "clannishness"—as circulators of their form of "enlightenment" among the workers—in favor of activities on a higher plane.

THE STRIKE OF THE PETERSBURG TEXTILE WORKERS

The strike against the St. Petersburg textile mills provided the opportunity for direct action. The factory managers reacted slowly and with serious consequences. All factories closed, as was customary, for three days during the coronation (14-16 May 1896), but the mill owners intended to pay

only for one day. Negotiations went on for a week, while the
workers remained on the job. On the 23rd workers at the
Rossiia cotton works approached the manager and demanded
pay for all three coronation days. The manager agreed, but the
workers immediately presented new demands, including a reduction of the work day. When they received no reply, they
went on strike. The movement spread quickly to other factories, and in about a week workers confronted every enterprise
in St. Petersburg with demands for a two-and-a-half hour reduction of the working day. (In the 1890s the workday everywhere—not only in Russia—was much longer than now. In St.
Petersburg work began at 6:00 a.m. and ended at 8:00 p.m.—
thirteen hours, including a one-hour rest; the workers were
asking for a ten-and-a-half hour day—from 7:00 a.m. to 7:00
p.m. with an hour-and-a-half break.)

Official statistics set the number of strikers at fifteen thousand, about half of what the workers claimed. Members of the
Union of Struggle for the Emancipation of the Working Class
were active in the strike from the beginning. They published
twenty-five different leaflets which they distributed in various
factories and even in Moscow. Foreign workers provided financial assistance to the Union, whose tactics were quite simple. They directed the workers' discontent to concrete issues
and explained how they could step up their demands. The success of the strike increased the workers' dependence on the
leaders of the Union. Success also magnified the workers'
awareness of their grievances.

WITTE'S POLICY

The rapid spread of the strike and its organized character,
which indicated planned leadership, caught the government
by surprise. Nicholas V. Kleigels, the Governor-General of St.
Petersburg, not only issued appeals but personally went into
the factories and talked to the strikers. Witte, whose jurisdiction as finance minister included the supervision of industry,
hastened to St. Petersburg from the exposition at Nizhni
Novgorod. He reproached the police authorities for failing to
adopt appropriate measures. The strike, however, was already
subsiding. Strikers held out only in the factories where better
conditions prevailed and where the workers therefore had

greater savings to sustain them. Expected "assistance from the German workers" failed to materialize. The strike movement lasted slightly less than a month, yet the government deemed it necessary to publish a full report.

The Petersburg strikes revealed an obvious danger, and two factors explained the disorders—the genuinely miserable working conditions in the factories and the revolutionary drive of a well-organized group of socialists. The authorities moved first against the socialists. During the summer and fall, they arrested more than a thousand. "There is a great epidemic here," members of the St. Petersburg Union reported to their comrades abroad. But the government's efforts did not stop there. It created a special commission to look more deeply into the reasons for the strike's success. Then, on 6 July 1896, the finance minister summoned the textile magnates and addressed them angrily: "You scarcely could conceive of a government more favorably disposed toward industry than the present one . . . . But you are mistaken, gentlemen, if you think our policies are designed exclusively to enable you to make greater profits. The government has a major interest in the welfare of the workers. Had you understood that, this latest strike would not have occurred. The proof of what I say is that strikes did not hit those factories where the owners have established more decent and humane relations with their workers . . . ." Witte cut short all objections: "What you are trying to tell me is not new. I gathered you here not to listen to you or to learn from you, but to give you my opinion."

The conservative publicist Ilya F. Tsion [Cyon], who from Paris issued one tract after another condemning Witte, did not fail to comment on this episode. "In the French Republic," he wrote, "Jean Jaurés and newspaper publishers are tried for issuing appeals to strike, but in autocratic Russia the speeches of the minister of finance himself unlawfully incite the workers to strike!" Witte, however, was invulnerable to the accusation that he neglected industrial interests. His attitude was that the government should not be a party but an arbitrator in labor disputes. He also held that the government could not condone concessions in politically motivated strikes.

Vestnik evropy, a journal of moderately liberal views, maintained that "agitators appeared on the scene only after the strikes already had begun," and it advised that "the causes of the strikes would be found in the working conditions." *Vestnik evropy* advocated reduction of the length of the workday. It asserted that the thirteen-hour day of the Petersburg cotton mills was excessive when a twelve-hour day prevailed in the majority of Russian factories. "Nearly everyone agrees that thirteen hours is too long." *Severnyi vestnik* published a table, but not the source of its information, alleging that cotton manufacturing profits ranged from 16 to 45 percent a year.

THE STUDENT MOVEMENT

Revolutionary groups also exploited the Khodynka tragedy in their agitation. Careless police work was not the monopoly of an autocratic system, but nevertheless the leftists successfully planned a demonstration in the Vagankov cemetery [where most of the victims were buried]. They chose the date of 18 November 1896 which coincided with the opening of the university for the fall term and also marked the sixth month since the disaster.

An official report of 5 December 1896 pointed to the existence of a "united council" of students that embraced some forty-five "territorial associations" *(zemliachestva).* In a letter to French students at the time of the Toulon festivities[13] the council had protested its indignation at the servility of a free nation before the representatives of an autocratic regime. The police arrested the council early in 1895, but others revived it and under one pretext or another attempted to foment riots in the fall. On 21 October [1896] the council resolved that "the main objective of the student associations must be the training of fighters for the political arena," because "in an era of intensified reaction an organized active protest will have great and wide-ranging educational significance." The resolution asserted the necessity "to struggle against the present university administration, which is a partial manifestation of official policy. In fighting the coercion and arbitrary rule of the university administration the student body will be steeling itself and educating itself for the political struggle against the entire governmental system."

STUDENT DISORDERS IN MOSCOW

To give effect to its resolution the council appealed to students to join a memorial service for the victims of Khodynka and "to protest the existing system which makes possible such grievous occurrences." On 18 November 1896 about five hundred students moved on the Vagankov cemetery. When they were denied entry, they took their demonstration into the streets. The police recorded the names of the demonstrators who refused to disperse and arrested thirty-six students suspected as ringleaders. For the next three days students staged protests at the university, and the police made arrests at each meeting until finally 711 students were taken into custody. Forty-nine were held as instigators, and authorities expelled the rest for a year. (A year later 201 received right to enter another university, and 461 were allowed to re-enter Moscow University.) The students were detained under guard for three or four days.

Moscow University was not the only institution to experience disturbances. "Many unruly demonstrations took place in several other universities and institutions of higher learning," according to the official report. "However, these meetings dispersed without police intervention, thanks to the persuasive influence of the administrators."

The press generally viewed the protests as without foundation—the demonstration at Vagankov was not "absolutely necessary." Although the government was well-informed on the student movement, complained *Moskovskie vedomosti*, it failed to do anything to prevent the demonstration. A.S. Suvorin observed in *Novoe vremia* that "all these disturbances indicate that adults either lack an understanding of life or misunderstand certain other things .... The government handled the situation with understanding by coping with the demonstrators as students and not as rioting conspirators." Prince Ukhtomsky's *Peterburzhskie vedomosti* warned that "repressive 'surgical' measures alone cannot obviate this sad event .... Boredom in the extreme and lack of excitement besets the provincial cities and their public, literary, and even their academic life."

The student disorders drew their basic strength, however, from the passivity of most of Russia's educated society. The absurd behavior of the students, and their petty rationale evoked no reaction from this section of the public. The intelligentsia maintained its own unique consistency. Significantly unlike the industrial strikes of 1896, the student disorders were purely political. They aimed to disrupt the existing order, yet no particular need or burden inspired them.[14] The student outburst of 1896 was merely another of the recurrent manifestations of the general political dissatisfaction of the Russian intelligentsia.

✎

CHAPTER FOUR

THE LIQUOR MONOPOLY AND THE CENSUS OF 1897

Emperor Nicholas II was not preoccupied with any preconceived scheme to reorganize Russia from top to bottom. He
had no ambition to become at any price one of those "architects" to whom Pobedonostsev referred in his *Moscow Collection.*[1] Nicholas believed that changes should be introduced
only if they led unquestionably to the betterment of the
country. Therefore his thoughtful conservatism never prevented him from instituting reform that seemed advisable or necessary for the general development of Russian life. He went
ahead with the reforms inaugurated by his father, and he began to complete some of the institutions created by Alexander
II. With each year the liquor monopoly extended into more
and more provinces. In 1896 Nicholas introduced the judicial
statutes of 1864 into Siberia and the province of Arkhangel,
and into other parts of the empire in the years that followed.

The liquor monopoly, like other government reforms, encountered bitter criticism from a broad cross-section of the
educated public who averred that the government "was turning the people into drunkards." The liquor monopoly, however, had no direct relation either to the spread or decline of
drunkenness. Under the old system, the government licensed
vendors who then collected and remitted the excise tax on
alcoholic beverages. The old system produced a special class
of people whose interests were bound up in the increased sale
of strong spirits. The government's monopolization of the
vodka trade attempted neither to restrict consumption nor to
stimulate demand artificially through advertisement, the extension of credit, or other means. The monopoly provided
more substantial revenues than previous fiscal measures, and
that was its main purpose. Revenues increased not because the
government increased consumption but because it claimed the
profits that previously went to middlemen. Indirect taxes such

as this, wherein all proceeds flowed directly into the state treasury, existed in all countries in one form or another. To a degree, of course, the monopoly imposed a restriction on private enterprise. This restraint was justifiable, however, as a fiscal measure and also as a means of eliminating the most flagrant abuses stemming from the on-premise sale of vodka, which invariably led to the exploitation of the consumers.

The first general census was taken on 28 January 1897. Previously, during the period of serfdom, the government had made some incomplete "revisions" (the last in 1858). The census of 1897 proved to be only another approximation. The government issued an "official" total of 120,000,000, but this was subsequently revised to 126,400,000 (and then did not include the 2,500,000 inhabitants of the Grand Duchy of Finland). The census produced a mine of information on the religious and national composition of the population, its occupational status, literacy, and other characteristics, but many years were required to analyze this data.[2]

"A CROSS OF GOLD" FOR RUSSIA

With the liquor monopoly successfully launched, S. Yu. Witte, the finance minister, turned to the monetary reform long in preparation. Russia had not enjoyed a stable currency since the Crimean War when the government suspended the redemption of paper notes for gold and silver. The [international] exchange rate of the credit or paper ruble fell considerably during the Russo-Turkish War of 1877-78. In the 1880s the ruble fluctuated widely, plunging to a low of 50 kopecks and rising only rarely to 80 kopecks.[3] Russians meanwhile lost the habit of using coins and turned increasingly to paper notes to settle accounts. The new coinage (of copper and low quality silver alloys) was adjusted to the value of the government notes, while gold and fine silver coins practically disappeared from circulation. Gold rubles were used only for the collection of international tariffs.

The instability of Russia's currency stemmed from its lack of any precise correlation with foreign currencies [based on the gold standard]. This instability created a serious obstacle to nineteenth-century Russian commercial and capital transactions. Russians had to pay higher prices for foreign goods and capital, since a risk premium was added to the regular price of any commodity. At the same time, fluctuations in the rate of exchange complicated the Russian export trade. A profit or loss in the sale of Russian grain or other commodities often depended on the current exchange value of the paper ruble in the international money market. Some of the more skillful Russian merchants profited from currency speculation, but in general the instability of the ruble impeded the development of trade and industry.

Ivan A. Vyshnegradsky, Witte's predecessor as minister of finance [1886-92], began the process of accumulating a gold reserve in order to stabilize the ruble. Witte accelerated this policy of accumulation, partly by using foreign loans to obtain gold. He put an end to the speculation in rubles in this manner: first, the finance ministry went into the Berlin exchange and bought up all available paper rubles (at the rate of 2.19 marks per ruble); next, Witte prohibited the export of rubles from Russia and concurrently warned Russian bankers that in the government's view anyone who sent rubles out of the country was speculating against the ruble. The Berlin currency dealers, who had sold practically their entire stock of rubles, then found themselves in no position to repurchase them at their "natural" price. In order to meet their ruble obligations and avoid bankruptcy, they had to turn to the finance minister himself for permission to purchase rubles at the very unfavorable rate of 2.34 marks per ruble. The operation cost currency speculators an estimated 20,000,000 rubles, a sum which entered the Russian treasury as a profit and increased its free cash reserve. Witte's coup practically ended efforts to undermine the value of the ruble, and henceforth without any special effort the finance ministry maintained the paper ruble at two-thirds parity with gold.

DIRE WARNINGS

Protests from various quarters followed the announcement of the pending devaluation in the 15 March 1896 edition of *Novoe vremia*. Opponents raised the most divergent arguments against the stabilization of the ruble at two-thirds parity. Some claimed that it would be a fraudulent admission of bankruptcy to exchange the ruble note for gold at any ratio

Sergei Yu. Witte

but one to one, despite the fact that over the past forty years the entire economic system had adjusted to the new, lower rate.[4] Others pressed the desirability of a currency based on both gold and silver (bimetallism), while still others claimed that the reform was doomed to failure and that it threatened to produce unimaginable economic upheaval. Some simply denied that the reform served any useful purpose. The Imperial Free Economic Society discussed the project in five sessions in March and April 1896. Opposition clearly prevailed over approval in the articles which filled the newspapers and magazines. Even the paper ruble had its defenders. One was Sergei F. Sharapov who maintained that the economy had adapted successfully to the notes, which offered added protection to Russian manufactures by making foreign goods too expensive. Sharapov went so far as to insist that soft currency promoted the Russian grain trade by injecting an element of risk into it. He recounted a conversation with a Kalashnikov grain merchant who had told him: "The way I see it, speculation offers the chance to make a killing! And that's why I trade. That may be a very stupid reason, but it's a fact!"[5]

Others, who acknowledged the virtues of the gold standard, maintained nevertheless that it could not survive in Russia. The country was too poor, they said, and eventually all the gold would end up abroad. Other opponents of the reform argued that the Russian people would hide the gold in money boxes, it would soon disappear from circulation, and the State Bank would have to cease the conversion of notes to gold. The same arguments put forward in the Free Economic Society by Russian intellectuals were repeated in the State Council. Two council members, Boris P. Mansurov and Dmitry G. Derviz, submitted detailed memoranda to demonstrate that devaluation would destroy the prestige of the government.

Witte and his financial assistants responded to every point raised by the opposition with equally detailed rebuttals. Against the "moral" objection to devaluation, the defenders readily demonstrated that devaluation had occurred forty years earlier. To fix the ruble at full parity with gold, they asserted, would create great difficulties in all areas of the economy, increase the size of all debts by fifty percent, create excessive price increases, and cause other problems. They argued, moreover, that even though silver formally had remained the legal currency, the price of silver had fallen drastically in recent years. Consequently the value of the gold ruble was not one-and-a-half but actually two times the value of silver. Witte and his aides denied the concern that gold would flow abroad by pointing out that Russia enjoyed a generally favorable balance of payments.[6] They scoffed at the idea that Russians would be able to squirrel away a hundred million gold rubles and ridiculed the reform's opponents: first the reform would not work because the people were too poor; now it would fail because of their boundless prosperity!

Under the terms of the monetary reform the new gold ruble, which was to become the basic monetary unit, was made to equal 1.50 old rubles. That is, the new ruble would equal [two-thirds of the value of] the credit ruble, whose rate was then fixed for one year at 7 rubles 50 kopecks for each "Half-Imperial" (the old five-ruble gold coin). The gold reserve of the State Bank stood at approximately 1,200,000,000 rubles (in new currency), whereas the paper rubles in circulation totaled about 1,100,000,000 rubles. Therefore the resumption of convertibility presented no difficulties.[7] If the ministry of finance were to be reproached for anything, it would have to be for overcaution—for its excessive outlays in accumulating the gold reserve and for purchasing silver in order to mint the one-ruble and the fifty-kopeck coins. The ministry considered full-value silver coinage psychologically necessary, however, to instill in the people the habit of using metallic money.

The State Council in general session discussed the monetary reform in April 1896. At the conclusion of his speech in defense of the reform Witte stated that personally he would be happy to see the project fail, for then it would become necessary to issue 300-400,000,000 credit rubles. "We would sober up in about ten years," he explained, "when we faced the complete collapse of the ruble. But then censure would not fall on the present financial officials. They would reap only praise for having stimulated trade and industry." The State Council postponed the question until the fall.

The struggle against the monetary reform did not cease, nonetheless, and indeed it took the most unexpected turns.

During the emperor's visit to Paris, for example, the French premier, Méline, tried to persuade the tsar that a gold currency would be harmful to Russia. Count Montebello, the French ambassador, pursued this line by submitting to the emperor two detailed memoranda on the question.[8] *Russkiia vedomosti*, a liberal paper published in Moscow, took a firm stand in favor of the reform. Its position drew sharp criticism from almost the entire press, which accused the *Russian Gazette* of ignorance, "lack of respect for the science of finance," and other inadequacies. Ilya Tsion, Witte's old enemy and irreconciliable critic on the right, fired off diatribes from Paris—pamphlets titled "Where is Witte Leading Russia?" and "Witte and His Plan of Fraudulent Bankruptcy" in which Tsion denounced Witte as "a worthy disciple of Karl Marx." During the second half of 1896, opposition to the reform increased, but still the State Council deferred its consideration.

NICHOLAS AT THE RUBICON

Yet the emperor remained steadfast in his attitude toward the reform. He forwarded the French notes to Witte with the notation: "Enclosed are the memoranda which have been sent to me; I have not read them—you can keep them!" Finally on 2 January 1897 Nicholas convened a special session of the State Council at which he himself presided. The council decided at this meeting to proceed with the implementation of the reform. The emperor's ukaz of 3 January 1897 ordered the beginning of a new gold coinage in which the old Imperials [ten ruble gold coins] would be replaced by coins of the same weight and purity but stamped "15 Rubles" instead of 10. Typically, this ukaz, which signified "the crossing of the Rubicon" by acknowledging the two-thirds devaluation, appeared in the newspapers in small print and prompted scarcely any public reaction.

So the monetary reform entered Russian life without fanfare and, contrary to the warnings of its opponents, without creating any tremors in the economy. For two years already the rate had remained stable. The speculation in rubles had ceased. The state had been selling gold at the rate of 1 ruble 50 kopecks for each ruble in gold, and the exchange of paper

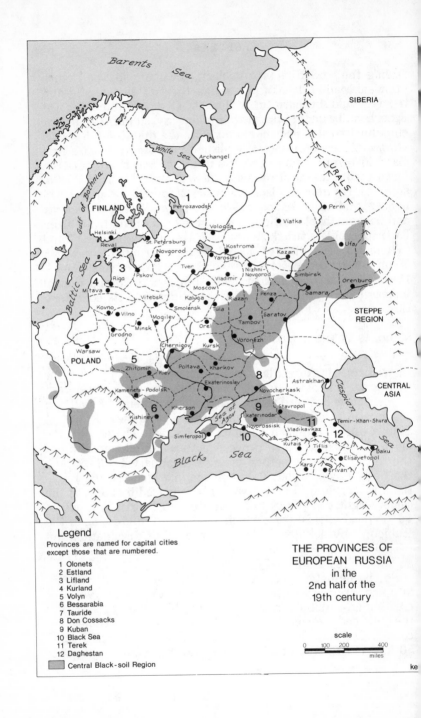

Barents Sea

SIBERIA

White Sea

Archangel

URALS

FINLAND

Perm

Petrozavodsk **1**

Viatka

Vologda

Helsinki

St. Petersburg

Kostroma

Kazan

Ufa

Reval

Novgorod

Yaroslavl

2

Nizhni-Novgorod

Simbirsk

Pskov

Tver

Orenburg

Riga

3

Vladimir

Penza

Samara

STEPPE
REGION

Mitava

4

Moscow

Kaluga

Riazan

Vitebsk

Smolensk

Tula

Saratov

Kovno

Vilno

Mogilev

Orel

Tambov

Baltic Sea

Minsk

Grodno

Voronezh

Warsaw

Chernigov

Kursk

POLAND

5

Poltava

Kharkov

Zhitomir

Kiev

8

Astrakhan

CENTRAL
ASIA

Kamenets-Podolsk

Ekaterinoslav

Novocherkask

6

Kherson

7

Stavropol

9

Kishinev

Sea of Azov

Ekaterinodar

11

Temir-Khan-Shura

Simferopol

Novorossisk

Vladikavkaz

12

Baku

10

Kutais

Tiflis

Elisavetopol

Black Sea

Kars

Erivan

Caspian Sea

Legend

Provinces are named for capital cities
except those that are numbered.

1 Olonets
2 Estland
3 Lifland
4 Kurland
5 Volyn
6 Bessarabia
7 Tauride
8 Don Cossacks
9 Kuban
10 Black Sea
11 Terek
12 Daghestan

Central Black-soil Region

THE PROVINCES OF
EUROPEAN RUSSIA
in the
2nd half of the
19th century

scale

0   100   200   400
                   miles

ke

rubles for gold at the same rate was no novelty. Gold did not flow abroad, nor was any significant amount of it hidden away. Russia meanwhile stabilized its international financial position by painlessly moving on the gold standard, which by then most of the great powers had adopted. (Japan followed Russia's example in March 1897.) The timing of the reform was fortuitous. Adoption of the gold standard followed four years of bumper crops (1893-96). Very possibly any further delay of the reform might have been fatal, for the years 1897 and 1898 brought poor harvests, and domestic and international complications followed soon afterward.

Some of the most prominent European economists—the Germans Adolph Wagner and Wilhelm Lexis and the Englishman George Viscount Goschen—unanimously recognized the timeliness and success of the Russian monetary reform. For his own part Witte recorded in his memoirs that "in the end I had only one force behind me, but it was a power stronger than all the rest—that was the confidence of the emperor. And therefore I repeat that Russia owes its metallic gold currency exclusively to Emperor Nicholas II." Indeed, confronted by the inertia of Russian opinion and by foreign interests hostile to stabilization, the currency reform probably would have failed except for the intervention of the emperor who compelled an end to the dispute by forcefully expressing his will at the meeting of the finance committee on 2 January 1897.

Toward the end of 1897 the government decided to produce new gold coins in values of 10 and 5 rubles. The new coins represented a one-third depreciation of the old Imperials and Half-Imperials. Wits in the capital sneeringly christened the new coins *matildory* (after Witte's wife) and *Witte-kindery* ["Witte's children"—slurring also his German ancestry].[9] Nevertheless the new gold currency rapidly acquired "citizenship rights," as Russians quickly adapted to it. Over the next fifteen years and for the first time since the introduction of paper currency (except for the brief period between the devaluation of 1842 and the Crimean War), Russia enjoyed the normal circulation of gold currency.

A NOVEL ANALYSIS OF THE AGRICULTURAL DEPRESSION

The debate on the monetary issue stimulated a strong general interest in economic affairs. A vigorous and open discussion of the future of the Russian economy emerged in the pages of the press and the meetings of various organizations. The rather rigid censorship that applied to "pure politics" offered little interference to the discussion of economic questions. Marxists and populists aired their views with relative freedom, and even the exiled Lenin contributed articles on the agrarian question to the "legal" journals.

One book published early in 1897 generated a bitter polemic. The minister of finance [in 1895] had invited a team of economic experts, headed by Professors A.I. Chuprov and A.S. Posnikov, to investigate the effect of declining grain prices. They published their detailed research as *The Influence of Harvests and Grain Prices on Some Aspects of the Russian Economy*.[10] The authors arrived at some unexpected conclusions—conclusions contrary to the opinion prevailing in agricultural circles. Agriculturalists took it for granted that the fall of grain prices (particularly the collapse of 1894) meant catastrophe for the villages. Chuprov and Posnikov, on the contrary, concluded that depressed grain prices actually were advantageous to the great majority of the Russian population.

The two authors found that the majority of Russian peasants either subsisted on their own grain or supplemented their production by purchasing additional grain. Higher grain prices, therefore, did not bring prosperity to the peasantry but on the contrary diminished their income. The effect was the same on the cities—city dwellers and factory workers naturally found it advantageous to buy bread as cheaply as possible. Chuprov and Posnikov calculated that only nine percent of the peasantry produced marketable surpluses. Only this peasant minority and the large landowners profited from higher prices, whereas the interests of the vast majority of the Russian nation required low priced grain.

Witte was well pleased with the conclusions of this study, and he made them the basis of his annual reports for 1895 and 1896. But the book was roundly attacked in the press.

Critics vigorously assailed the conclusions of the study as well as the statistics on which they rested. A debate in the Free Economic Society in March 1897 revealed the intelligentsia's wide diversity of opinion on economic affairs. The so-called "Marxist" economists, P.B. Struve and Michael I. Tugan-Baranovsky,[11] vigorously attacked the book. They insisted that the favorable conditions associated with low prices tended to coincide with abundant harvests. Good harvests, they continued, were obviously advantageous to the villages not *because of* low prices but *in spite* of them. Depressed grain prices hindered agricultural development, but they were equally detrimental to other economic sectors such as handicrafts and even industry.

Chuprov responded to this argument by taking the position usually raised in defense of the obshchina: "That form of economic system whereby man consumes what he himself has produced on his own land and with his own tools—that system is preferable to one in which the independent proprietor becomes a farm laborer or a factory worker. A natural economy has served Russia well. It explains why we have borne with considerable ease the agricultural crisis that has gripped the whole of Europe. We have a great number of farms that are unaffected by the price of grain. Who can say, under the current conditions of stress, that to a certain extent we should not bless fate for preserving our natural economy." Chuprov's remarks provoked a sharp rebuttal. "In my opinion," replied Struve, "Mr. Chuprov's hymn to our natural economy scarcely deserves a response. His optimistic sentiments are contradicted by the economic wretchedness so obviously apparent in time of famine and also by our cultural and political backwardness. To me the connection between these aspects of Russian life and our natural economy is irrefutable."

This heated controversy produced a curious alignment in which Marxists sided with landowner groups against populists who found themselves in Witte's camp. The acid debate between these factions of the intelligentsia typically erupted in mutual recrimination. The populists denounced their opponents for defending the interests of the landlords—for demanding higher prices for grain when "the progressive parties in the West" are advocating lower prices. The Marxists countered by condemning the populists for relying on the minister of finance and his selected data. The intelligentsia reached no common ground on the fundamental problems of the Russian economy, but their polemics examined the problem from every angle and occasionally furnished the government useful material for its legislative work.[12]

CAPITAL, LABOR, AND GOVERNMENT

For the intelligentsia the workers' condition was no less complex, but it was less controversial. Nearly all of them agreed that Russia needed to industrialize in order to assert its economic independence. Russia's status as a great power depended on that. They generally agreed that the persistence of rural Russia's natural economy actually did insulate the country from the effects of the world agricultural crisis (and thus also aggravated the negative impact of poor harvests). But a natural economy also hindered the development of the domestic market and retarded the movement of workers into the cities. The government instituted various measures to assist industrial development—notably railway construction and protective tariffs—but Russia lacked capital, and the tempo of industrialization picked up only at the end of the eighties and in the nineties.

The milieu of the intelligentsia was not wholeheartedly in favor of industrialization, as demonstrated by the Congress of Trade and Industry in Nizhni Novgorod.[13] The populists maintained that the condition of the Russian people deteriorated with the development of capitalism: alongside the treasury appeared a new "exploiter" to sap the energies of the people. The Marxists regarded industrial development as a progressive phenomenon to be exploited primarily to form the proletariat into a "revolutionary vanguard." Only a moderate segment among the Marxists, men like Struve, believed that Russian capitalism needed time to grow and develop before it could be engaged in a decisive struggle.

Russian workers clearly earned less and lived in poorer conditions than the industrial workers of Western Europe. On the other hand, they retained their village ties and therefore had less fear of unemployment. But lower earnings also signified the lower productivity (and less intensive application) of Russian labor. The average profit of a Russian industrialist (expressed as a percentage of turnover) was higher than in Western Europe, and on a national basis this profit was quite important for it represented practically the sole source (besides the influx of foreign capital) of funds for industrial development. The industrialists did not squander their profits on "champagne binges" but instead put them to work financing that expansion of manufacturing so necessary to Russia.

The intelligentsia were all but oblivious to the costs of production, and they inevitably backed the workers' extreme demands for the improvement of conditions. Populists and Marxists closed ranks on this question. Government authorities, recognizing that workers' benefits increased productive costs, had to proceed more cautiously. The administration had to seek the middle ground between the interests of workers and employers and to focus above all on the general interests of the nation and its future. After the great strikes of 1896, the government adopted a series of regulations covering working conditions. A special committee of five ministers studied new evidence on the problem but concluded that workers were no worse off than peasants. The committee therefore found no basis to recommend extraordinary measures that would require new state expenditures. Nevertheless, [Witte pushed through] the new law of 2 June [1897] which established a maximum eleven-and-one-half hour day for adult males with a ten-hour maximum on Saturdays and days preceding holidays. It also established a ten-hour limit on full or partial night work. This legislation failed, of course, to satisfy the leftists even though it provided a shorter work day than did the laws of Russia's competitors. France imposed a twelve-hour limit, but England, Germany, the United States, and Belgium had legislated no maximum for adult males. Italy adopted a twelve-hour day but applied it only to women. Legal limits lower than Russia's existed only in Austria (eleven hours) and Switzerland (ten-and-one-half hours). In many countries, in fact, the work day was actually shorter, as in England for example. There the struggle between labor and management rather than legislative action determined the outcome.

In Russia the government, fearful of disorders and their exploitation by revolutionary elements, considered strikes (or "crowd actions" as they were called) to be quite unacceptable. Consequently the authorities sought to prevent open economic

warfare between owners and workers, and the government intervened in the economic sphere with legislation and an enforcement agency, the factory inspectorate. The law of 2 June
1897 considerably increased the number of factory inspectors.
This provision, an indirect response to the strikes of 1896, was
designed to show that while the government opposed undesirable forms of labor protest, it was concerned to protect
workers' rights.

IMPASSE ON THE VISTULA

The sovereign paid a visit to Warsaw at the end of the summer
of 1897. Before his journey, he introduced several measures
to testify to his desire to soften the animosity in Russian-
Polish relations, severely strained since the uprisings of 1830-
31 and 1863. He revoked a special tax, imposed after the revolt of 1863, on landowners of Polish extraction in the western provinces. He allowed the Poles to collect funds to erect
a monument in Warsaw to Adam Mickiewicz (until then his
name was considered "seditious"—the work of this great Polish poet was overshadowed because he was an enemy of Russia, an organizer of the Polish legions during the Crimean
War).[14] The tsar appointed the gentle and courteous Prince
Alexander K. Imeretinsky to succeed the ailing Count Paul A.
Shuvalov as Governor-General of Warsaw. Finally, the government repealed the law that required non-Orthodox children
to attend Orthodox religious services (a measure that had
applied only to the Kingdom of Poland).

Among the Poles arose a movement toward compromise
with Russia, a position disdainfully labelled "appeasement"
by its opponents. The Franco-Russian Alliance had some bearing on this question, since Poland had a long-standing French
"orientation." A Polish publicist, Bagnitsky, wrote a pamphlet
that set forth the conditions under which Polish society could
accede to a reconciliation with the Russian Empire. Poland,
he wrote, was prepared to accept fewer rights than Finland
and to demand neither a separate army nor a separate tariff
zone. The Poles were willing to forsake their demand for independence of the western provinces and to limit their claims
to elected municipal and zemstvo self-government and to
discontinuation of russification in the Polish provinces.

Bagnitsky's program had one other point, the hope that Russia would reunite in the Polish Kingdom the Polish provinces then under German and Austrian rule. (To this condition the populist organ *Russkoe bogatstvo* responded: "To pay this price for reconciliation with the Poles would earn us a sworn and irreconcilable enemy in Germany.")

Their highnesses entered Warsaw on 19 August 1897 to a reception never before accorded a Russian monarch in Poland. The vast majority of the population, led by the local aristocracy, turned out for a welcome that went far beyond the official display of flags, illuminations, and cordons of troops. "We have passed through a hard school to reach the conclusion that one can be a good Pole and still remain a loyal citizen of the Russian state," wrote one of the influential Polish papers, adding that "our enthusiasm harbors no illusions and no wild hopes or dreams."

The emperor spent four days in Warsaw, receiving representatives of Polish society and thanking the people for their generous greeting. In a rescript to Prince Imeretinsky he wrote that his "concern for the welfare of the Polish people is equal to that for all loyal Russian subjects in their inseparable unity with the state." This remark indicated that while ameliorating the repression and revising the tone of Russia's relations with Poland, the tsar desired no basic change in that relationship. Like Alexander III and Pobedonostsev, Nicholas II stood for the centralized concentration of power and against the autonomy of the distinctive sections of the empire. The very least the Poles would accept as a basis for reconciliation with the Russian state was some degree of autonomy and some relaxation of central control. But would not such concessions prove to form an inclined plane leading to the complete secession of Poland? In any event, the Warsaw days of 1897 represented a step along a road beyond which History could not proceed.

NICHOLAS II AS FOREIGN MINISTER

During the first half of his reign, Nicholas II, like his father, served as his own foreign minister in more ways than his contemporaries perceived. After the death of Prince Lobanov-Rostovsky and during the tenure of his deputy Shishkin and other successors, the emperor guided Russian foreign policy along a route and toward an end known only to himself. His personal contacts with other rulers and personal interviews with ambassadors gave him access to information that was often different and frequently more reliable than the intelligence received through regular channels. The appointment of Count Michael N. Muraviev (the Russian ambassador to Copenhagen) to the post of foreign minister on 1 January 1897 injected nothing new into the foreign policy of Russia.[15] Before assuming his new position, Muraviev called at Paris (and on the way home at Berlin) to assure the French government of the permanence of Russian policy and to advise the Germans of Russia's peaceful disposition.

Three heads of state visited the emperor in Petersburg in the course of 1897: in the spring the Emperor Franz Joseph, in July the Emperor William II, and two weeks later President Felix Faure. The visit of the Austrian emperor, the least heralded of the three, nevertheless held the greatest political significance.

THE AUSTRO-RUSSIAN AGREEMENT OF 1897

The Austro-Russian agreement concluded on [18/30 April] 1897 determined the course of events in the Near East for some time. The interests of Russia and Austria-Hungary had clashed repeatedly in the Balkans and seemed beyond composition. All governments regarded the Austro-Russian rivalry as a self-evident political fact. Ultimately this perception was probably correct. In 1897, however, the two powers discovered the basis for a temporary agreement—to the great alarm of the British. Nicholas became convinced that the plan for the seizure of the Bosphorus, advanced by the Russian ambassador in Constantinople with the support of the army, would create dangerous complications. Despite the British "advances," Hanotaux told Muraviev quite plainly that such a move by Russia would produce a general European war. Nicholas decided, therefore, to accept the existing situation on a more or less permanent basis. To that end he sought an agreement with Austria for even though they pursued different long range objectives in the Balkans, both powers equally were interested in deferring any solution to the remote future. The Austro-Russian agreement proved immediately useful in the relatively painless liquidation of the Greco-Turkish war that erupted on [5/17 April] 1897. The Greeks were saved from the consequences of their military defeat, and Crete, while nominally remaining under Turkish sovereignty, submitted to administration by the concert of Europe.[16]

TETE-Á-TETES WITH GERMANY AND FRANCE

Splendid ceremonies attended the visit of Emperor William II from the initial reception at Kronstadt to the grand illumination at Peterhof, the military reviews at Krasnoe Selo,[17] and finally the commissioning of the kaiser as an admiral of the Imperial Russian Navy. This meeting was similar in many respects to their earlier meeting at Breslau [1896]. The German monarch, counting on his close personal relationship with the tsar, still hoped to bring him under his political sway, while the tsar responded with cautious restraint to the zealous toasts of his guest.

Two weeks later, the Russians gave French President Faure a similar reception. Nicholas welcomed the president at Kronstadt and treated him to the illuminated gardens of Peterhof and to parades and maneuvers at Krasnoe Selo. This duplication created some dismay among the French, but the end of the visit gave them good cause for satisfaction. For the first time the two leaders openly avowed the existence of the Franco-Russian Alliance. The occasion was a farewell breakfast aboard the cruiser *Rothnau* on 14/26 August 1897. Each head of state inserted into his speech the particular nuance that characterized his interpretation of the alliance. Nicholas referred to the "friendly united goal, inspired by our equal determination to assist with all our might, in the maintenance of peace." President Faure asserted that the two allies were "guided by the common ideals of civilization, right, and justice."

The citizenry of the Russian capital received their allies with great cordiality, stirring demonstrations for the sailors of the French fleet, and applause for the strains of the *Marseillaise*. The intelligentsia, especially, savored this sweet taste of the "forbidden fruit" of republicanism. The French visit carried no special political importance, however, and the liberal *Vestnik evropy* warned against excessive enthusiasm on this count. "French publicists," it observed, "are well known for their propensity to ascribe to the Russian people aspirations and joys which the people themselves scarcely comprehend. If our educated people disregard good sense and overflow with the exuberance of the French, then why should these Frenchmen not accept it as genuine coin?" For once this liberal journal agreed with the government's policy, warning that "the alliance with France can be useful to us only if it is not directed against Germany," and that generally "the Franco-Russian Alliance undoubtedly holds greater importance for France than for us."

ENGLAND'S RETREAT FROM SPLENDID ISOLATION

Although the emperor failed to bring about a reconciliation between France and Germany, the period 1895-98, during which Hanotaux occupied the office of French foreign minister, wore some of the edge off the old antagonism. This greatly alarmed the British whose policy of splendid isolation was predicated on the assumed inevitability of continental rivalries. Meanwhile Russia and Austria arrived at a working agreement, and the good offices of Russia threatened to ameliorate the enmity between France and Germany. Actually Russia was far from accomplishing this, but "fear has big eyes." Nevertheless, events in the Far East—the occupation of Kiaochow and then Port Arthur[18]—seemed to show that the continental powers of both Triple and Dual Alliances shared a common colonial policy and could act in Asia without British concurrence. The Salisbury-Chamberlain government made several efforts to prevent the establishment of a "concert of European continental powers." (Their secret maneuvers became public knowledge many years later.)

The British had still another reason for concern. An imperial ukaz of 24 February 1898 ordered the treasury to release 90,000,000 rubles for the construction of naval vessels. These funds were to be "independent of the increased allocation for the naval ministry for the period 1898-1904." In the Baltic Sea at that time Russia maintained seven battleships and three armored cruisers less than ten years old. In 1898 Russia set out to double the size of its navy.[19] Almost simultaneously the German Reichstag approved a new naval construction program valued at 250,000,000 marks.

A British note to Russia on 31 January/12 February [1898] suggested the partition of China and Turkey into British and Russian spheres of influence (which Russia refused). At the end of March the British government proposed a formal alliance to Germany, which Berlin received with suspicion. The Germans assumed that England and Russia could never reach an understanding and that the British, at any rate, could no longer count on anyone except an Anglophile faction in France. But Berlin reasoned that if France moved toward England, Germany doubtlessly would be compensated by a Russian rapprochement. Giving little credit to the British offer, the kaiser disclosed it to the tsar in a personal letter in which he also sought some recompense for his little "favor." In his letter of 18/30 May 1898 the kaiser wrote[20] that before replying to the British, "I frankly and openly come to you most esteemed friend and cousin to inform you, as I feel that it is a question so to say of life and death." England wanted to conclude an alliance with the Triple Alliance "and with the addition of Japan and America with whom pourparlers have already been opened! What the chances are for us in refusing or accepting you may calculate yourself! Now as my old and trusted friend I beg you to tell me what you can offer me and will do if I refuse? Before I take my final decision and send my answer, in this difficult position I must be able to see clearly, and clear and open without any backthoughts must your proposal be. . . . You need not fear for your Ally in any Proposal you make should she be placed in a combination wished by you."

Nicholas, however, correctly appraised the situation. If the kaiser wanted an alliance with England, he would not be seeking the tsar's advice. Obviously Germany hoped to extract some compensation for its refusal. The tsar sent back a cordial response, but fine irony punctuated his remarks. First, he noted that England also had made Russia a "very tempting offer which indicated that London seeks our friendship in order secretly to counter the growth of our influence in the Far East." As to the possibility of Japan and America joining an Anglo-German alliance, Nicholas observed that "as you know, we have reached an agreement with Japan regarding Korea and recently established excellent relations with North America. To tell you the truth, I don't see why the Americans would suddenly turn against their old friends just for the sake of England's beautiful eyes. It is very difficult, indeed impossible, for me to tell you whether it would be useful for Germany to accept England's offer. I do not know what it is worth. Therefore you yourself must decide since you alone know what is better and necessary for your country." Events confirmed the tsar's judgment. No Anglo-German alliance materialized and soon [6/18 August 1898] William wrote again to Nicholas: The British "are trying hard, as far as I can make out, to find a continental army to fight for their interests! But I fancy they won't easily find one, at least not *mine*!"[21]

The spring of 1898 saw still another great power enter the military and colonial field—the United States with its insignificant army but already powerful navy. War erupted between Spain and the United States, and as a result the Americans for the first time acquired possessions outside the North American continent. These were the circumstances in which Nicholas II conceived and proclaimed his historic appeal to restrict the growth of armaments that might lead to a war of unprecedented proportions.

THE EMPEROR'S APPEAL FOR ARMS LIMITATION

The origins of the tsar's circular remain an unsettled historical question. In March 1898 General Alexis N. Kuropatkin[22] presented to the emperor a tentative agreement to postpone the introduction of rapid-firing artillery into the Russian and Austrian armies. Meanwhile Ivan Bloch published a six-volume work that demonstrated the impossibility of waging war successfully under modern conditions.[23] The inspiration for a general limitation of armaments has been attributed also to foreign minister Muraviev and even to Witte, although the finance minister never stood in the ranks of the "ideologues." The most likely explanation is that the initiative belonged solely to the emperor. In order to divorce the idea from identification with any great power, it had to be proclaimed with a combination of boldness and frankness and outside the normal diplomatic channels.

Europe had known peace for more than a quarter of a century. Taking peace for granted, the peoples of Europe had begun to mistake the exceptionally long lull between volcanic eruptions for the extinction of the volcano itself. Their governments, however, understood the fragile nature of the peace, and they annually expanded their armaments. England responded to the vastly expanded Russian and German naval programs with a naval budget that exceeded both continental powers. The Austro-Russian agreement to delay their artillery rearmament was only a limited agreement, and even that encountered major obstacles. The result of the prolonged absence of military conflict was the unprecedented accumulation of the forces and instruments of war. The war of the future inevitably would assume unimaginable and incalculable proportions. Ordinary citizens believed that vast armaments precluded war. But their rulers—not only the tsar—knew that the sources of conflict had not diminished and that a mechanism for the peaceful settlement of problems still did not exist. Efforts to create an international system to prevent war only produced complicated chess moves, mines and countermines, alignments and illusory realignments. An example of this was the British proposal, first to Russia and then to Germany, a ploy designed to wreck the suspected alliance of the continental powers. The Franco-Russian Alliance offered advantages to each partner in case of war, but the alliance itself held no promise of peace for Europe.

Although many others besides the tsar foresaw the danger of a great holocaust, only the tsar, by virtue of his status and personal qualities, was in a position to step forward and lay before the world the imminent danger that confronted it. His communique exposing the dangers of an armed world deviated from normal diplomatic practice in that it bluntly asked the world's governments: you see the danger; are you willing to bend all your efforts to avert it, and are you capable of doing so? If one believes that life is regulated by laws as inflexible and independent of mankind as the laws governing the motion of planets, then the tsar's question must seem fruitless and naive. But anyone who believes that free will is inherent in individuals and nations must acknowledge that Emperor Nicholas II, who first demanded effective measures to prevent war and reduce the burden of armaments, inaugurated a momentous historic enterprise that has earned him the right to immortality.

Constantine Nikolaevich

Michael Nikolaevich

Vladimir Alexandrovich

Alexis Alexandrovich

Grand Dukes, Uncles of the Tsar and Brothers of Alexander III

THE CIRCULAR OF 12/24 AUGUST 1898

The emperor apparently conceived the idea in March 1898. Foreign minister Muraviev drafted the proposal. Nicholas stuck to his original plan despite the objections of [his uncle] Grand Duke Alexis Alexandrovich,[24] and the communique took final shape in August. Spain and the United States concluded a treaty of peace on 31 July/12 August 1898, and Count Muraviev invited the corps of ambassadors to his office two weeks hence, on 12/24 August. (The French ambassador, Count Montebello, was invited to appear two hours earlier than the others out of courtesy to Russia's special relationship with France.) The tsar already had given his approval to the final text. In his report to the emperor Muraviev observed: "Whatever the outcome of the proposal, the mere fact that Russia, fully armed with unconquerable forces, was the first to advocate the preservation of universal peace—that alone will serve as a pledge to ease the concern of the peoples of the world. This appeal will offer tangible evidence of Your Imperial Majesty's lofty altruism, greatness, and charity toward mankind. It will cause Your August Name to be engraved over the threshold between the expiring age of iron and the dawning new century in which, with God's help, may Russia be surrounded with the renewed splendor of peaceful glory." The text of the tsar's proposal reads as follows:

The preservation of universal peace and a possible reduction of the excessive armaments that weigh heavily upon all nations are, under present conditions, an ideal toward which the efforts of all governments should be directed.

This view corresponds fully to the humanitarian and benevolent intentions of His Majesty the Emperor, my August Sovereign. In the conviction that this lofty aim corresponds as well to the basic interests and legitimate aspirations of all powers, the Imperial Government believes that the present moment would be quite propitious to begin the search, through international discussion, for the most effectual means to guarantee to all peoples the benefits of a genuine and durable peace and, above all, to put an end [peredel—also "a limit"] to the progressive development of modern armaments.

In the course of the past twenty years the longing for peace has become especially pronounced in the consciences of civilized nations. Governments have proclaimed the preservation of peace as an object of international policy, and in the name of peace they have forged powerful alliances. To make peace more secure they have developed armed forces to proportions hitherto unprecedented, and they continue to increase them without regard for any sacrifice.

All these exertions nevertheless have failed to yield the beneficent results of the desired appeasement. An ever-expanding financial burden strikes at the very source of the commonweal. The intellectual and physical capacities of nations, labor, and capital are substantially diverted from their natural application and are dissipated unproductively. Hundreds of millions are spent to obtain the terrible engines of destruction which today represent the last word in science but tomorrow lose any value in consequence of some new development. National culture, the public good, and the production of wealth are stunted or diverted to worthless ends.

Each increment in armaments corresponds less and less with the aims that governments have set for themselves. The derangement of the economic system, caused largely by excessive armaments, and the continual danger, created by the cumulation of war material, are transforming the armed peace of our time into a crushing burden that is increasingly oppressive to the people who bear it. It appears evident, then, that to prolong this state of affairs will lead inevitably to the very cataclysm that all men seek to avoid and to horrors before which all thinking men must recoil.

To put an end to these incessant armaments and to seek the means to avert the disasters which threaten the entire world—such is the supreme duty now imposed upon all governments.

Imbued with this idea, His Majesty the Emperor has been pleased to order me to propose to all governments whose representatives are accredited to the Imperial Court to convene a conference for the purpose of discussing this grave problem.

With God's help, this conference should become a happy omen for the century that is about to begin. The conference would concentrate into one powerful focus the efforts of all states which sincerely strive to make the great idea of universal peace triumph over the elements of upheaval and strife. It would confirm, at the same time, their dedication to the solemn principles of justice and right on which rest the security of states and the welfare of nations.

This document was published in the *Pravitelstvennyi vestnik* [Government Messenger] on 16/28 August [1898] and circulated that same day throughout the whole world.

"SOME KIND OF DEVILTRY IN THIS"

The response was rapid—and negative. In practical political terms to renounce any further armaments meant a consolidation of the status quo, since armaments were necessary mainly to revise existing conditions. In other words, those who rejected the status quo had to oppose any limitation of armaments.

Vestnik evropy bluntly asserted that the weakness of the proposal lay in the fact that it emanated from the ally of France. "The proposed conference offers little hope of success as long as the attitude of France remains unchanged with regard to the lost provinces. As long as the problem of Alsace-Lorraine remains on the horizon and is not settled to the satisfaction of Germany, there can be no discussion of a durable peace nor any real relief from the unbearable burdens of the armed peace."

Meanwhile, an editorial of the semi-official *Times* of London (18/30 August 1898) immediately responded to the Russian circular by underscoring the same point: ". . . the principle of eternal justice received in 1871 a blow which has not yet been atoned for. So long as the scandal of this violation of right shall not have been effaced, the descendants of the men of 1789, the faithful heirs of that Revolution which found once more the title deeds of the human race should not subscribe to the application of the principles invoked by Count Muravieff . . . save after having ensured, with the very existence of France, the reparation of the past and the righteous adjustment of the future." Since "redressing the past" meant the return of Alsace-Lorraine, the *Times* meant that the French response to the Russian proposal would have to be negative. France, however, was not the only country to find the tsar's proposal unacceptable, although the alliance required that France be the first to "dot the i." The British and German press responded generously. *The Times* even conceded that the proposal would "bring glory to the Tsar and his reign." But the British government showed no inclination to take the Russian note seriously, and the German government was greatly alarmed by it.

If the first thought in France was whether "they mean to force us to accept the Treaty of Frankfurt" [1871], in Germany the question was whether some concession regarding Alsace would be demanded as a token of reconciliation. Foreign minister Bernhard von Bülow instructed the German ambassador in Petersburg to reject in advance any such possibility. The kaiser was irritated to distraction. He scribbled his angry comments across the reports and memoranda that crossed his desk on 16/28 August—"This effusion of prose is born out of bitter necessity . . . . Up to now Europe has been paying for Russia's armaments . . . . Intoxication with

humanitarianism led to his incredible step . . . .   There is
some kind of deviltry in this!" Nevertheless, the kaiser wired
the tsar that his proposal "clearly illuminates the loftiness and
purity of your motives." William added, however, that "it is
difficult to carry out . . . . Can one imagine a monarch dis-
missing regiments consecrated by centuries of history?"

RUSSIA'S DIOGENES IN SEARCH OF PEACE

The first month produced positive responses only from Italy
and Austria. Nicholas therefore sent Muraviev and war minister Kuropatkin abroad for consultations. The emperor instructed them to place the following interpretation on the
circular of 12 August: the proposal envisioned a limitation of
armaments, not a general disarmament; that principle should
suffice to begin the conference without committing any government to full compliance with any decision. The Russian
ministers arrived in Paris at the height of the Fashoda crisis.[25]
The British had routed the Mahdist forces at Omdurman and
laid claim to the entire valley of the Nile. They were threaten-
ing forcibly to remove from Fashoda a small French detachment commanded by [Captain] Jean-Baptiste Marchand. The
French force had reached the Nile from the Atlantic coast
after an arduous trek through the uncharted and dense jungles
of Equatorial Africa. The deterioration of Anglo-French relations was so serious that President Faure and Théophile
Delcassé, Hanotaux's successor as foreign minister, informed
Muraviev that "our enemy is England, not Germany."

The initial conversations between the allied ministers were
far from amiable. Kuropatkin was informed by the new
French war minister, General Jules Chanoine (with the Dreyfus affair at a climax in France, war ministers changed rather
frequently), that "your government's announcement of 12
August had a most depressing effect on the French Army. Officers of the French Army hung their heads. The thought of
disarmament after twenty-seven years of great effort and sacrifice deprived them of all hope for the return of Alsace and
Lorraine . . . .   Frenchmen cannot forsake this aspiration,
because it unites the best forces of France irrespective of their
membership in different political parties . . . . The suspicion
spread that the Russian emperor made this move in agreement
with the kaiser."

The French government complained that it had received no prior warning of the proposal. Kuropatkin explained that "in order to ensure that this great message proclaimed from the tsar's throne would be received by all peoples and governments as his magnanimous desire for the good of all, it was necessary not to offend any country and to offer the arms limitation proposal equally to all." Of course if France had been notified beforehand, the emperor would have been forced either to cancel the project, or to proceed with it over French objections, or at least to modify the proposal and deprive it of its impartiality and altruism. When the French finally realized that the circular contemplated no concrete political concession and that it represented only a basic statement of principle, they recovered their equanimity and agreed to take part in the conference. General Chanoine, who had quickly familiarized himself with the project, recommended specific proposals to neutralize hospital ships and restrict the use of new types of explosives. He suggested that the conference devote itself to a "statistical survey" of the benefits that might accrue to agriculture, industry, and commerce as a result of decreased armaments.

Count Muraviev also had the task of explaining the proposal to the German leaders. He tried to convince Eulenburg that France was wealthier than either Germany or Russia and that each of them would exhaust their capacities more rapidly. "A lie!" wrote the kaiser on the report of Eulenburg's conversation. "The Russians have already reached their limit." The Germans steadfastly insisted that an acute deficit in the Russian treasury had prompted the tsar's proposal. In fact, the Russian foreign debt decreased between 1897 and 1900.[26]

Kuropatkin and Muraviev returned from abroad to report on the results of the Russian initiative. Kuropatkin's report to the emperor on 23 November proved most interesting. "The people responded enthusiastically," he asserted, "but their governments reacted distrustfully." A reduction of armaments was politically unacceptable to the French, "who bear the cost more easily than others and who, for the sake of Alsace, will never cease to rearm." Germany, too, "bears the cost easily. But no nation considers military preparedness such a desperate necessity as the French: France lives for the moment of revenge." Austria and Italy would be receptive

("Austria fears anyone and everyone, real and imaginary," according to Muraviev). England would support arms limitation—except for the *fleet*! The reaction of the smaller countries would be positive if their inviolability could be guaranteed. The war minister set forth the following preconditions for general disarmament: 1) the breakup of the Austrian Empire; 2) Russian occupation of the Bosphorus; 3) French occupation of Alsace-Lorraine and, as compensation, the incorporation of Austria's German provinces into the German Empire.

By this time the Anglo-French confrontation at Fashoda had been resolved. The British government, however, continued to flirt with Germany in order to create the impression that London could count on German support in case of war. Chamberlain made a provocative speech against France at Manchester on 3 [15] November.[27] The situation seemed to favor a continental alignment against the British, but the Germans wavered between England and Russia. In any event Berlin failed, or decided not to exploit the Anglo-French conflict to improve relations with France. Delcassé backed down and ordered Marchand to surrender Fashoda to the British. Throughout this crisis Russian diplomacy favored reconciliation.

From Damascus [during a visit to the Holy Land] Kaiser William II wrote to inform Nicholas that "if it is true, what the Papers say, that Count Mouravioff councelled France to take this foolish step he was singularily and exceptionally ill advised, as it has given your *"friends and allies"* a mortal blow here [in the Near East] and brought down their ancient prestige here never to rise again!"[28] The tsar, however, followed his established policy of avoiding European complications, while Delcassé, an irreconcilable foe of Germany, was paving the way to the *Entente cordiale*: it was much easier to forget Fashoda than Sedan.[29]

THE TSAR'S SECOND APPEAL

As for the international peace conference, the generally discouraging replies to the tsar's proposal offered little promise of success. St. Petersburg had the possibility of citing this general disinterest as the reason for the failure of the proposal.

That course would have offended the sensibilities of friendly
countries and in no way furthered the aims of appeasement.
At one point the Russian government considered a new communique to emphasize that a conference would be inoppor-
tune "in the presence of developments so highly contradictory to the desire for peace." The original draft of this note
levelled accusations directly against England, but the government reconsidered the injustice of making England alone the
scapegoat. Still, it was inadvisable to let the matter drop.
Untold numbers of people in all countries, who fervently had
welcomed the call for universal peace, could not believe that
it was unattainable. To have disappointed their hopes inevitably would have given rise to disillusionment and aspersions.
The Russian government, therefore, made a second attempt
in December 1898. The revised appeal took account of the
reaction to the original proposal and reformulated the general
wording of the first appeal into several specific points. The
second circular read [in part]:

Despite the strong current of opinion that exists in favor of the ideas of
general pacification, the political horizon recently has undergone a decided change. Several Powers have undertaken fresh armaments in efforts to strengthen their military forces. In the face of this uncertain
situation, it might be asked whether the Powers consider the present
moment favorable for an international discussion of those principles
set forth in the circular of 12 August . . . .
    Should the Powers consider the present moment opportune to con-
vene a conference for the aforementioned purposes, it would be patent-
ly useful for the Governments to reach concurrence on the items to be
included on the agenda of the conference . . . .
    It is well understood that all questions relative to political alignments
and treaty obligations among States, as well as all other matters not
specifically included on the agenda, will be excluded unconditionally
from discussion during the conference.

Having mollified French and German fears of the possible
injection of political questions into the conference, Russia
proposed the following agenda:

(1) agreement to maintain at present levels for a fixed
period all land and naval forces and military budgets;
(2) prohibition against the introduction of new weapons
and explosives;

(3) limitation on the use of existing explosives and a prohibition against hurling projectiles from balloons;

(4) prohibition against the use of submarines in naval warfare (at the time only the first experimental tests were underway);

(5) application of the Geneva Convention of 1884 to naval
warfare;

(6) recognition of the neutrality of ships and boats engaged in life-saving operations during naval battles;

(7) revision of the 1874 declarations on the laws and customs of warfare;

(8) adoption of principles for the acceptance of good offices, mediation, and facultative arbitration; an agreement to
accept these instruments and to establish uniform procedures
in using them.

In this document the original proposal for a reduction and
limitation of armaments became simply "the first" among
several other proposals. Thus the second appeal for a world
conference translated the general program of the first into
several rather concrete items. Some thirty years later at Geneva, the World Disarmament Conference [1932] took up the
"tag ends" of the Russian proposal.

The second Russian note received an even cooler response
than the first. Some saw it as a retreat from the earlier position, but others blatantly expressed their scorn for the newly
advanced program. *The Times*, which had praised the general
tone of the August circular, denounced the program of 30
December as impracticably utopian: "It is incumbent upon
us not to deviate from obligatory courtesy with regard to
Russia nor to alter the humanitarian idealism that is our tradition; but within these limits we reserve all freedom of action."

In a conversation with Kuropatkin the tsar, remarking at
the second unfavorable response, regretted that he had ever
embarked on such an undertaking. Nevertheless, despite the
unpromising atmosphere, the peace conference finally got
underway. In a history of the conference Albert de Lapradelle[30] recorded that "the world was startled when the

powerful monarch, the leader of a great military power, proclaimed himself an advocate of disarmament and peace in his messages of 12/24 August and 30 December. The world was even more surprised when, thanks to Russian persistence, the conference was prepared, came into existence, and opened." The Hague was the site chosen for the conference, because Holland was one of the more "neutral" countries (though not formally "neutralized" like Belgium and Sweden).

To ensure the participation of all the great powers, they agreed to exclude certain governments. No African state was invited because of the Anglo-Boer conflict, nor was the Vatican because of Italian sensibilities, nor any Central or South American government. All twenty European states participated (with Bulgarian representatives included in the Turkish delegation), as well as four Asian (Japan, China, Siam, and Persia) and two American states (the United States and Mexico). The Hague Conference met from 6/18 May to 17/29 July 1899 under the presidency of the Russian ambassador to London, Baron Egor E. Staal.

A SMALL STEP FOR MANKIND

The struggle within the conference centered on two issues—arms limitation and compulsory arbitration. The debate on the first question took place in the plenary session of the First Commission (22, 26, and 30 June 1899).[31] Baron Staal argued that "the main purpose of the conference is the limitation of military budgets and armaments. We are not speaking of utopias: we do not propose disarmament. We seek to limit, to halt the growth of armaments." The Russian military representative, Colonel Jacob G. Zhilinsky, offered a three-fold proposal: (1) a pledge not to increase the existing peacetime strength of armies for a period of five years; (2) the size of armies to be determined precisely (but to exclude colonial forces);[32] (3) a pledge not to expand military budgets for the same period. Russia's naval delegate proposed a three-year limitation on naval budgets and the complete publication of naval statistics.

Several representatives (including the Japanese) claimed that their governments had sent no instructions on these questions. The German military representative, Colonel Gross von Schwarzhoff, took upon himself the unpopular role of official oppositionist. He ridiculed those who protested that the cost of armaments was excessive. "I permit myself to dispel these well-intentioned concerns," he declared. "The German people do not suffer under a yoke of taxation, nor do they stand on the edge of an abyss. They are prospering, and their living standard is increasing. Universal military service is a sacred duty, not a burden." In addition, he argued, military strength was not measured in numbers. Colonial troops, substantial in some countries and insignificant in others, were a source of inequality, but "I maintain that a country can increase its military power without expanding the size of its army."

The First Commission referred this question to a subcommittee of eight military delegates representing Austria-Hungary, England, France, Germany, Italy, Russia, Rumania, and Sweden. With only the Russian representative Zhilinsky dissenting, the committee reported that it would be difficult to limit the size of armies even for a period of five years without simultaneously regulating all other elements of the national defense systems. Further, since the other components of national defense varied from country to country, it would be no less difficult to regulate these through international agreements. Consequently, the committee regretted that it was unable to accept the Russian proposal. The commission and then the general conference endorsed the committee position. Leon Bourgeois, the French representative, seconded the German delegate. Citing technical problems, Bourgeois recommended that the report be supplemented by the following purely platonic declaration: "The conference considers that a limitation of the military charges which now weigh upon the world is *greatly to be desired* in the interests of the material and moral welfare of mankind."[33] When the delegates also protested the absence of instructions on naval armaments, the chairman of the First Commission, [former Dutch foreign minister] Hermann van Karnebeeck, announced that "with instructions hardly to be expected before the end of the conference, we will handle naval armaments in the same manner as land armaments."

The proposed establishment of a court of arbitration came under heavy fire. The German position reflected the inflexible views of Baron Friedrich von Holstein, councillor of the German foreign office, who was the leader behind the scenes of the German delegation: "One can envision small states and insignificant problems becoming the subjects of arbitration, but great powers and important questions—never! The greater the state the more it sees itself as an end in itself, not as the means to some remote higher objective. The state has no object more vital than its own self-interest. For a great power, however, national interest is not necessarily coincidental with the maintenance of peace. National interest sometimes is served by overwhelming an enemy or competitor by means of a skillfully contrived, more powerful coalition."

The conference ultimately reached a compromise by abandoning the principle of compulsory arbitration (even in matters having no bearing on the honor or vital interests of individual states). In return the German delegation agreed to the establishment of a permanent court. William II, incidentally, regarded the court a great concession to the tsar. On the margin of Bülow's report on the conference the kaiser wrote: "So that he will not appear the fool before the whole of Europe, I agree to that nonsense! But in practice I will continue to rely and depend only on God and my own sharp sword." Although couched in more considerate language, those were also the sentiments expressed by other national leaders.[34]

Of the Russian proposals of 30 December the conference completely rejected only the first article. The delegations adopted prohibitions against explosive ("dumdum") bullets, projectiles dropped from balloons, and gas warfare. They agreed to extend the Geneva Convention to naval warfare (the protection of hospital ships) and to revise the articles of war [on the treatment of prisoners and wounded]. They adopted a declaration on the peaceful settlement of international disputes through mediation by third parties. The details of this agreement developed by the Russian delegate, Professor Feodor F. Martens, led to the establishment at The Hague of the Permanent Court of Arbitration. All these accomplishments, however, paled beside the original vision of the emperor.

Throughout the entire period, from the appeal of 12 August to its conclusion, the Hague Conference received little attention from the Russian public. Compassion intermingled with skepticism and a touch of derision characterized the public's attitude. The tsar's proposal surprised the intelligentsia, because it contrasted sharply with their rigid opinion of the "imperialistic" and "militaristic" government of Russia. They attempted to rationalize the circular of 12 August as trivial or as emanating from some *raison d'état*, and invariably they alluded to its "insincerity." By the time the conference opened, Russia's educated elite was so engrossed with domestic politics that they scarcely noticed the work at The Hague.

EMPEROR OF RUSSIA, APOSTLE OF PEACE

Nevertheless the tsar's circular of 12 August 1898 and the First Hague Conference played a major role in world history. They demonstrated the remoteness of universal peace and the instability of the international truce, but at the same time they asserted the possibility and desirability of ensuring peace through international agreements. From these events sprang all subsequent efforts to secure universal peace—not only the Second Hague Conference of 1907 but also the Geneva institutions. "This idea will take root," declared Count Muraviev in August when he submitted the proposal to the ambassadors, and events subsequently confirmed his prophecy.

Men who regard war as inevitable, necessary, or even useful undoubtedly would label this a noble but unproductive utopian scheme or a useless if not deleterious initiative which only created treacherous illusions. But those convinced of the possibility of international peace and all those who later endorsed the idea of a League of Nations and the disarmament conferences could not fail to acknowledge that the quest for peace originated with the Russian emperor, Nicholas II. The wars and revolutions that plague our times cannot erase this achievement from the pages of history.

When the Washington Conference on naval armaments opened on 9 November 1921, the President of the United States, Warren G. Harding, paid tribute to the man who provided the original inspiration: "Arms limitation through international agreement is not a new idea. On this occasion it would be appropriate to remind ourselves of the noble aspirations expressed twenty-three years ago in the Imperial Rescript of His Majesty the Emperor of All the Russias." Then, having read almost all of the "clear and moving" words of the Russian circular of 12 August, President Harding added: "It was with such a sense of duty that His Majesty the Emperor of All the Russias proposed the convening of a conference, which should have addressed itself to this important problem."

꧁ꕥ꧂

CHAPTER FIVE

RUSSIA AND ASIA

Kaiser William II with his passion for sententious slogans once declared that "Germany's future is on the seas." If Nicholas II had not possessed an intense dislike for tumidity and theatrical posturing, he would have distilled his policy into the assertion that "Russia's future is in Asia." Many signs directed Russia along this new (and yet very old) path. Traditional nineteenth-century tsarist ambitions in the Balkans and the Austrian and Ottoman Empires could be realized only through a general European war. Even under optimum conditions the acquisition of the Straits would have committed Russia to a continuing struggle for mastery in the Mediterranean Sea, which the British firmly bolted at each end. The unification of the West and South Slavs with their "elder Northern Brother" indeed would have enabled Russia to thrust its outposts into Europe.[1] But this Slavic salient would not have made Russia invulnerable or inaccessible to foreign onslaughts, and it offered no inexhaustible source of strength and resources. It was Asia that promised all these advantages, if Russia could establish its supremacy there.

Other nations competed for parcels of land at the antipodes of the earth. Then they built navies to protect their colonies which stretched around the globe. Russia, however, continuing the original example of its own conquerors of Siberia, followed a course far superior to this race for colonies. For Russia, empire meant a process of organic growth—expansion into Asia behind an advancing frontier. Russia's empire represented the enlargement of Russian territory, not the conquest of remote foreign lands. This process was a legacy of earlier reigns: the Ussuri region and Vladivostok were added to the empire in 1859, the southern part of Sakhalin Island in 1873, the Central Asian khanates on the borders of British

India in the 1880s during the reign of Alexander III.[2] Asia, a continent of enormous polities each with fully developed national cultures, was quite unlike Africa [the other major target of late nineteenth-century European imperialism]. Russia had acquired dominion over the northern rim of Asia. (Russia's possessions appeared enormous on maps, but the inhospitable northern taiga and tundra restricted the habitable area to a very narrow corridor.) St. Petersburg had yet to solve the fundamental Asian problem—the China question.

"Immovable China," as Pushkin described it in 1831, had been wracked continuously by internal upheavals since the middle of the nineteenth century. Civil war had raged incessantly through the fifties, sixties, and seventies—for nearly thirty years!—erupting in the very heart of China in the valley of the Blue [Si] River (the Taiping Rebellion [1848-64]), in southernmost China (in Yunnan on the borders of Indo-China [1855-73]), and in the extreme west (the Tungan revolt in Chinese Turkestan [1862-78]).[3] Europeans already had begun to despoil the collapsing Celestial Empire, and in 1860 at the height of the civil war an international expedition occupied Peking and forced the government to open twenty-five ports to foreign trade. (At that point Russia annexed the Ussuri region without a war.) The power and influence of the Manchu dynasty was ebbing rapidly. But then by the will of fate there emerged an energetic woman, widow of Emperor Hsien-feng [1851-61], the "iron" Empress Tzu-hsi. During the next two reigns, from 1861 until 1908, Tsu-hsi was the real ruler of China.[4] Although unsuccessful in restoring China to its international position, she managed at least to reunite the country.

In 1871 during the Tungan rebellion in Chinese Turkestan, Russia occupied the Kuldja district in order to preserve it from pillage and ruin. Russia restored the territory to China in 1880 but retained a small part of it as "recompense."[5] The other great powers anticipated the disintegration and partition of China, but Russian policy generally sought to preserve the integrity of China. This policy was not a contradiction but rather a direct application of the "great Asian program."

TOWARDS A CHINA POLICY

Alexander III committed Russia to the construction of a trans-Siberian railroad. This in itself revealed that the emperor's father thought in terms of Russian domination of Asia, since it made no sense to expend such enormous resources and energy simply for the sake of direct communication with the sparsely settled periphery of the empire. It was the reign of Nicholas II, however, that saw the crystallization of Russia's Asiatic "mission" into the pre-eminent policy of the state.

Prince E.E. Ukhtomsky, the emperor's companion on his tour of Asia, was an expert and passionate admirer of the Buddhist East and a collector of precious oriental art. He undoubtedly remained a confident of Nicholas, who was thoroughly acquainted with his views. Although Ukhtomsky's published opinions had some effect on the course of events in the Far East, he actually did not exert any decisive influence on Russian foreign policy. His opinions stemmed from his belief in a profound spiritual affinity between Russia and Asia. Between the peoples of Western Europe and Asia was an abyss, he once said, that became more obvious as contact between them increased. No such gulf separated Russians and Asians however.

Beyond the Altai and the Pamirs stretches a vast unexplored land, unknown to any thinker and identical with pre-Petrine Rus in its uninterrupted traditions and its boundless love of miracles, in its humble submissiveness to the natural and unnatural calamities inflicted on man for his sins, and in the austere grandeur that permeates its spiritual mien.

The Ghenghises and Tamerlanes led vast warrior hordes with which they forged invincible empires and created spiritually strong, tolerant governments which in turn molded and impregnated pre-Petrine Russia with a political theory rooted in the refined conservative wisdom and wiles of China. Russia has yet to reverse the migration and organize the movement of our western peoples into the depths of Asia where we find ourselves at home—where long the harvest has waited while the reaper tarries . . . .

To skeptics who protested, "So what? We already have enough land," Ukhtomsky replied: "The All-Russian state has no alternative. Either it must fulfill its ancient destiny as mediator in the merger of West and East or, ignominiously and imperceptibly, it must follow the path to oblivion. For

in the end Europe will overwhelm us with its superiority, or
Asia's peoples aroused by others will become an even greater
menace to us than foreigners out of the West."

Other advocates no less influential than Ukhtomsky offered
still another view of Asia. In 1895 the kaiser sent Nicholas a
notorious cartoon which depicted the nations of Europe fear-
fully regarding a statue of Buddha illuminated by a bloody
glow in the East. "People of Europe!" warned the caption,
"Defend your sacred property!" This same vision terrified the
philosopher Vladimir S. Soloviev who imagined another Mon-
gol invasion of Europe in which, again, Russia would become
the first victim. In a famous poem titled "Pan-Mongolism"
Soloviev prophesied:

> O Rus, forget your past glory:
> The double-headed eagle is smashed,
> And for their games, yellow children
> Are given the shreds of your ensigns!

The French thinker, Count Joseph de Gobineau, whose writings greatly influenced the development of "racial" thought
in Germany, entertained quite the opposite view—the image
of tsarist Russia leading Asia in an assault against "Aryan"
Europe. Whether one regarded Asia as a dreaded danger or a
source of Russian might and the foundation of our future,
one thing was unmistakably clear: Russia had to be strong in
Asia. The Siberian railway was an essential but insufficient
means to that end.

In 1895, when Russia intervened with Germany and France
in the Sino-Japanese War to prevent Japan from gaining a
foothold on the continent, Nicholas II noted on a report of
the foreign minister (2 April 1895): "A port ice-free and
open year round is absolutely indispensable to Russia. This
port must be somewhere on the mainland (southeast of Korea)
and it is imperative that it be linked to our earlier possessions
by a strip of land." The situation did not permit immediate
attainment of this goal. Russia with inadequate forces in the
Far East had to act jointly with the other powers. The liberal
Novosti urged that "now is the opportune moment to polish
off China, immediately and without trouble, and to divide it
among the powers mainly concerned." But Russian policy
was more complex than that.

Russia had no desire to partition China. To the contrary, Russia sought to maintain China's integrity and to exert the dominant influence over the Manchu empire. For that reason St. Petersburg cultivated the friendship of China after the Treaty of Shimonoseki of 1895.[6] The Chinese delegation led by Li Hung-chang was accorded special treatment at the time of the tsar's coronation. Subsequently Russia and China concluded a treaty granting Russia permission to extend the Great Siberian Railway through Manchuria, the ancestral land of the imperial dynasty (but almost unpopulated by that time). Russia in return promised to support China.[7]

THE KOREAN COCKPIT

Even closer relations developed between Russia and Korea. As a result of the Sino-Japanese War, Japan established its hegemony in Korea and proceeded to create a "reform party." Queen [Min Chii-rok] and her courtiers, however, opposed this faction. On 9 October 1895 Japanese supporters burst into the palace, murdered the queen, and made King [Yi Kojong] their prisoner. A national protest movement formed in the wake of this outrage, and the popularity of the reform party disintegrated. The Russian consul appealed for two hundred sailors to protect the Russian mission in Seoul. The arrival of this force was sufficient to cause a drastic turn of events in late January 1896. The king escaped and took refuge in the Russian legation. From there he ordered the execution of his prime minister and other officials serving the Japanese. The royal decree was carried out. With the Russians as his protectors, the King of Korea was disposed to accede to their wishes, but Russia, without the support of a fleet or railway, was unable to take advantage of its good fortune. Consequently Petersburg compromised with Tokyo. Each antagonist recognized the independence of Korea and the sovereignty of its monarch. They agreed to maintain equal forces of about one thousand men to protect their diplomatic missions and commercial interests.[8]

THE CRAFTY KAISER TAKES KIAOCHOW

The surge of Russian influence in the Far East upset the western powers no less than Japan. The Siberian railway, advancing several hundred versts a year, was about one-third completed (extending about 2,300 versts [1,525 miles] beyond Cheliabinsk), when new events at the end of 1897 greatly altered the situation.

As the tsar's guest at Peterhof in the summer of 1897, Emperor William II broached the question of German harbor and coaling facilities in China. He wanted to know in particular whether Nicholas would object if Germany shared Kiaochow Bay, where Russian naval forces already had acquired the right to winter. According to Bülow, who accompanied the kaiser, Nicholas replied that "Russia wanted to retain access to the bay since at the moment it lacked rights to a more northerly port . . . . In response to the German emperor's inquiry, Emperor Nicholas II said he would not object if out of necessity a German ship entered the bay with the permission of local Russian authorities."

That fall [23 October/4 November 1897] Chinese rioters killed two German missionaries in Shantung Province not far from Kiaochow.[9] Germany seized the opportunity to intervene forcefully in China. The kaiser demanded that warships be sent to Kiaochow, but Chancellor Hohenlohe advised that he first consult with Russia. William II telegraphed the tsar directly for Russia's permission to dispatch ships to Kiaochow to punish the murderers, "since it is the only point from which to reach these brigands." Nicholas replied (26 October/7 November 1897): "It is not my place to approve or deny the deployment of your squadron to Kiaochow. Our vessels used these waters only temporarily [during 1895-96]. I fear that severe measures will only widen the gulf between Chinese and Christians."

The tsar's intent was clear. He had no right *"to permit"* Germany to send a force into the port of another sovereign state, and indeed he advised against it so as to avoid deepening the hostility between Europeans and Chinese. In a supplement to the tsar's cable foreign minister Muraviev indicated that he had advised the Chinese government to punish the murderers and thereby satisfy German demands and make intervention superfluous. But with the aid of a little "pressure on the texts" the German government interpreted Nicholas's telegram not only as assent to sending a squadron to Kiaochow but also as endorsement of a permanent German naval base!

This created the first major disagreement between the emperor and William II. Nicholas was indignant at the distorted interpretation of his telegram. The Russian government pointed out that in any discussion of rights in Kiaochow Bay, Russia enjoyed the right of "first anchorage." The fact that Russia currently was not exercising that right could not be interpreted to mean that St. Petersburg was ceding it to others.

Germany, however, decided to proceed in spite of Russia. "Russia and France could instigate Chinese resistance and require us to commit large forces and expenditures," wrote the German ambassador, Count Paul Hatzfeldt, from London. That prospect apparently failed to move the Germans. Even though China agreed to all German demands respecting the murder of the two missionaries, a German ship entered Kiaochow Bay and landed a detachment. This was a "new factor" of enormous import and one that forced Russia to clarify its position. From the standpoint of Russian-Chinese friendship, the extreme but logical position was to fight Germany for China's rights. War against Germany, however, implied a struggle against the entire Triple Alliance, and Russia moreover would be confronted by the hostile attitude of England and Japan. Even France could find scant appeal in the prospect of war under those conditions, and the possibility was not considered for long. On 18/30 November, following a conversation with Russian ambassador Count Nicholas D. Osten-Sacken, Bülow recorded his "impression that the Russians will not attack us because of Kiaochow and do not want a quarrel with us at this time."

Friends of China like Prince Ukhtomsky recommended that Russia temporize and back China in a policy of passive resistance. The fruits of such a policy, they maintained, would be realized in only a few years, after completion of the Siberian railway. Witte's position was similar. But this approach could not promise certain success. In international affairs, where time is an essential ingredient, there was no guarantee that time would work in Russia's favor. The partition of China might outstrip every calculation. The Manchu dynasty, on whose friendship this policy depended, might have been overthrown at any time. In the ensuing struggle for the Chinese inheritance Russia would find itself isolated in the far north without an ice-free base for its fleet. Was Chinese friendship worth the risk? Could the "spiritual affinity" between Russia and China serve as a realistic basis for Russian policy? The decision that finally emerged from these contending views was to secure a base in China without disrupting the friendship of the Chinese government. This line seemed to offer insurance as well against any further partition of the Chinese Empire.

PORT ARTHUR AND THE INTEGRITY OF CHINA

On 3/15 December 1897 Russian naval vessels entered Port Arthur and Talienwan [Dalny], the same ports on the Liaotung Peninsula that Japan had been forced to renounce two and a half years earlier. For the next two or three months a complicated diplomatic scenario unfolded. With great fanfare at Kiel the German emperor took leave of his brother, Prince Henry of Prussia, who was leading the squadron bound for the Far East. In an unexpected move, England sent Russia a proposal to take up negotiations for the partition of Turkey and China. Faithful to the agreement with Austria on maintenance of the status quo in the Balkans, Nicholas authorized Muraviev to discuss only the Far East, but he also gave special instructions that "it is impossible to divide an existing sovereign state (China) into spheres of influence."[10]

In late December 1897 an interesting commentary appeared in one of the Peking newspapers.[11] The Chinese writer predicted that Russia, with the very best of intentions, would occupy Port Arthur and Talienwan until China was strong enough to defend them without foreign assistance. "But I fear that the day of their return to China will never come. Having assumed such an awesome responsibility, Russia will not get rid of it, even if it wanted to . . . . All that will remain Chinese in these two ports will be their hollow names." The gloomy seer continued: "Our situation is identical to that of a large family waiting with folded hands for its total annihilation by bandits who have broken into the house. Of course, whether it is a passive death at the hands of the villains or death coming after a struggle against them, it is death all the same, but an unequal death . . . . Even a chained animal resists, and a man all the more, but at present China is worse off than any animal." The publicist concluded with an appeal to resist the Germans—but only Germany and not Russia, since the writer regarded the seizure of Port Arthur as a chess move to counter the German landing at Kiaochow.

If China had risen to become more than "a chained animal" and had summoned the energy and determination to fight for its existence, Peking's friends in Russia, Prince Ukhtomsky and others, might have found support for their policy. But China stirred no more than a corpse. Aided by substantial bribes to several leading Chinese politicans with Li Hung-chang at their head, Russia concluded a new Sino-Russian agreement in Peking on 15/27 March 1898. The treaty reaffirmed the inviolability of Russian-Chinese friendship, proof of which was a lease to Russia for twenty-five years of "Port Arthur and Talienwan including the adjacent territories and waters, as well as permission to construct a branch railroad to connect these ports to the Great Siberian main line." The Russian government in reporting the agreement observed that "as stipulated in the diplomatic act of 15 March, the peaceful occupation by Russian naval forces of the ports and territory of a friendly nation could offer no better indication that the government of the Chinese emperor has understood, quite correctly and in the proper perspective, the significance of the agreement concluded between us."

Western Europe and also a considerable segment of the Russian public regarded the occupation of the Liaotung Peninsula as natural and unavoidable. The liberal *Vestnik evropy* wrote for example that "the timing of our movement undoubtedly was quite fortunate. Our acquisition of Port Arthur and Talienwan in no way violates established international procedure, but on the contrary conforms to it fully. In satisfying its genuine need for a suitable ice-free port on the Pacific Ocean, Russia merely fulfills its duty as a great power." Organs of opinion further to the left, such as *Russkoe bogatstvo* (having already condemned French colonial policy in Indo-China), maintained an unfriendly silence. Only the partisans of China voiced discreet objections. In an interview with a German journalist in the spring of 1898 Prince Ukhtomsky declared: "I now oppose our foreign ministry. I am against the occupation of Port Arthur. I condemned the German occupation of Kiaochow. We must do everything possible

Kiahkhta, a Russian Outpost on the Mongolian Frontier

to strengthen the Peking regime. If disorder erupts in China, the Manchu dynasty will be overthrown, and a fanatic national reaction will succeed it . . . . Peking in fact is already without a government. Under the circumstances anyone could conclude an agreement without resistance, but when the dynasty collapses, foreigners will be butchered."

SOMETHING FOR EVERYONE

At the time of its agreement with China, Russia also made certain concessions to Japan in Korea. In 1898 the government recalled its military and financial advisers and announced that "henceforth Russia can refrain from active participation in Korean affairs in the hope that its young government, which grew strong with Russia's support, will be able to maintain domestic order and national independence." Nevertheless, the communique also warned that if Korean tranquility and integrity were jeopardized, "the Imperial Government will adopt measures to safeguard the interests and rights incumbent on Russia as a great power bordering on Korea."

The occupation of Port Arthur, so recently taken from the Japanese, created deep bitterness in Japan. Following its easy victory over China in 1895, Japan had been on a collision course with Russia in Asia. Thenceforth a conflict appeared unavoidable unless Russia remained so powerful that Japan would not dare to attack it. The Siberian railroad was under construction simultaneously in several sections, but as the pace of events quickened in the Far East, continuous track extended only as far as Lake Baikal. Following the lead of Germany and Russia, England also acquired a naval base in China, the port of Weihaiwei (which the Japanese had occupied as security for China's payment of the indemnity for the war of 1894-95).[12] England tried strenuously to reach agreement with Russia on spheres of influence. Meanwhile London and Berlin agreed to extend the open door principle to the Yangtze Valley. Finally in 1899, after two years of negotiation, an Anglo-Russian accord was signed. The Russian government agreed not to seek railway concessions south of the Yangtze River, and the British gave the same assurance with respect to northern China. The status of the Peking-Mukden Railroad, financed with British funds and already under construction, remained an open question.

PEACE THROUGH STRENGTH

The Hague Conference and especially the attitude of the great powers to the Russian circular of 12 August had demonstrated clearly that elimination of war was impossible in the prevailing international situation. Russia, like every other country, had to be prepared to assert its position in the world, such as it was. Enemies of the Russian crown (including Count Witte) later insinuated that this attitude contradicted the tsar's peace initiative. Such was not the case, for this position derived logically from the failure of the Hague Conference. The world recognized only force; it had greeted the tsar's proposal for arms limitation with nothing but skepticism and scorn. Russia therefore had no choice but to be strong—strong to maintain the peace and strong for security in the event of war. Despite the near inevitability of war in the Far East, Nicholas II never deviated from his love of peace. In the eyes of advocates of "preventive war" he perhaps even missed a golden opportunity to strike at England.

The war in South Africa, which occupied the British after [October] 1899, proved far more difficult than anyone had imagined. A nation of a few hundred thousand practically without artillery managed to tie down the military forces of the British Empire for nearly three years. So great was England's unpopularity throughout Europe that volunteers by the dozens and hundreds flocked from everywhere to join the Boers. The Russian emperor shared the popular attitude toward this struggle between "David and Goliath," as it was known. This was the same attitude that moved a member of the Moscow city duma, Alexander I. Guchkov, to volunteer for service in South Africa. Nicholas expressed his sympathies in letters to his relatives. In a letter to [his sister] Grand Duchess Xenia Alexandrovna he described the pleasure he derived from the thought that he could have a decisive effect on the outcome of the war by moving troops into India. But the emperor realized the difficulty and risk of such an undertaking, which might have led to a general European war, and the thought extended no further than a few remarks in his personal correspondence. Some of his ministers, nevertheless, definitely favored the idea that Russia take advantage of England's tribulation. For their part the British made some effort to accommodate Russia. On 31 August 1899 London agreed to accept a Russian consul in Bombay, thus for the first time permitting official access to India which the British had preserved so carefully from Russian influence.

A WARNING TO THE GERMANS

In November 1899 the tsar, returning from a visit to Hesse, passed through Potsdam for the first time since his accession. There he held a very important interview with the German Secretary of State for Foreign Affairs, Bernhard von Bülow (soon to be appointed Reich Chancellor). The tsar spoke frankly and precisely. While admitting his sympathy for the Boers, he nevertheless declared that Russia would not intervene in African affairs. Russia desired peace. It did not want a conflict between England and France. *Had Russia wanted it, the conflict would have broken out a year ago.* (This statement confirmed widespread rumors concerning the role of Russian diplomacy in resolving the Anglo-French crisis over Fashoda.) "There is no problem," Nicholas continued, "that finds the interests of Germany and Russia in conflict. There is only one area in which you must recognize Russian traditions and take care to respect them, and that is the Near East. You must not create the impression that you intend to oust Russia politically and economically from the East, to which we have been linked for centuries by numerous national and religious ties. Even if I myself handle these matters with somewhat more skepticism and indifference, I still would have to support Russia's traditional interests in the East. In this regard I am unable to go against the heritage and aspirations of my people."

The full impact of this warning was to be felt some fifteen years later in 1914. It was uttered at a time when Russo-German relations were relatively amicable, when the Russian foreign minister, denying he had said that Alsace should be returned to France, exclaimed, "Do they take me for a fool?" This conversation with Bülow indicated that although preoccupied with Far Eastern affairs the emperor had not forgotten Russian interests in the Near East and did not wish to disturb the temporary maintenance of the status quo established in the Russian-Austrian pact of 1897.

The first two years after the occupation of Port Arthur and Kiaochow (from early 1898 to early 1900) passed without incident in the Far East. China appeared to go on "sleeping." Russia followed its previous course of maintaining good relations with the Chinese government. The entry of the United States into the Far East (with the occupation of the Philippines) passed almost unnoticed. It was nevertheless an event of momentous importance for it blocked Japan's southward expansion and its plans for the creation of an insular empire. American annexation of the "unclaimed" Hawaiian Islands in 1899 provoked no objection from any quarter. Russia devoted intense effort to its naval program. Franco-Russian relations lost some of the ardor associated with Hanotaux's tenure as foreign minister. France was not especially sympathetic to Russia's Far Eastern ambitions, which if successful would have freed Russia from involvement in Western Europe. Moreover, the Dreyfus affair brought leftists to the fore in France, and they were less disposed to rely on Russian support. Neither ally, however, expressed any thought of terminating the alliance.

"SLEEPING CHINA" AROUSED

During the spring of 1900, agitation against foreigners began to mount in China, but the great powers, accustomed to Chinese passivity, paid it little heed. Elusive rumors circulated about a Society of Righteous and Harmonious Fists (or "Boxers" as they came to be known), an organization that was fomenting riots against the "devils from across the seas."[13] Soon this powerful movement was spreading everywhere like water surging from an underground spring. The spontaneous power of the movement caught the diplomatic corps in Peking by surprise. On 8/21 May the delegations presented a note to the Chinese government demanding that it arrest all members of the Boxer society and all property owners who allowed them to meet in their homes. The note also demanded the execution of all persons responsible for assaults against the life and property of foreigners and the execution of those who "lead the Boxers and provide them with financial means." On 13/26 May the Russian minister, Michael N. Giers, notified St. Petersburg that "foreign representatives have no reason to consider the central government powerless to suppress the Boxer uprising," and accordingly

he had ordered back to Port Arthur the Russian gunboat that
had been sent to Taku.[14] A force had been landed to protect
the mission, but it consisted of only seventy-five men. On
18/31 May Bülow inquired of his minister in Peking whether
the growing disturbance presaged the final partition of China.
The revolt could signify only one thing—the crumbling power
of the Manchu dynasty!

On 20 May (2 June) the Russian envoy reported that
Peking had grown calmer since the arrival of the detachment.
"But within less than a week," according to the government's
report of 25 June, "an alarmed Giers cabled that the role
of the ambassadors had ended and that matters should now
pass into the hands of the admirals. Only the prompt arrival
of a strong military force can save the foreigners in Peking."
But it was already too late: Peking was cut off from the sea,
and Chinese troops besieged the diplomatic quarter. While
the diplomatic representatives pressed their demands for
"punishment of the guilty parties" and tried to get action
from the Chinese government, it was apparent from the outside that the authorities had become one with the "rebels."
China, suppressed and silent for so long, had ceased to be a
"corpse" or a "chained animal." The Chinese rose up against
the foreigners, and while the government was not convinced
fully of the wisdom of this rebellion, it gave in to the people's
movement. It was rumored—no one knew for certain—that
Prince Tuan, a kinsman of the emperor, had seized power,
that the Dowager Empress Tzu-hsi had fled, and even that the
empress herself had ordered the destruction of the foreigners.[15] The rumors, as usual, exaggerated the "Chinese atrocities," but without question hundreds of Europeans including
women and children perished during this dramatic revival of
Chinese nationalism.

Communication with Peking was interrupted (there was no
wireless telegraph at the time), and reports reached Europe
that all diplomats had died with their families under dreadful
torture. Meanwhile the Chinese, so unwarlike and even scorn-
ful of the military arts, suddenly had become fearless and
faced death practically unarmed. A British column which set
out under Admiral Sir Edward Seymour to rescue the missions
not only failed to reach Peking but even when reinforced by
Russian sailors barely managed to fall back to Tientsin. At

the height of these events, on 8/21 June 1900, Count M.N. Muraviev, the Russian foreign minister, died. The tsar appointed Deputy Minister Count Vladimir N. Lamsdorf[16] to succeed him. The change in ministers in no way affected the course of Russian foreign policy.

WHITHER RUSSIA?

Now all the Cassandras who had foretold of the "yellow peril" vociferously proclaimed that doomsday was at hand. The western powers, united by the common danger to their legations, resolved to dispatch troops to China. But first they turned to the neighboring countries, Russia and Japan, with requests for military assistance. Once again Russia faced the difficult choice of whether to join the European powers in the destruction and partition of China or to adhere to its policy of friendship with China and frustrate as far as possible the actions of the other powers. In their rebellion against foreigners the Chinese made no distinction between Russians and other Europeans. The advocates of Russian-Chinese amity explained that these indiscriminate attacks stemmed from the occupation of Port Arthur, which signalled Russia's alignment with the partitioners of China, but they maintained their faith in the possibility of Russo-Chinese cooperation. In the introduction to a book that he published, *On Events in China*, Prince Ukhtomsky wrote (in July 1900): "The movement, which thus far embraces only part of China, threatens to reach unprecedented proportions. The movement has fallen with full force upon Russians because of, one can only hope, the temporary and incidental identification of our interests with the rapacious and treacherous interests of others. We must recover our historic road and never for a moment lose sight of our true mission in Asia, which is intimately rooted and cherished within our soul." Prince Ukhtomsky did not conceal his sympathies for Chinese nationalism even to the point of asserting that the Chinese "have taught the West a good lesson."

F.F. Martens, the professor of international law who played a prominent role at the Hague Conference, took a similar position in an article on "Europe and China" (also in July 1900):

The Chinese will be defeated, but no victory can crush a nation of 430,000,000 people. This revolt against all foreigners has deep roots. In 1880 I wrote: 'The weaker the Chinese government and the more enemies that it acquires within its own frontiers, the more the civilized world must remember that any pointless propaganda as well as any interference in China's domestic affairs can produce only two results: either they will precipitate the fall of the present Peking regime, or they will force it into a league with its own people for the destruction of all foreigners.' The first alternative offers no guarantee that a new dynasty would be more favorably disposed toward the outside world. The second—the annihilation and proscription of all foreigners—would make it quite difficult to recover the lost position.

Professor Martens offered the following principles for a Russian policy in China: 1) an absolutely unique position of Russian preponderance; 2) the inviolability of China; 3) only moral and financial compensation to be demanded for the massacre of foreigners; 4) a stable Chinese government as an essential condition. ("If the presently ruling Manchu dynasty proves unfit, another Chinese emperor must be found and supported if necessary.")

INTO THE JAWS OF THE DRAGON

Meanwhile the movement spread into sparsely populated Manchuria, and Chinese nationalists attacked Russian engineers and laborers on construction sites along the railroad. Acting with the connivance of local authorities, the rebels severed overland communications between Port Arthur and Siberia. Inflamed by the reported slaughter of foreigners, the West mounted a crusade against China. With customary bombast Emperor William II grandiloquently exhorted an expedition bound for the Far East to wield the "mailed fist" and "show them no mercy."[17] Vladimir S. Soloviev, who lived in constant dread of the "yellow peril," celebrated the kaiser's speech with a poem that he completed just before his death:[18]

The Fire of Christ is in your Sword,
And your menacing speech is holy!
. . .
You know that before the Dragon's jaws,
The Cross and the Sword are one!

The Russian public, inspired neither by Soloviev nor by Ukhtomsky, followed events in China with only languid interest.

("Due to the progressively misanthropic and uncivilized illusions of our better classes, we are losing any political sensi-
bility for eastern affairs," wrote the author of *Events in
China*.)

The Russian government, however, pursued a middle course.
It had no alternative but to take part in the action against
the Boxers, if only because Russians were among the diplomats besieged in Peking and because Chinese assaults in Manchuria struck directly at Russian enterprises. Yet at the same
time St. Petersburg clung to a rather artificial diplomatic
position by insisting that the Boxer movement was a rebellion
[against legitimate authority] and that Russia sought to
retain the friendship of the Chinese government.

Japan, on the other hand, wasted no time in placing itself
at the service of the European powers for the purpose of
suppressing the Chinese revolt. A formidable international
force began to assemble around Tientsin in July: 12,000
Japanese, 8,000 Russians (transported by sea from the vicinity
of Port Arthur), and 2-3,000 troops from other European
countries. After a prolonged diplomatic negotiation, Field
Marshal Count Alfred von Waldersee was placed in overall
command, since Germany had suffered the greatest injury.
(By then, rumors of the murder of the German minister in
Peking had been confirmed.) Petersburg had no desire to have
a Russian at the head of a punitive expedition against China.

Meanwhile, panic broke out along the Russo-Chinese frontier. The Russian border town of Blagoveshchensk came under
sustained rifle fire, undoubtedly from Chinese regulars. Just
before this assault, the Russian garrison had moved further
down the Amur River and left the city practically defenseless.
The terrorized population and authorities of Blagoveshchensk
wreaked terrible vengeance on the local Chinese. Fearful
that the Chinese residents of the city would stage an uprising
in the rear and overwrought by reports of atrocities, the local
authorities herded all the "yellows" to the banks of the Amur
and ordered them to swim to the Manchurian side. Only a
handful managed to cross the broad river, and several hundred
drowned. This tragedy, understandable enough in the prevailing atmosphere of terror, revealed the difficulty of actually
carrying out the policy of Russo-Chinese friendship. (The
local intelligentsia approved of this panic-inspired reprisal,

much to the indignation of the liberal press in cities far removed from the borderlands.)

The international relief column, which had beaten off several attacks around Tientsin, began its advance on 23 July/5 August 1900, long before the arrival of Marshal Waldersee. On 2/15 August Russian troops under General Nicholas P. Linevich occupied the Chinese capital. Simultaneously a Russian column under General Paul K. Rennenkampf moved southward into Manchuria and encountered scant resistance. The relief column discovered that the diplomatic quarter in Peking was untouched; Chinese forces had done little but blockade the legations. Russia immediately reverted to its policy of goodwill toward China and hastened to separate itself from the other powers.

Certain that the military intervention was over, the tsar on 8/21 August ordered a halt to the introduction of Russian forces into China. A few days later, on 12/25 August, Russia proposed that the international force withdraw from Peking and also recommended that the legations be moved out of danger to Tientsin. Russian representatives explained that there was no longer any government in Peking, that the government could not return to Peking as long as foreign troops were stationed there, and that even if it did return, the people would regard it as a captive of the foreigners and refuse to obey it. Germany vigorously objected to this point of view and accused the Russians of violating the European united front. Before long, however, the other governments were persuaded that under the circumstances the Russian proposal was well-founded.

The next question was with whom to negotiate. The whereabouts and composition of the Chinese government, which had fled to Sian, was unknown. The European detachment occupied the capital and held the line Peking-Tientsin-Taku. European marauders plundered the palaces of the Forbidden City [the imperial residence and government buildings]. But the occupied zone was no more than an island in a yellow sea, and China had not surrendered. On 15 September the powers presented their demand for the extradition of those responsible for the rebellion, including Prince Tuan. In response came notification on 25 September that Prince Tuan had been appointed chairman of the state council. The consular corps at Tientsin desperately suggested that in retribution the powers should threaten to destroy the ancestral graves of the Manchus, but even western governments could not condone such an infamy. Meanwhile [200,000] Russian troops occupied all of Manchuria lying between the Russian frontier and the Liaotung Peninsula, and work on the railroad resumed.[19]

The great powers too set to work to devise a plan for liquidating the "Boxer incident." (In the end they subscribed to the fiction that there had been a war with China.) Throughout these negotiations, Russia pressed for terms as advantageous as possible for China, and Petersburg in particular stubbornly opposed the extradition and execution of leading Chinese officials who had collaborated with the Boxers. Finally, after a year of negotiation, the powers presented their demands to the Chinese government, which in the meantime they had been able to locate. The Chinese promptly agreed to every demand, and the international occupation of Peking came to an end.[20]

RUSSIA: NOT GUILTY

As a result of two events beyond its control—Germany's seizure of Kiaochow and the Boxer Rebellion—Russia found itself in possession of an ice-free harbor on the Pacific and a strip of land (indeed, a broad overland corridor) that connected this port with its earlier acquisitions. Thus the objectives set forth in the emperor's memorial of 2 April 1895 had been fulfilled, even though Russia's possession of this territory still awaited formal recognition. Nevertheless, the situation had grown very complex. The "great Asian program" had been predicated originally on good relations with the Chinese government, whose authority was now seriously undermined. The Manchus still had the capacity to preserve Chinese national unity. In conducting its foreign policy, however, Peking constantly had to respect the distrustful nationalist movement, which made no distinction among foreigners and which regarded any concession to outsiders as treason against the state.

No action taken by Russia had vitiated the authority of the Manchus. China's defeat at the hands of the Japanese,

Germany's unchallenged seizure of Kiaochow, and, as some
Europeanized Chinese intellectuals perceived it, Peking's em-
phatic rejection of reform—these were the reasons behind the
swelling opposition to China's traditional authority. All these
factors occurred quite apart from Russia's occupation of Port
Arthur. To have stood aloof from the China question and to
have foregone the acquisition of these borderlands scarcely
would have improved Russia's position in the struggle for
supremacy in the Far East. More likely, disengagement would
have been construed as a sign of weakness. In any event the
Chinese people would not have distinguished Russians from
any other "white devils," and the goodwill of the crumbling
Manchus already counted for very little.

A NEW DEAL FOR SIBERIA

At the end of the nineteenth century Manchuria was a sparsely settled land. In an area of about one million square versts
lived only three or four million people. As the ancestral lands
of the Chinese imperial family, this province had been closed
to settlers. The tracks of the Chinese Eastern Railway were
being laid through vast areas all but completely barren of
inhabitants. Manchuria was a direct extension of the better
and more fertile sections of Siberia.

Russia greeted the dawn of the twentieth century from a
favorable position in the Far East. Siberia had entered a
period of rapid growth. A migration bureau, organized early
in the reign of Nicholas II, sent torrents of "scouts" (khodoki)
and settlers from European Russia to areas more suitable for
farming. The Siberian railway stretched uninterrupted to
Irkutsk, and sections of the line were operating in the Ussuri
region. Growth of the Siberian population accelerated in the
last half decade of the century. The judicial reform of 1864
was extended to Siberia in 1896. In his ukaz of 12/25 June
1900 the emperor introduced another important reform, this
one prohibiting the settlement of exiles in Siberia. The elimination of the "Siberian exile system," known so well abroad
through hearsay,[21] by no means abolished the stern system
of repression that the "fearsome" name of Siberia conjured
in the lurid imagination of Western Europe. The imperial
ukaz was designed to prevent the valuable outlying regions of

A Siberian Convict

Russia from being "littered" with undesirable elements. It
was not that Siberia was not good enough for convicts, but
rather that convicts and exiles were not good enough for
Siberia! As the ukaz declared, the tsar had decided "to lift
from Siberia its heavy burden as an area filled through the
ages with vicious people."[22] Only Sakhalin Island remained a
place of exile. Of course prisons for holding convicted crim-
inals were not abolished in Siberia (or elsewhere for that
matter). *Vestnik evropy* drew a very sound parallel between
the abolition of Siberian exile and developments in China:

In the not too distant future we must anticipate either a genuine reorganization of China or a struggle among the powers over its ruins. In
either case so vast a part of our country as Siberia, lying directly along
the borders of ancient China, should become more than the slender
thread that now links European Russia with the shores of the Pacific
Ocean. We must hope that Siberia will witness the rapid and extensive
development of its native resources. This in turn will attract from the
homeland the best and most enterprising colonists—energetic settlers in
contrast to the dregs that European Russia until now has conferred
upon Siberia, a type of emigration which [the tsar's decree] now has
brought to a most timely conclusion.

CHAPTER SIX

NEW DIRECTIONS IN LITERATURE AND ART

The end of the nineteenth century formed "the Chekov years" in Russian literature. With the successive deaths of A.N. Maikov (1897), J.P. Polonsky (1898), and D.V. Grigorovich (1899), Anton P. Chekov, a keen psychologist and perceptive observer, assumed first rank among Russia's writers.[1] Radical critics forgave him his lack of positive social views because his portrayal of the dullness and boredom of Russian provincial life indicated his "striving for the ideal." Among the newer writers Maxim Gorky achieved almost instant fame in 1898.[2] His tales of "vagabonds" who neither had nor required anything were something new in the stale intellectual atmosphere of despair and disbelief [*Weltschmerz*]. *Severynyi vestnik*, a mirror of new literary trends, ceased publication. In its place there emerged the representatives of "decadence"—as symbolism, a new mode in search of spiritual values, then was called.[3] Merezhkovsky produced his trilogy *Christ and Anti-Christ*, Zinaida N. Hippius her first collections of stories and poetry, and Feodor Sologub his first poems and the novel *Bad Dreams* (1896). Balmont was beginning to attract attention, and Briussov published his first collection of poetry [1894] which Vladimir Soloviev ridiculed with intemperate gusto.[4]

New directions were even more apparent in art than in literature. A group of artists gathered around Sergei P. Diaghilev first organized exhibits (toward the end of 1898) and then began to publish the journal *Mir iskusstva* (World of Art). Alexander N. Benois, Constantine Somov, Mstislav V. Dobuzhinsky, Constantine A. Korovin, and V.A. Serov (who won first prize at the Paris World Exhibition of 1900 for his portrait of Grand Duke Paul Alexandrovich) were all members of the *Mir iskusstva* school. The leftist stereotype in art was beginning to grow boresome. Programs of the Society of

Circulating Exhibitions no longer seemed interesting, and their attendance began to fall off. *Mir iskusstva*, asserting the cause of pure art, now locked horns with the radical journals.

"They call us children of an age of decline," wrote Diaghilev, "and coolly and without complaint we bear the senseless and insulting title of 'decadents.' But what should we consider our golden age? Where are our Sophocleses, our Leonardos and Racines, who could see our work only as a feeble perversion of the art that they created? The reign of Chernyshevsky, Pisarev, and Dobroliubov has been fashionable for too long in Russia." Diaghilev scorned the precepts of the "anti-art theory of socialism that consigns art to the role of an obedient student in braces." The editor of *Mir iskusstva* concluded that "the great virtue of art is that it is an end in itself, that it is useful to itself, but above all, that it is free!"

It was noteworthy that in Russia the demand for artistic freedom was not directed against the tsarist authorities, who in no way infringed upon the freedom of artists, but rather against the moral oppression of radical intellectual critics. Following the well-established monarchist tradition, Russian imperial authorities provided a broad range of support to the fine arts. Alexander Benois, for example, managed the art exhibit at the Nizhni Novgorod exhibition; Bakst and others were employed by the imperial theaters or the art publishing house (Society of St. Eugene) of the Russian Red Cross. A number of Serov's works were portraits of the tsar's family. Among them was the finest and best known portrait of the emperor, painted in 1900 at the request of Empress Alexandra Feodorovna.[5] Serov also did paintings of the coronation. The Russian Museum in honor of Emperor Alexander III opened in the Mikhailovsky Palace in St. Petersburg on 7 March 1898. The works of Russian painters and sculptors in the Hermitage all were transferred to the Russian Museum. Subsequently the Russian Museum was enlarged to accommodate new acquisitions from contemporary exhibits of Russian art.

Together with the flowering of the Imperial Ballet, Russian theater witnessed innovation and experimentation. The Moscow Art Theater opened in 1897, and under the direction of Constantine S. Stanislavsky it acquired an outstanding reputation in Russia and abroad.[6] Vera F. Komissarzhevskaia, an

Portrait of Emperor Nicholas II by Serov

actress of the late nineties, won rapid and ardent acclaim among the public. Motion pictures too developed rapidly, although at that time they were far removed from the world of art. As early as 1898, however, the censors found it necessary to prohibit the projection on to screens of images of the Saviour, St. Mary, and the saints.

The allocation of funds for public education expanded without interruption year by year, and the public school system developed at a remarkable pace. The ministry of finance had created its own special School of Commerce and was preparing to open the St. Petersburg Polytechnic Institute. Two years of bad harvests, 1897 and 1898, and the crisis that was affecting all of Europe slowed somewhat the rapid rate of Russian economic development. Industry and the railroad network continued to expand despite these difficulties. Receipts from indirect taxes and taxes on amusements and entertainments showed steady increases. One of the liberal journals observed in reporting this fact that "as you see, we are living more merrily."

ORGANIZING THE REVOLUTION

At the same time the ranks of the enemies of the existing order also were increasing and forming "illegal" organizations. Following the example of the Polish Socialist Party which originated in the early nineties (and had among its founders one Joseph Pilsudski),[7] the Russian Social Democratic [Labor] Party was formed in Minsk (in 1898) at a congress called by the Jewish Bund.[8] The League for the Emancipation of Labor and several other organizations participated in the congress. The police surprised the gathering and arrested most of its participants. Nevertheless, both Bolsheviks and Mensheviks celebrate this date as the "birthday" of their parties.[9] Only much later [1901] did the populist revolutionaries organize as the Socialist Revolutionaries. Even so, some of their independent groups, whose origins extended back to the notorious People's Will, acted together with the Marxists. In general, despite a wide array of theoretical differences between revolutionary and even oppositionist elements, a considerable degree of unanimity actually existed during those early years. "The fierce and difficult struggle against the

autocracy," announced *Sovremennik* [The Contemporary],
an illegal organ published in London (1897), "requires all
available forces, regardless of the color or shape of their
banner or the title they have chosen for whatever reason. The
only symbol of our destiny—the only essential requirement
that we recognize—is hostility toward the principle of autocracy. Once you truly accept this thesis, you are our ally.
What you consider the best way to injure and destroy it is a
matter for your own conscience and understanding."

Secret revolutionary organizations found support mostly
among students. Kiev University, in particular, had strong
Bund and Polish Socialist groups. Of course, only an insignificant minority of students belonged to these organizations, but
other political movements were not organized at all. Prince
V.P. Meshchersky, an unwavering proponent of the "aristocratic principle," wrote of the new year 1898:

New voices resound, new ideas are born, new wishes and aspirations
emerge, new wills make themselves heard. From the turbid sedimentary
muck of the past sprout new problems . . . and out of all this confusion
something like a mood takes shape . . . . The appearance—the clothes
and the style—is the same, but those who notice only this similarity
between the present and past fail to see that the clothes are gradually
wearing out at the seams . . . . Our friends, the French, often tell us:
'You, you are happier than we. We have five hundred wills attempting
to guide France, but only one will directs Russia. In Russia God is a
necessity: in France He is only a luxury.' I must confess, I would have
preferred that it would not be the French to tell us this out of envy, but
rather we who would announce it to the French with pride . . . .

CONTINUING THE GREAT REFORMS

Nicholas II was aware, of course, of the hostility of the urban
intelligentsia to the existing order, but he deeply believed that
the attitude of the peasant masses was totally different. In a
conversation in the summer of 1898 with Prince Peter N.
Trubetskoy, the marshal of the nobility of the province of
Moscow, the emperor touched on the question of limiting the
autocracy. He was quite prepared, he said, to share his power
with the people, but that was impossible. The people would
assume that the intelligentsia had forced their tsar to share
his power, whereupon they would wipe the upper classes from
the face of the earth. (The fate of the intelligentsia and
bourgeoisie since the overthrow of tsarist authority has confirmed the validity of that argument.)

Always desirous not to break with the past and to build anew incessantly, the emperor continued nevertheless to "complete and repair" the structure of the Russian Empire. Gradually he surrounded himself with collaborators of his own choice. By the end of the century eight of the twelve ministers in office at the time of his accession had been replaced (three as a result of death).[10] Of the ministers appointed by Alexander III there remained only Pobedonostsev, Witte, the Minister of Justice Nicholas V. Muraviev (who was appointed in the last year of Alexander's reign), and Minister of Agriculture and State Domains Alexis S. Ermolov. To replace Ivan D. Delianov, who died at the age of seventy-nine after sixteen years as Minister of Public Education, the tsar at the beginning of 1898 appointed Nicholas P. Bogolepov, a professor of Roman law. "I know," Bogolepov told his subordinates upon assuming office, "that life has raised demands for improvement and innovation in all areas of public education. But I am of the opinion that both should be undertaken gradually and with great care. I am not in favor of abrupt changes."

Under the general formula of "completion and repair" the ministry of interior was responsible for extending the zemstvos into those provinces that still lacked them. The extension of the judicial statutes of 1864 furnished the precedent for this operation. News of the project provoked an immediate reaction from the conservative press. The authoritative *Moskovskie vedomosti* even denied the rumor when it first appeared. The announcement came during the course of a campaign by Meshchersky's *Grazhdanin* in which that paper severely criticized zemstvo programs as useless and beyond the capacities of zemstvo taxpayers. A friend informed me that "embezzlers had been uncovered in about ten zemstvos," wrote Prince Meshchersky. " 'Thank you, Oh Lord,' I said and beaming with joy I crossed myself. I only regret that embezzlers were not caught in all thirty-four provinces. Then they would not introduce the zemstvo into places where there have been none, and they would not drown the nobility in a pool of zemstvos."

Nevertheless, interior minister Goremykin obtained the emperor's approval to place before the State Council a project to introduce zemstvos into the nine provinces along the western frontier and also into the provinces of Arkhangel, Astrakhan, Orenburg, and Stavropol. (The three Baltic provinces and the territory of the Don Cossacks were still excluded.) Meanwhile the Tiflis nobility applied for the introduction of the zemstvo system into the Caucasus. The government polled the governors and marshals of the nobility before introducing the zemstvo, and all of them responded favorably. Because of special local conditions—the predominance of Polish landlords in the western provinces—many councillors feared that the zemstvos might be used for anti-Russian purposes. Consequently they advised against the immediate creation of district establishments and, instead, to establish only the provincial assembly and to appoint [rather than elect] from one-fourth to one-third of the representatives. It was found, however, that some districts had sufficient numbers of Russian landowners so that district zemstvos could be established immediately.

Concurrent with, but independent of this zemstvo project, the ministry of interior also considered the possibility of concentrating all education programs in the hands of the central government so that henceforth no school would be under zemstvo authority. Before that measure could be implemented, the expenditure for public education had to be augmented considerably in order to associate the measure with a general upsurge of enrollments. The ministry of finance, however, saw no way to increase the educational budget in view of the bad harvests and the industrial crisis.

The business of "completing" the zemstvo system was pushed into the background of public attention by new complications that arose early in 1899. One of these problems was related essentially to the zemstvo program in that it too concerned the establishment of more uniform institutions throughout the Russian Empire. But contrary to the zemstvo project, which broadened the area of self-government, in this case the problem was its limitation.

THE ATTACK ON FINNISH AUTONOMY

Nicholas II inherited the issue of limiting the competence of the Finnish diet from his father who had established a special commission to look into the matter. Alexander III had charged the commission to work out a plan to bring the Finnish law on conscription into line with Russian statutes. Controversy centered on whether the concurrence of the diet was necessary to accomplish that. Finnish legal experts appealed to Alexander I's declaration to the diet at Borgo and to a series of statements by Alexander II.[11] Buttressed by those declarations, the Finns argued that the fundamental laws of the Grand Duchy of Finland, solemnly confirmed by the emperor upon his accession to the throne, did not permit passage of a new conscription law without the consent of the diet. In rebuttal noted Russian scholars like Professors Nicholas M. Korkunov and Nicholas S. Tagantsev maintained that the all-imperial power of the emperor implied a constituent right to revoke any decision previously made by the crown.

In the summer of 1898 the tsar appointed General Nicholas I. Bobrikov[12] to succeed Count F.L. Heyden [died 1897] as Governor-General of Finland. This act alerted Finnish society, and rumors swept the country that the revocation of the Finnish constitution was imminent. (On that point among the Russian press the moderate *Novoe vremia* was even more certain of its position than *Grazhdanin*.) When the diet convened in January 1899, it received a modified draft of the proposed Russian military regulations for Finland. The Finnish army numbered about ten thousand men who, according to Finnish law, were required to serve only within the boundaries of the grand duchy. The new legislation proposed to increase the size of the army by fifty percent and to allow Finns to be sent to other parts of the empire to serve their terms of service. (In Russia, as in France, draftees customarily served in their native provinces.) The diet referred the project to a commission. Expansion of the imperial armed forces by five or six thousand men was not in itself a matter of exceptional importance. However, it did produce a collision between two juridical views of the nature of the relationship between Russia and Finland.

Nicholas did not deny that long precedent required the consent of the diet but he maintained that he possessed the legislative power to alter that procedure. "You and I have received an inheritance in the form of a lop-sided house," he wrote to Bobrikov, "and now a difficult task has fallen to us —to reconstruct that building, or rather a wing of it. To do that, one question obviously must be answered: will the wing collapse during the reconstruction? No, I do not think it will collapse if we follow the correct techniques as we go about replacing the old parts with new ones and if we use reliable methods to strengthen the entire foundation."

The emperor's manifesto of 3/15 February 1899 gave force to these considerations. "Separate from local legislative affairs peculiar to any social component," it read, "there arises in the governmental process other legislative matters closely related to the needs of the entire state. Such matters cannot be left exclusively to the jurisdiction of the [legislative] institution of the Grand Duchy . . . .   While leaving in force existing regulations concerning the adoption of local legislation pertaining exclusively to the needs of the Finnish region, We find it necessary to reserve to Our discretion the future disposition of subjects that pertain to general Imperial legislation." Together with this manifesto the tsar promulgated the "Fundamental Regulations on the Drafting, Consideration, and Promulgation of Laws Issued for the Empire, including the Grand Duchy of Finland." The new regulations prescribed that general legislation was to be issued by the imperial power [the tsar]. But legislation that affected Finland was subject to preliminary consideration by the highest authority [Russian State Council] and also by the Finnish diet. Any resolutions produced by these deliberations, however, were to be advisory. Moreover, the authority to differentiate between imperial and local legislation, which required the concurrence of the diet, was reserved to the crown.

In welcoming the manifesto *Novoe vremia* opined that "the new regulations do not infringe upon the autonomy of the region and have not diminished the so-called Finnish constitution one iota. The fact that the diet cannot have a decisive voice in general imperial questions should be understandable even to the most pretentious Finnish statesmen."

CONSEQUENCES OF A DISASTROUS POLICY

The manifesto created unusual consternation in Finland, however. Even the senate, which was composed of persons appointed by the emperor, nearly refused to promulgate it. Ten senators voted for its publication, ten against, and only the chairman's vote created the majority for publication. At the same time both senate and diet resolved to petition the emperor to repeal his manifesto of 3 February. The diet's appeal declared that "the Finnish people, high-born and low, are compelled to interpret the manifesto as a disregard of their constitutional rights which, as far as the people understand, is not merited by any of their actions." Finnish leaders immediately began to collect signatures for a petition to the tsar, and within a few days more than five hundred thousand persons had signed. A delegation of five hundred persons, mainly former ministers and peasants, was selected to take the petition to St. Petersburg. In Helsinki and other cities protest demonstrations assumed the character of memorial services in honor of Emperor Alexander II. His portrait framed in black appeared in windows, and a mountain of wreaths accumulated at the base of his monument in the Senate Square in Helsinki. According to the new regulations, the diet was to offer its advice on the proposed military regulation. Instead it referred the project to a committee with instructions to debate the project in accord with the former statutes and to offer amendments in the traditional manner. The aroused opposition made the emperor indignant, and his first thought was that, as in Russia, this protest originated with "an intriguing political minority." On 5 March he wrote to the state secretary for Finnish affairs: "Please declare to the members of the delegation of five hundred that I, of course, will not receive them, even though I am not angry with them, for they are not responsible . . . . I see in this [petition] the evil intent of the Finnish elite to sow distrust between Me and My good people."

Nicholas's instructions to Governor-General Bobrikov indicated that he did not anticipate any disruption of the tenor of local life. Some expansion of the governor-general's power and the reorganization of the gendarmery and police were necessary. "Having solved these problems and having finished with the military law, it seems to me that we should be satisfied by the results: Finland will be integrated solidly with Russia." The character of the conflict, however, reflected the basic issue at stake. It was not a question of the nature of the laws to be issued but the process by which they would take effect. Over the course of several decades the Finns had

Senate House Square, Helsinki. Monument to Alexander II at left

grown accustomed to certain legal procedures, confirmed by three previous emperors, even if one ignored the original promises of Alexander I. (Throughout the reign of Emperor Nicholas I, the diet had not been convened even once.) Nicholas II may have sensed the tragedy of this conflict for the first time when State Secretary Prokope (whose personal devotion he did not doubt) burst into tears in his study and begged him not to forbid the Finns to petition the throne. Nicholas heard him out, but the policy on Finland remained unchanged.

The effort to establish a closer union of Russia and Finland by consolidating their institutions ultimately proved to be counterproductive. The campaign stimulated the unity of Swedes and Finns within the grand duchy, and it created a separatist movement where none had existed before. Viewed in terms of the needs of the state, the revocation of a constitution originally granted by the crown hardly could be construed as an unlawful act. But judged as a matter of political expediency, it was a disaster. Instead of integrating Finland with Russia, it estranged the Finns from Russia. Abroad, the Finnish question provided the *cause célebre* for a journalistic campaign against Russia. Some critics asserted that the projected five-thousand man increase of the Finnish army violated the principles of the tsar's circular of 12/24 August which called for a reduction of armaments. The manifesto of 3 February also had a chilling effect in the Kingdom of Poland where, following the emperor's visit to Warsaw, hopes had been raised for self-government along Finnish lines. Russian society, as was its custom, opposed the government on the Finnish question. Problems in the grand duchy, however, soon receded into the background as student riots, unprecedented in duration and intensity, suddenly erupted.

RUSSIA'S STUDENTS ON STRIKE

The composition of the Russian student body was far more "democratic" than in the West European democracies. Thousands of students from poor families entered Russia's universities and received substantial state support. A survey of the financial status of the Moscow University student body, which was the largest and probably the poorest, revealed that in a

total of four thousand students two thousand were classi-
fied as poor students and enrolled without paying tuition.
Of these about one thousand received additional stipends in
varying amounts. The government provided about a half million rubles annually in subsidies to students.[13] The picture
was roughly the same in the other universities. Dominated by
an "educated (as well as half-educated) proletariat," the student body was notorious for its radical tendencies, and no
extraneous measures, such as loyalty oaths or strict police
surveillance, altered this basic fact. Student organizations were
prohibited, and this left the field open for the formation of
illegal organizations. Students developed a spirit of comradery
that created enormous difficulties for the authorities in their
struggle against the revolutionary elements in the universities.

Five semesters of tranquillity followed the student riots of
the fall of 1896. Only minor disorders at Kiev University at
the end of 1898 disturbed the calm. That outburst grew out
of Polish student demonstrations against the dedication at
Vilna of a monument in honor of Michael N. Muraviev, who
had suppressed the Polish revolt in the western provinces in
1863.[14] (He was the same man whom the intelligentsia, accepting the Poles' characterization, referred to as "the hang-
man," and about whom the great Russian poet Tiutchev had
written: "He had few enemies, were it not for yours, O
Russia.") But no one in his wildest dreams could have forseen
the turmoil that erupted quite by accident in 1899.

The disorders began with the St. Petersburg University
commencement on 8 February 1899. Prior to the ceremony,
the rector of the university, Professor Vasily I. Sergeevich,
had issued a warning to the student body. His notice recalled
that in previous years groups of students, frequently drunk,
had disturbed the peace by invading restaurants, theaters, and
other public places. The rector bluntly declared that such
conduct was unacceptable, and he warned that the police
intended to prevent such disturbances "at all costs." Many
students regarded this warning as an insult. Rumors began to
circulate about an impending protest demonstration. At the
commencement the students hissed the rector and would not
permit him to speak. Then they began to drift away from the
university. Police blocked the way to the Bourse and Palace
Bridges so that, whether they wanted to or not, the students

were driven in a body along the embankment to the Nikola-
evsky Bridge. When mounted police attempted to separate
the students from the public, the students would not let them
through. Finally they began to throw snowballs and anything
else that was handy. One of the objects struck a police officer
directly in the face. At that point the police moved into the
crowd and dispersed it with whips. No student was injured
seriously in this encounter.

To many witnesses other than students it seemed that the
entire incident had been caused by clumsy police work which
had created a crowd that finally had to be dispersed with
force. Indignation caused by that event laid the groundwork
for revolutionary organizations to begin a serious campaign.
The students spent the remainder of 8 February at parties,
and the rest of the day passed quietly. From the next day on,
however, intense agitation began to develop in the university.
One faction insisted that the student body had been insulted;
another compared the dispersal of the crowd to the infliction
of corporal punishment (to which the Russian public felt
aversion); still another discussed the need for a protest. About
half the students (as many as two thousand) attended a
meeting that lasted for two days (9-10 February). They heard
and rejected proposals to lodge a formal complaint against
the police with the courts and also to petition the emperor.
Those procedures offered no prospect for continuing the
disorder. A resolution to cancel classes finally carried the day.
The resolution denounced the "violence which offends one's
dignity and which is felonious even when applied against the
most ignorant and most stupid segment of the population."
It continued: "We declare that St. Petersburg University is
closed, that [compulsory] attendance at lectures is terminat-
ed, and that those of us present at the University will prevent
from attending lectures anyone, whosoever they may be . . . .
We will continue this program of obstruction until our demands have been satisfied: 1) Publication, so that all may
know, of the instructions governing the police and the [uni-
versity] administration in their relations with the students.
2) A guarantee of the physical inviolability of our persons."

The student demands were composed skillfully. They appeared to contain nothing "political" in nature, and yet it
could always be claimed that they had not been fulfilled.

What, for example, was meant by "a guarantee?" If it referred to groundless, illegal violence, that already was prohibited. If it was meant to ban counteraction against illegal activity, what government could guarantee that its police henceforth would submit passively to a barrage, shall we say, of stones rather than snowballs?

Rector Sergeevich courageously confronted the meeting on 10 February. "I will confront you with your own common sense," he said. "The only sensible act is one that offers some hope of success. You can demand anything you want, even a bird of paradise, but such demands will not survive in our circumstances . . . . You have announced that you will prevent the reading of lectures, that authority in fact will be done away with, and that a provisional government is being created in the University. At this moment everyone is indignant. It so happens that in their official zeal the police did go overboard . . . . But a revolution in a closed room is an absurdity. You read the rules when you entered the university, and you promised to obey them."

The students ignored the rector's advice. On 11 February they obstructed the lectures of those professors who chose to ignore their resolution. On the 12th the movement began to spread to other institutions under the cry "Students, Your Comrades Are Being Beaten!" In one day student strikes seized the Institute for Women, the Military Medical Academy, the Institute of Mines, the Institute of Forestry, the Electrotechnical Institute, and the Academy of Arts. Only at the recently opened Women's Medical School did a brave minority refuse to yield to coercion. Everywhere else students clamored for the same vague but effective demand for "guarantees." They organized a strike committee to supervise the walkout. The movement spread to Moscow on 15 February, when lectures ceased at all institutions of higher learning, and to Kiev and Kharkov on the 17th. Soon every Russian university was in the grip of the strike. The speed with which the movement spread was all the more remarkable in that until 21 February the press did not carry a single line about it. The newspapers reported the sudden death of President Faure and Déroulède's attempt to summon the army to a coup d'état, but they were prohibited from writing about the strike. In some places the strike did not take place without a struggle.

The bulletin of the Organizational Committee reported that "in Kiev the obstruction [of lectures] turned violent because of the stubborn counteraction of a minority."[15]

UNSUCCESSFUL CONCILIATION–THE VANNOVSKY COMMISSION

Most of educated society endorsed the student point of view. A number of eminent St. Petersburg University professors appealed to the minister of education to protest the action of the police on the 8th. There was disagreement within the government itself. Some ministers even characterized the action of the police as "somewhat tactless." Academicians A.S. Fomitsyn and Nicholas N. Beketov (a former tutor of the tsar) obtained an audience to give the emperor their opinion of the reasons for the students' indignation, and they maintained that politics had nothing to do with it.

Nicholas sought his ministers' views and learned that a majority favored the creation of a special investigative commission. The ministers most concerned—N.P. Bogolepov [education], I.L. Goremykin [interior], and A.N. Kuropatkin [war]—objected. The minister of war, who had spoken with students of the Military Medical Academy, insisted that the strike was being guided by "dark political forces alien to knowledge, and even though they may stand in the background, they nevertheless direct everything." On 21 February the newspapers carried the following announcement:

His Imperial Highness has ordered Adjutant-General Vannovsky to make a comprehensive investigation of the causes and circumstances of the disorders, which began on 8 February at St. Petersburg University and spread thereafter to other institutions of higher learning, and to submit the results of this investigation to the Emperor for His consideration. In conjunction with the above, His Imperial Highness points out that the responsibility for adopting measures necessary to the restoration of normal order in the previously mentioned educational institutions rests with the chief administrators of those institutions.

The importance of this step was heightened by the fact that General Vannovsky, a former war minister, was rumored to have been sharply critical of police conduct on 8 February. The emperor wanted to treat the students with respect, and therefore he entrusted the task of determining the cause of their dissatisfaction to a man favorably disposed toward them. Likewise Nicholas entrusted the restoration of order in the universities to the academic authorities, who usually were more lenient, rather than to administrative agencies outside the universities.

The students appeared to have achieved more than they themselves could have expected. Nevertheless, the Organizational Committee decided to continue the strike. The appointment of investigators, it declared, "will not produce any guarantees." The striking students at Kiev University turned to the workers for support. Their appeal proclaimed that although they already had "won concessions," they intended to continue the struggle. Society, too, rejected the conciliatory measures of the emperor, and sympathy for the strikers remained strong. Only A.S. Suvorin, publisher of *Novoe vremia*, dared to stand against the tide: "If the government were to let the present student strike follow its natural course—that is, if it were to say to them, 'If you don't want to study, then don't'—the government would not be harming itself or higher education. But it would be putting the students into a sad position, leaving them without education and without the possibility of pursuing those public careers on which they counted." Nearly every other organ of the press attacked *Novoe vremia* for its position, and many faithful readers cancelled their subscriptions. Some time later Suvorin wrote with some pride that he had diverted the thunder of society to himself.

THE REIGN OF "DARK FORCES ALIEN TO KNOWLEDGE"

The strike entered a new phase as students within the movement began to press for an end to the strike. As the situation changed, administrators allowed almost all those expelled for participating in the strike to re-enter their universities. Classes resumed at the Military Medical Academy on 21 February and there were no more disruptions. When the universities reopened after the Shrovetide vacation, a majority of students voted to end the strike at St. Petersburg, Moscow, and Odessa Universities. At Kharkov and Kazan, too, the strikes came to an end. At Kiev, however, the "United Council" adopted a sharply worded resolution reproaching the St. Petersburg students. The Kiev strikers continued to obstruct lectures while some of the Russian students organized a "Party of Nationalists" to confront the strikers. Enraged by this resistance, the extremists resorted to violence. On 9 March a pitched battle took place at Kiev University, where students fought it out with furniture and laboratory equipment. On the following day the authorities expelled the entire student body and then began to readmit students on a selective basis. (Eventually 2,181 out of 2,425 were readmitted.)

The events in Kiev and the appeals of the "United Council" gave new impetus to the strike. Once again the extremists appealed for fraternal solidarity—"Comrades are being beaten! Comrades are being expelled!" In St. Petersburg on 18 March the students met and decided to resume the obstruction of lectures. Students in Moscow and Odessa followed their lead. But the obstruction of classes grew difficult, for the obstructionists ignored the will of the majority. At the Institute of Mining, for example, a majority of students protested against the strike, but the strikers continued nevertheless. At St. Petersburg University the dining hall became the strike headquarters, and from there the leaders issued instructions and bulletins on the course of the strike.

By the end of March it was clear that university administrators and moderate students were powerless against organized obstruction. Still the police did not interfere. The movement spread to the polytechnical institutes at Warsaw and Riga. The policy of expulsion and readmission by application proved fruitless: the strike committees ordered the students to sign anything but to continue to block classes. By the end of March nearly every institution of higher education had been closed until fall. Examinations, which the students also boycotted, nonetheless took place in a few places. An official announcement, published on 2 April 1899, summarized the results of the past two stormy months.

The strike made a great impression on the emperor. He had set out to meet the students half-way but had become convinced of their ill-will and of the indisputable political basis of their demands. The Vannovsky commission, originally formed on the assumption that the student demands were lawful, pursued its investigation but completed its work under entirely new circumstances. The commission acknowledged that the police had acted [im]properly on 8 February, but that event had been all but forgotten. The commission offered a series of recommendations designed to allow students more freedom, but these proposals were meaningless since the universities had been closed by the violence of radicals and the passiveness of moderates.

An official report, published on 24 May, was based in part on the work of the Vannovsky commission. It pointed out that the clash of 8 February had been attended by violence on both sides. Students had instigated the conflict and had been repulsed by a small detachment (thirty-eight men) of mounted police who "without actual need employed the most extreme measures against the crowd." The report attributed subsequent disorders to extremists who carried the crowd with them. "The inquiry has disclosed furthermore that the very structure of the institutions of higher education contain general conditions which contributed to the development of the disorders," and the commission cited in particular the lack of contact among students and faculty, the overcrowding of students, and the lack of supervised study.

The conclusions to be drawn from the second phase of the strike were apparent in the concluding section of the report. First, the emperor had deemed it necessary to express his dissatisfaction to the concerned academic authorities and faculties; the ministers should take stronger proscriptive measures and, if necessary, resort to stricter enforcement. Second, police officials should be reprimanded for their clumsy and contradictory contingency instructions. Third, "the behavior of students and bystanders, who forgot their duties of obedience to and maintenance of established order, is not to be excused . . . . None of them can or should evade his duty to strive in quest of the knowledge essential to the welfare of the fatherland." "Regretfully," the report concluded, "during these disturbances the local citizenry not only failed to assist the efforts of the authorities but in many cases supported disorder. Citizens incited excited youths by approving their actions and by allowing themselves to interfere improperly in activities within the official domain. Disturbances of this type cannot be tolerated in the future, and they must be crushed by strong official action exercised without indulgence."

Ceremonies to commemorate the centennial of the birth of Pushkin took place on the day following the publication of the official report. Occurring at a time when society and government were divided so sharply, the celebration lacked a

great deal if not in outward magnificence then at least in
candor and sincerity. "Why was literature all but absent from
the celebration, and why did society fail to show much enthusiasm?" asked *Russkaia mysl*, and then diplomatically suggested that "the answer lies in the last two decades of our
social development." In honor of the Pushkin Jubilee the
Imperial Academy of Sciences was authorized to create a
section devoted to fiction and to elect a number of honorary academicians from the ranks of Russia's distinguished
authors.[16]

REFORM AND REPRISAL

The measures outlined in the government report of 24 May
were enacted during the quiet summer vacation of 1899. The
new regulations reflected the recommendations of the Vannovsky commission as well as conclusions drawn from the stubborn obstruction of classes. In order to overcome student
alienation, the circular of the minister of public education
dated 21 July 1899 recommended more contact based on academic needs, establishment of non-theoretical courses in all
schools of the universities, formation of scholarly and literary
circles under faculty guidance, and the opening of more dor-
mitories. On the other hand, any form of general student representation such as class or school presidents was considered
not only superfluous but even harmful.

Simultaneously six ministers[17] met together to work out
"temporary regulations" on military conscription for students
who had been expelled from educational institutions for their
part in the disorders. Witte recommended the idea and defended it by pointing out the educational benefit that military
discipline would have on students. War minister Kuropatkin
vigorously objected: he saw no virtue in turning the army
into a collection of convict work-gangs. Nevertheless the
"temporary regulations" created special boards, chaired by a
school district trustee, to determine who was to be expelled
and for how long (one, two, or three years). Expelled students
were assigned to the army for a designated term of service,
even though they were not subject to conscription. Those
physically unfit were assigned to non-combatant duties. The
regulations provided that the term could be shortened for

good conduct, after which the student could return to his educational institution.

Following the Vannovsky commission findings of over-crowding in some universities, the minister of education established maximum enrollments for each first-year class in all universities and schools. The maximums were calculated on the basis of the average total enrollment in each institu-tion. As a result the number of vacancies in provincial uni-versities increased while positions decreased in the universities located in the capitals. Finally, the minister suspended from teaching several professors at St. Petersburg University who in his opinion had "connived" with the students during the disturbances. All of these measures reflected the emperor's deep disappointment with the attitude of students and society toward the creation of the Vannovsky commission.

A CASE OF JACKALS AND WILDCATS

Concerned that wide discussion of the student strike and government measures would inflame the public, the govern-ment maintained a tight rein on the periodical press. Only conservative publications were allowed to express their views in relative freedom. This tactic provoked a bitter response from Prince Sergei N. Trubetskoy. Writing in one of the philosophical journals, Prince Trubetskoy evoked Isaiah's image of the desolation of Idumea (Isaiah, XXXIV:11-15)—a land in which human persuasion had been overwhelmed by "the howl of jackals and the shriek of kites, the screech of owls and wildcats, the cawing of crows and the hissing of vipers." He compared this to Russia, where "the attitude of wild beasts on matters of domestic policy is sufficiently well-known. They discuss tranquillity and order simply as a matter of discipline, as if it were the lack of discipline that allows jackals and wild cats, having lost their fear of man, to attack anyone who happens to pass by. In their view the tranquillity of a well-ordered society is the same as the silence of a wilder-ness inhabited by beasts."

The poet-philosopher Prince Dmitry N. Tsertelev answered this attack in *Peterburzhskie vedomosti*, a newspaper which with difficulty was trying to maintain a moderate course. "The press," wrote Tsertelev, "has ceased long since to be an instrument of enlightenment and has become instead a tool for the enrichment and factious competition of political parties . . . . How many human voices are heard in the French press, amidst that concert of jackals and wildcats? I grant that complete freedom of the press would form a guarantee against the tyranny of censorship. But to demand freedom in the hope of being able to hear a human voice over the cacophony of the beasts is like jumping into a river to get out of the rain. No Demosthenes is powerful enough to outshout a hyena or a domesticated ass once it has found an eager audience." Nevertheless, Prince Trubetskoy's image of "jackals and wildcats" circulated through the Russian press with comments of approval.

AUTOCRACY AND ZEMSTVO

This turbulent atmosphere formed the context for an important decision on a basic question of Russian domestic policy, namely the government's policy toward the zemstvos. The proposal of the ministry of internal affairs to introduce zemstvo institutions into the western region and four other provinces came under heavy fire in the top levels of the government. It was natural to find C.P. Pobedonostsev in opposition to the project. "It is not difficult to imagine what harm it will bring to the Russian cause and what evil will befall the interests of Russian authority in the northwestern and southwestern regions," he wrote. The Minister of Finance, Count Witte, whose role in this matter was somewhat puzzling, also spoke out no less emphatically against the project. This debate of principle—this "competition before the throne" in which the emperor served as arbitrator—deserves serious consideration, not only for its intrinsic interest, but also as an example of how historic debates were conducted at the highest level of the state.

Interior minister Goremykin, referring to the general course of policy established in the first years of the reign of Nicholas II, maintained that it was necessary, "without haste and without being carried away by the logic of one system or another, to continue the established course. Even though it may be a deliberate pace, it is by far the more certain way to improve existing institutions gradually." From personal experience Goremykin was quite familiar with existing zemstvo organizations, and they were not the least of his concerns: "The question is raised as to whether the principle of local self-government conforms to the foundations of the Russian state, whose cornerstone is political autocracy concentrated in the person of a tsar who shares the fullness of his power with no one. That question is no more important than any question relative to the legality of almost any aspect of the Russian administrative structure." Alluding to Russian Slavophiles and to foreign authorities, Goremykin argued that local self-government was fully compatible with the principle of unlimited monarchical power and that, since ancient times, various forms of self-government had been present in Russia, from village assemblies to non-Russian institutions. Conflicts between the central government and its local organs, he continued, could be resolved by particular adjustments to the system. He pointed as an example to the revised zemstvo statutes of 1890 and indicated that further adjustments could be made for the western region.

The essence of Goremykin's position, however, was an open avowal of the zemstvo system. Self-government, he wrote, develops independent action among the people. It gives them "the experience and instinct for organization which can come only through long practice with independent institutions and self-determination." On the other hand, the total suppression of independent social action or the complete elimination of all forms of self-government will turn the nation into "faceless, incoherent mobs of humanity—into human dust."

In rebuttal of Goremykin's proposal, Witte published his well-known treatise on *Autocracy and Zemstvo* in the summer of 1899.[18] Witte attempted to prove that elective local institutions of self-government were incompatible with autocracy. Witte's double-edged arguments already have been noted, and here again, while asserting the incompatibility of independent public activity with monarchical authority, he also furnished powerful ammunition to opposition groups. It was not by chance that this memorandum was published originally in Stuttgart by the "Liberation" press, an agency of emigre constitutionalists.

At any rate, the memorandum was composed in such a way that the dogma of autocratic immutability stood beyond question. From that premise he argued that in every country self-governing institutions reflecting all social classes were harmonious with popular representation. But Witte had no difficulty in selecting from the history of the Russian zemstvo since its inception a whole series of examples to illustrate a ceaseless struggle to expand zemstvo rights and the no less persistent efforts of the government to combat those pretensions. "I am not compiling an indictment against the zemstvos on the basis of evidence and proofs assembled against them," he wrote. Nevertheless, he proceeded to cite a whole series of zemstvo actions that reflected their constitutional aspirations—in 1878, and then in 1880 the constitution of Count Michael T. Loris-Melikov, the refusal of the Samara zemstvo to address Emperor Alexander III on the occasion of his accession to the throne, the failure of Count Ignatiev's Slavophile projects, and finally the zemstvo petitions of 1895 to which Nicholas II responded in his speech of 17 January 1896.[19]

Simply to count all those zemstvos that directly or indirectly petitioned for permission to participate in the legislative process reveals that it was not just a few local districts, but more than half of all the zemstvo provinces. The movement among the zemstvos for a zemstvo congress is far more serious than some 'empty, noisy opposition to provincial authority.' At the head of this movement, of course, stand a few herdsmen (demogogues and politicians, as your [that is, Goremykin's] memorandum characterizes them). But if the vast majority of noble and loyal landowners choose so willingly to follow these "politicians," is that not proof that something is wrong in the very nature of the zemstvos? Does that not prove that the zemstvo itself contains some kind of absurdity, some political discrepancy that sets it apart from the entire governmental structure?

Witte concluded by attacking Goremykin directly. You yourself are fighting the zemstvo, he wrote, by cutting back its rights and "emasculating" it. Why then, he asked, do you propose not only to protect it but also to extend it into new provinces, when it would be better to deal with the question through administrative reform?

In republican or monarchical regimes, administrative government and self-government can be either good or bad instruments of rule . . . . Each process is useful in the system to which it corresponds but useless in the system to which it corresponds but useless in the system to which it does not respond. Zemstvos can be excellent instruments of government in a constitutional state, for there they constitute a link in a chain forged of the same metal. But in an autocratic state the zemstvo is and always will be in an entirely anomalous position.

One should not put all his chips simultaneously on the red and the black. One should not, on the one hand, discuss the development of independent social action, the beginnings of self-government, and its territorial expansion; and then, on the other hand, go about suppressing independent action and restricting self-government . . . . One cannot institute liberal reforms and then fail to give them the content they require.

Such a course, warned Witte, leads only to strictures and repression, and "nothing undermines the prestige of authority more than the frequent and widespread application of repressive measures."

Witte sent his memorandum to Pobedonostsev with a note that his motive was to expose "a position predicated on insincerity and a desire to reconcile the irreconcilable—both to gain popularity for its author and to preserve his innocence." The director-general of the holy synod observed in response that while Witte's criticism was well-founded, he had failed to draw the proper conclusions. "What is the use of discussing the eradication [of the zemstvos], when everyone wants to extend it to the whole of Russia?" Witte was only attempting to vindicate himself. "Frankly, show me just one highly placed person who in one way or another does not harbor a hearty inclination toward self-government. The majority clings to the zemstvo from the conviction that economic life is better wherever the zemstvo exists. The minority probably assumes that if we continue along the zemstvo road, the emperor can be compelled gradually to cross the sacred line that separates autocracy from republicanism."

Rumors of a campaign against the zemstvos soon reached the public and the press. The monthly journals responded with series of articles praising the zemstvos. Professor Boris N. Chicherin. defended the institution in *Peterburzhskie vedomosti*. "Russia," he warned, "perhaps more than any other country, needs to deal carefully with its social forces, for they are its weakest component . . . . In that respect the attitude of the ruling bureaucracy can only create an insuperable barrier between the government and society. To the enemies of Russia such an attitude is quite desirable, for it threatens our fatherland with discord and sedition."

THE TURNING POINT

To the emperor fell the responsibility of deciding the issue. Convinced of the ill will of society and the intelligentsia by their attitude toward the student disorders, made aware by the example of Finland of how difficult it was to retract privileges once granted, and sobered by Witte's indictment of the zemstvos, Nicholas found it impossible at that moment to complete the zemstvo reform of 1864. For five years he had pursued a domestic policy rooted in the traditions of the reign of Alexander II. But in 1899 Nicholas reverted to the policy of his father. The success of the "great Asian program" required complete freedom to make decisions as well as the prestige of unlimited power. Consequently every measure aimed at a rapprochement with society was either muted, as in the case of the Vannovsky commission, or inadvertently interpreted as a portent of more drastic changes, which the emperor did not desire.

In consequence the plan to extend the zemstvos to the peripheral provinces was cancelled. Moreover, by an imperial ukaz of 20 October, its author, interior minister Goremykin, was appointed to the state council. That was an honorable form of retirement. Dmitry S. Sipiagin, Head of His Majesty's Private Chancellery to Receive Petitions, was named Acting Minister of Internal Affairs. Since the responsibilities of that ministry included supervision of the police, the incumbent enjoyed little public favor. Goremykin had been unable to avoid the unpopularity inherent in the position, and therefore some restrained malevolence greeted his retirement.

The newspapers pondered the meaning of the ministerial change. *Novoe vremia* held that since Russian ministers did not make policies, speculation about the continuity of the government's program was unnecessary. *Grazhdanin*, on the other hand, attributed major political significance to the change: "The fact that the appointment was announced on the day of the late sovereign's death gives it great political import: it seems to indicate that the past five years of his reign have convinced the emperor of the need to bind his reign more firmly and forcefully to the legacy of his father, who was beloved by all of Russia." *Grazhdanin* was right. In the person of D.S. Sipiagin the tsar had found an ideological conservative dedicated to the ideal of unlimited power. In that respect he was a rare person for those times, and his appointment signified a policy of retrenchment.

Witte meanwhile had hoped to establish himself as watchdog over the legacy of Alexander III. Compared to Sipiagin, however, Witte was a liberal. Witte therefore undertook to debate the new minister on the principle of implementing the power of the throne. "You are saying, then," he wrote to Sipiagin, "that the tsar is autocratic, that he creates laws for his subjects but not for himself: I am nothing, only a spokesman. Since the tsar will decide, rules are unnecessary. He who demands rules restricts the tsar. He who doubts that the tsar, and not I, will decide assumes that the tsar himself is incapable of deciding. He who wants to circumscribe the number and form of decisions seeks, therefore, to separate the tsar from his subjects .... Your theory my precious, sweet, dearly beloved Dmitry Sergeevich, has much in common with the doctrine of papal infallibility."

Sipiagin, however, was not the only minister who wholeheartedly and conscientiously obeyed the will of the tsar. Count Lamsdorf, who was appointed foreign minister in the middle of 1900, expressed his conception of his role in this way: "My duty consists of giving the emperor my opinion on every subject and then, after he has decided, to obey him unconditionally and to make every effort to see that his decision is carried out." Contrary to the widely held opinion that the tsar was easily influenced, the facts indicate that he made all major decisions by himself and that his ministers, Witte included, accommodated themselves in one way or another to his views.

In that most significant year of 1899, which witnessed a conservative turn in the course of domestic policy and the failure of the Hague Conference, the emperor's brother, Grand Duke George Alexandrovich, died [28 June 1899]. The tsar's younger brother, Grand Duke Michael Alexandrovich, was proclaimed heir to the throne. In the following year, the emperor became gravely ill with typhus—the only serious illness he suffered through his entire reign. His illness prompted the imperial court to consider whether the fundamental laws permitted the possibility of proclaiming Grand Duchess Olga Nikolaevna [eldest daughter of Nicholas II] heiress to the throne. The emperor's recovery disposed of the question.

ONE TSAR, ONE FAITH

Toward the end of the nineteenth century, a radical religious sect known as the Dukhobors[20] spread mainly among the Russian population of the Caucasus. The Dukhobors, among other things, refused to accept military service, and this refusal inevitably brought them into conflict with the authorities. What government could ignore a group that propagated the belief that one could abjure his obligations to the state? The plight of the Dukhobors attracted the attention of the Tolstoyans, who shared their views and who, through their connections abroad, were able to find a way out of the dilemma. Canada agreed to accept the Dukhobors, to exempt them from conscription, and to provide them land in the unsettled western plains.

The Russian government raised no obstacle to their emigration. The Dukhobors were given the opportunity to dispose of their property, and large sums of money were raised for them in Russia and abroad. In this instance Leo Tolstoy renounced his decision to accept no money for his new novels, and he sold the Russian rights to *The Resurrection* to the journal *Niva*. Another unabridged edition was published abroad, and Tolstoy donated all proceeds to the Dukhobors to assist their migration to North America. Several groups departed for Canada in 1899, and overall about fifteen thousand Dukhobors left the country.

The foreign edition of *The Resurrection* ridiculed the sacraments of the Orthodox Church and led the holy synod to its sensational decision to excommunicate Count Tolstoy. Its judgment published on 22 February 1901 declared:

A writer known to the entire world, a Russian by birth, an Orthodox Christian by baptism, Count Tolstoy in his overweening pride rose impudently against his Lord and his Christ and against His sacred domain . . . . In his works and writings, which his pupils spread throughout the world and especially within our beloved fatherland, he preaches with fanatic zeal the subversion of all dogmas of the Orthodox Church and the very essence of the Christian Faith . . . . He . . . did not shrink

The Moscow Kremlin

back from blaspheming the greatest of all sacraments, the Holy Eucharist . . . . The Church does not count him among her members and cannot do so until he repents and resumes his communion with her.

The enemies of the Russian state and church understandably seized upon this decision to renew their attacks on those institutions. But repressive measures by secular authorities did not follow in the wake of the excommunication, nor could one deny the church its right to take a stand in the face of a clear defamation of its sanctity. Tolstoy's status in prerevolutionary Russia attested to the autocracy's proclivity toward forbearance, a characteristic hardly descriptive of many contemporary regimes.

CHILL WINDS IN HELSINKI AND PARIS

Apart from events in China, the year 1900 passed quietly on the whole without any significant change in the general situation in Russia. The manifesto of 3 February gave force to the new conscription law in Finland. In opening the new session of the Finnish diet, Governor-General Bobrikov warned that the actions of the preceding diet had "injected distressing and useless misgivings into the minds of the population. A repetition of those acts would raise doubts as to the ability of the diet to legislate in conformity with contemporary circumstances." On 7 June 1900 the tsar issued an ukaz proclaiming the gradual introduction and regular use of the Russian language in all official correspondence of the Grand Duchy of Finland. The ukaz gave effect to general statutes in force on that date, although the reform was not to be fully completed until 1 October 1905.

The new conscription law, which was the source of the conflict with the Finns and which the diet had refused to accept, was issued as an imperial statute in the summer of 1901. In view of the general opposition in Finland and within the Finnish army, the Russian government at the same time gradually began to disband the Finnish military units (first the infantry and then the regiment of dragoons). "We regard it as a boon to the Finnish people to make easier the transition to a new form of military service," declared the tsar in his manifesto of 29 June 1901, and the first call to military service was scheduled for the fall of 1903. Except for the few hundred men who served in the Finnish guard battalion, the Finns in fact had been exempt from military service. Nicholas hoped that as time passed the Finns would accept the new state of affairs, and he wanted to avoid the use of coercion.

An obvious coolness developed between France and Russia. The recovery of power by the French left, the election of President Émile Loubet, the formation of the government of Pierre Waldeck-Rousseau, and the conservative course of Russian policy—all these, even though matters of domestic policy, could not fail to influence the tone of Franco-Russian relations. Nicholas, moreover, failed to attend the Paris World Exhibition of 1900 and the opening of the Alexander III bridge, the cornerstone of which he had laid. His absence grieved the French greatly, but there were several reasons for it—the increasing activity of anarchists in Western Europe (they had assassinated Empress Elizabeth of Austria and King Humbert I of Italy and had made an attempt on the life of Kaiser William II),[21] the condition of the emperor's health, and finally attacks by part of the French press which demonstrated that the French left had little regard for the Franco-Russian alliance.

THE DEFECTION OF THE "LEGAL OPPOSITION"

In Russia, meanwhile, society's ever-present animosity toward the government began to emerge more sharply. "Russia has scarcely six conservative publishers for every hundred liberals, while in the zemstvos liberals outnumber conservatives twenty to one," wrote Prince Meshchersky. "For the welfare of Russia and the preservation of her future from dreadful catastrophes, the power of the monarchy has been summoned to maintain the state in its forward course. The main object is to restore the balance—the monarchy must assume the role of a conservative force, since the liberal element with its insoluble contingent of indifferent characters is too large, and the conservative element among the people is too small." Beginning in 1899, the monarchy took up the cudgels of conservatism, but the effect of this was only to exacerbate the differences between the crown and the moderate social elements.

Boris Chicherin, a figure far removed from revolutionary

circles, wrote a pamphlet titled "Russia on the Eve of the Twentieth Century." Written anonymously, it was published abroad in 1900. The fact that it was published was more important than its contents, for it captiously criticized every major act of the reign of Nicholas II. It signified, however, that the "legal opposition" had chosen the path of illegality! The contents clearly revealed that it was the work of an essentially moderate man and a confirmed enemy of socialism. "Up to now," he wrote, "many people have included Chernyshevsky, Dobroliubov and Company among the figures of the age of reform. But they ought to be regarded like flies who foul the canvas of a great artist. Even so, fly specks are easily rinsed away but socialist propaganda, which originates in the journalism of St. Petersburg, has infected and still continues to infect a considerable segment of Russia's youth." The author took note of the peculiar character and effect of contemporary censorship: "The socialists more or less enjoyed freedom of the press. The government regarded liberalism as the danger, whereas socialism seemed harmless as long as it was presented theoretically. As a result, books and pamphlets containing the teachings of Karl Marx circulated more widely among students."

Professor Chicherin believed that the problems that confronted Nicholas II were not as weighty as those faced by Alexander II: "The greatest changes had been accomplished. All that remained was to reinvigorate them . . . . That would have been no act of disrespect to the memory of his father but merely an acknowledgment that different times and different reigns face different problems. Had the young tsar, without even taking one step forward, simply followed the route marked out by his grandfather, Russia's sensible people would have been delighted." To the dismay of consistent conservatives like Pobedonostsev and Meshchersky, the first five years of Nicholas's reign had conformed exactly to Chicherin's prescription. Nevertheless, "Russia's sensible people" had proved to be either powerless or more demanding than the renowned scholar who wrote on their behalf.

In any case Nicholas II put a halt to the "completion" of the reforms of Alexander II without stretching them to the limit. The most critical step in limiting the rights of the zemstvos was the law of 12 June 1900 which curtailed the zemstvos' capacity to tax. The law, recognizing that tax-payers already were overburdened, restricted the zemstvo tax on immovable property to an increase of three percent per year. (Where taxes had not increased for several years, the rate could be raised in one cumulative increment—by fifteen percent, for example, after five years, etc.). A zemstvo that wanted a greater tax increase had to obtain the government's permission. This rather modest measure (inspired primarily by the plight of agriculture) was all but overlooked in discussions of the "impending" abolition of the zemstvos.

THE REVIVAL OF TERRORISM

Meanwhile, enemies of the regime stepped up their propaganda. In 1899 the governor of the city of Odessa reported that "the revolutionary party has staked its future on attracting workers to its cause . . . . To win the sympathy of the masses it has organized its propaganda around study groups that stress the people's lack of material and spiritual necessities." In the spring of 1901 the governor of Vilna had similar developments to report: "Within the past three or four years, our good-natured Russian folk have turned into a peculiar type of semi-literate intellectuals who consider it their duty to reject their families and religion, to ignore the law, and to disobey and mock authority . . . . This meager handful is terrorizing and leading the rest of the inert mass of workers."

Following the mass expulsions and conscription of expelled students, the institutions of higher education enjoyed three semesters of tranquillity. At the end of 1900, however, disorders again erupted, and again they began at Kiev University. The cause, quite absurdly, was the arrest of two students for a criminal offense (extortion involving some female dancers). A meeting was held (in itself a violation of the law) at which speakers demanded autonomy for the university in order to prevent a repetition of "such occurences" [the arrest of students]. This demonstration merged with a protest against the objectionable Professor Eichelman, the replacement for Prince Eugene N. Trubetskoy who was on leave, and produced a new confrontation with the university administration. This time, however, the revolutionaries were ready to take their protest into the streets. The police were forewarned of the impending demonstration but not the date on which it was to take place.

On 14 February 1901 Peter V. Karpovich, a former student twice expelled for his participation in student disorders, shot and mortally wounded N.P. Bogolepov, the Minister of Education.[22] This was the first act of terrorism in several years, and it signalled the adoption of new tactics by the revolutionary organizations. The victim was a minister who inspired no personal hostility in anyone: the shot was fired at the imperial government itself.

Bogolepov was still fighting for his life when on 19 February, the fortieth anniversary of emancipation, the first street demonstration erupted in St. Petersburg in the square opposite the Kazan cathedral. Timely precautions by the police, however, limited the size of the crowd. Between two and three hundred demonstrators singing revolutionary songs marched toward the Nevsky Prospect. The police herded them into the courtyard of the city duma where they recorded all of their names; 148 of the 244 protestors were women, mostly students in the higher courses. Similar street demonstrations took place in Kharkov on the 19th, one during the day and another that evening. Again the police dispersed the crowd. An official report noted that "eight complaints were submitted against police brutalities, but only one was verified medically."

In Moscow more serious disorders took place, and they continued for five days (22-26 February). A mob attempted to release the arrested students, and the rioters smashed street lamps on Nikitsky and Strastny Boulevards. The most violent demonstration took place on 4 March in Petersburg, again in front of the Kazan cathedral. This time the police failed to prevent the gathering (for which it was later accused of "provocation"). The crowd taunted the mounted police and eventually began to throw various objects at them. An officer was struck in the head by a hammer. As the police began to disperse the mob, some of the demonstrators burst into the cathedral. The police surrounded the demonstrators, however, and drove them off in groups to the police stations. Traffic on Nevsky Prospect between Sadovaya and Moyka Streets was interrupted for several hours. In all the police arrested

760 persons, half of them women. The official report of this encounter disclosed that several people were injured—two officers, twenty policemen, four cossacks, and thirty-two demonstrators. No one was killed.

The sight of mounted forces breaking up a crowd is always a distressing picture, and for Russia it was a new phenomenon. Many casual passers-by witnessed the clashes on Nevsky Prospect and the Kazan cathedral square, and these spectacles created fertile ground for revolutionary agitation. Radical propagandists portrayed the demonstrators as innocent "victims of police brutality," and they fully exploited that line for the first time in connection with those events. The writers' union in an ardent protest appealed for assistance to the public in Russia and abroad. The signatures on the appeal contained the names of only two writers with any literary standing (Maxim Gorky and Eugene Chirikov). The rest were either professors or contributors known more or less to the readers of radical journals. The leftist press in France took up the cause. Georges Clemenceau's *L'Aurore* carried the letters of eminent West European writers who added their names to "the appeal of the Russian writers" and joined in protest against the "murderous insanity" of Russian "tsarism." (The verbiage was all the more remarkable in that the encounter in question entailed no deaths and the police suffered almost as many casualties as the demonstrators.)

THE PATIENT TSAR

Nicholas II did not answer these demonstrations with more intense repression. The minister of interior naturally issued a circular prohibiting street assemblies, and he instructed the police to prevent (and not simply to stop) the disorders. He disbanded the writers' union and ordered the arrest of several of its organizers. At the same time, the tsar appointed General P.S. Vannovsky as Minister of Public Education to succeed Bogolepov (who died on 2 March). Because of his work in the commission of 1899, Vannovsky's name symbolized a conciliatory attitude toward student demands. The imperial edict of 25 March announced that "past experience has revealed such a basic deficiency in our educational system that I have deemed it appropriate to inaugurate its radical

re-examination and improvement.... It is my firm conviction that you will strive directly and steadily toward the
end that I have outlined and that you will bring to the task
the wisdom of your experience and your heart-felt concern
for the education of our Russian youth."

Although conservative newspapers welcomed Vannovsky
as a "man of military discipline," the satisfaction expressed
by the liberal press deserved more credence. General Vannovsky (seventy-eight years old at the time) continued to demonstrate his sympathy for the students and held to the belief
that conciliation was the best policy. One of his first ministerial acts was to permit a mass meeting at St. Petersburg
University. This legal assembly took place without incident
on 9 April. The ministry of interior clung to the "hard line"
in its struggle with disorder, and strict censorship of the press
was one of its methods. "There used to be an equality of
silence," complained the liberal *Vestnik evropy*, "but now
only the conservative press is able to discuss university affairs."

In contrast, the ministry of public education followed the
new course of appeasement. It mitigated the punishments of
students who had participated in the disturbances of recent
years. It requested the faculties to propose measures to
normalize university life, and some of them undertook detailed inquiries into the matter. Finally, in view of the vital
relationship between the gymnasia and the institutions of
higher learning, the ministry developed a program to reform
the secondary curriculum. (The late minister, Bogolepov,
already had begun to plan such a reform.) The reform envisioned some reduction of gymnasia courses (mainly the
study of ancient languages). The ministry's basic objective,
however, was to restore the health of the universities by
singling out the purely political reasons for the disorders and
by eliminating as far as possible all other causes of discontent.
The problem was that political factors had provided the basic
impetus for the student revolt. Those "dark political forces
alien to knowledge," to which Kuropatkin had referred, and
the "secret student organization," whose existence was acknowledged by a commission of Moscow University professors, fought the existing regime solely for political profit.
Prince E.N. Trubetskoy concluded that propaganda of that

type could not be suppressed, but he was hopeful that the student body could be made less susceptible to it. That was what the emperor sought to accomplish with the appointment of General Vannovsky. Nicholas neither over-estimated the strength of the revolutionary forces nor did he seek to deal with them by repression alone.

NOTES

SEARCHING FOR THE LAST TSAR

1. Quoted by Alexander, Grand Duke of Russia, *Once a Grand Duke* (Doubleday, 1932), pp. 168-69.

2. *Nicolas De Basily Memoirs* (Hoover Institution Publications, 125; Hoover Institution Press, 1973), p. 173.

3. George Katkov, *Russia 1917: The February Revolution* (Harper & Row and Longmans, Green & Co., 1967; Wm. Collins Sons & Co., 1969) depicts the tsar as a saintly, statesman-like leader. Mohammed Essad-Bey, *Nicholas II: Prisoner of the Purple* (Funk & Wagnalls, 1937) is a sympathetic but impressionistic biography.

4. For a critical survey of this material in various editions see Warren B. Walsh, "The Romanov Papers: A Bibliographic Note," *The Historian*, 31:2 (February 1969), 163-72. Since that article was written there has appeared *The Nicky-Sunny Letters: Correspondence of the Tsar and Tsaritsa, 1914-1917* (Academic International Press, 1970), a reprint in one volume of *Letters of the Tsar to the Tsaritsa, 1914-1917* (1929) and *Letters of the Tsaritsa to the Tsar, 1914-1916* (1923).

5. Atheneum, 1967; Dell, 1969.

6. Behaviorism presumes to create a science of society based on objective observation and measurement along the lines of the physical sciences. Its goal is to determine how society really works by creating an empirical and quantitative social science. Ideally then, social engineers will be able to predict and modify human behavior and thus, through the manipulation of people, to shape the course of individual and social development. Social engineering, unfortunately, sometimes works. It is sometimes dangerous, often irrelevant, but usually lucrative (for the engineers). In the United States since World War II, it has led to irrational activism and produced such niceties as mindless bureaucratization, contractual relations with children, and "the arrogance of power." Its greatest accomplishment is the "voter profile analysis," which gets us to bed early on election nights.

All social scientists, it should be noted, have not been overwhelmed by behaviorism. Moreover, at the annual meeting of the American Political Science Association in September 1974 a contingent—the vanguard, one may hope—of anti-behaviorists made a formal appearance, staging a series of panels titled "Toward a Post-Behavioral Political Science." The participants, younger radical and older conservative scholars, were students or followers of Leo Strauss (1899-1973) who, despite his relative obscurity, was one of the foremost political thinkers of the twentieth century. Best known for his magnificent studies of the philosophy of "natural right," Strauss resisted the mainstream of modern political science by insisting that values and moral issues could not be separated from the study of politics (but insisting too that they could and had to be studied objectively). His exhaustive analysis of ancient and modern political theorists led Strauss to emphasize the viability of classical rationalism as a philosophic alternative to modern rationalism.

7. For general authoritative expressions of the official interpretation followed by Soviet historians see B.N. Ponomaryov, ed., *History of the Communist Party of the Soviet Union* (Moscow, 1960), A.L. Sidorov, ed., *Istorii SSSR*, Tom II: *Period kapitalizma, 1861-1917* (History of the USSR, Volume II: The Period of Capitalism, 1861-1917), 2nd edition (Moscow, 1965); or M. Gorky, V. Molotov, K. Voroshilov, S. Kirov, A. Zhdanov, J. Stalin, eds., *The History of the Civil War in the U.S.S.R.*, Volume I: *The Prelude of the Great Proletarian Revolution* (Academic International Press, 1974) which is a reimpression of the London edition of 1937, translated from the Russian edition of 1936, with an added new introductory essay, *Stalinist History and Russia's Rendezvous with Bolshevism*, by Robert D. Warth.

8. Although Soviet historians have produced several significant and heuristic monographs, none has strayed successfully beyond prescribed sectarian limits to challenge any basic Marxist-Leninist assumption or conclusion. Among the more important Soviet monographs treating the reign of Nicholas II are A. Ya. Avrekh, *Stolypin i tretia duma* [Stolypin and the Third Duma] (Moscow, 1968); V.S. Diakin, *Russkaia burzhuaziia i tsarizm v gody pervoi mirovoi voiny* [The Russian Bourgeoisie and Tsarism during the First World War] (Leningrad, 1967); and S.M. Dubrovsky, *Stolypinskaia zemelnaia reforma* [The Stolypin Land Reform] (Moscow, 1963).

9. Investigation of this question was stimulated by the Carnegie Endowment for International Peace. James T. Shotwell served as general editor of a series titled *The Economic and Social History of the World War.* Twelve volumes on Russia were published in 1928-31 (Yale University Press) and summarized in Michael T. Florinsky's *The End of the Russian Empire* (Yale University Press, 1931).

10. Edited by R.H. McNeal (European Problem Studies; Holt, Rinehart and Winston, 1970). As used here, the term "evolution" signifies peaceful democratic change. Despite the implication of only two alternatives, McNeal's collection contains excerpts from the works of two conservatives, Oldenburg and Leonid I. Strakhovsky, and thus implies the possibility of other alternatives.

11. For a general historiographic guide see Arthur Mendel, "On Interpreting the Fate of Imperial Russia," in Theofanis George Stavrou, ed., *Russia Under the Last Tsar* (University of Minnesota Press, 1969), pp. 13-41. Stavrou's edition consists of several original essays and includes a basic bibliography of works in English. McNeal's *Russia in Transition* illustrates Soviet and Western interpretations with selections from the literature.

See also George F. Kennan, "The Breakdown of the Tsarist Autocracy" and the ensuing commentary in Richard Pipes, ed., *Revolutionary Russia* (Doubleday & Company; Anchor Books, 1969), pp. 1-19 and 19-32. In 1965-66 the *Slavic Review* carried an important debate that raised some fundamental questions about the interpretation of the reign of Nicholas II: Leopold Haimson, "The Problem of Social Stability in

Urban Russia, 1905-1917," Part I, *Slavic Review*, 23:4 (December 1964), 619-42; Part II, ibid., 24:1 (March 1965), 1-22; Arthur P. Mendel, "Peasant and Worker on the Eve of the First World War," ibid., 23-33; Theodore H. Von Laue, "The Chances for Liberal Constitutionalism," ibid., 34-46; Haimson's "Reply," ibid., 47-65; George L. Yaney, "Social Stability in Prerevolutionary Russia," ibid., 24:4 (September 1965), 520-27; and Alfred Levin, "More on Social Stability," ibid., 25:1 (March 1966), 149-54.

   Since these discussions, several important works, bearing on the interpretation of the fate of Imperial Russia, have appeared: Geoffrey A. Hosking, *The Russian Constitutional Experiment: Government and Duma, 1907-14* (Cambridge University Press, 1973); Richard Pipes, *Russia Under the Old Regime* (Charles Scribner's Sons, 1974); Donald W. Treadgold, *The West In Russia and China: Religious and Secular Thought in Modern Times, Volume I: Russia, 1472-1917* (Cambridge University Press, 1973); and George L. Yaney, *The Systematization of Russian Government: Social Evolution in the Domestic Evolution of Imperial Russia, 1711-1905* (University of Illinois Press, 1973).

   12. All cited above, Note 11. Von Laue builds a case for the inevitability of totalitarianism on a deterministic basis that most historians resist. Nevertheless, he makes the strongest case on the pessimistic side, and his analysis has all the substance that is lacking in the forlorn hopes of western optimists. Von Laue's argument that totalitarianism was the inescapable outcome of Russian industrialization can be found in *Why Lenin? Why Stalin?* (Lippincott, 1964); see also his "Problems of Industrialization" in Stavrou, ed., *Russia Under the Last Tsar*, pp. 117-53; and his consideration of the world-wide impact of industrialization in a modern classic, *The Global City: Freedom, Power, and Necessity in the Age of World Revolutions* (Lippincott, 1969).

   Pipes' *Russia Under the Old Regime*, a survey concluding with the 1880s, indicates that totalitarianism was the logical but not inevitable outcome of Russia's unique historical development.

   13. Yaney, "Social Stability in Prerevolutionary Russia" and *The Systematization of Russian Government;* Rogger, "Russia in 1914," *Journal of Contemporary History*, 1:4 (October 1966), 95-119; Mendel, "On Interpreting the Fate of Imperial Russia," esp. pp. 35-36 and 40.

   14. Ibid., pp. 13-40.

   15. "Social Stability in Prerevolutionary Russia," 523. The problem of "Russia and the West" is riddled with difficulties. Russia resembled Western Europe more closely in certain periods than in others and sometimes in some aspects but not others. See Marc Szeftel, "The Historical Limits of the Question of Russia and the West" in Donald W. Treadgold, ed., *The Development of the USSR: An Exchange of Views* (University of Washington Press, 1964), pp. 378-85, and related articles in the same collection. Yaney's statement is generally valid, therefore, though somewhat subject to time and circumstance. Although most western historians obviously disagree, Yaney's caution seems especially applicable to the question of politics and constitutionalism in the reign of Nicholas II.

   16. With variations the contemporary theory of convergence asserts that Soviet and American societies will grow more similar as they continue to develop, and this will reduce the chances of conflict between them.

17. For recent expressions see Massie, *Nicholas and Alexandra*, p. ix: "If Nicholas had not been instructed from childhood that constitutions were anathema, he would have made an excellent constitutional monarch . . . . In England where a sovereign needed only to be a good man in order to be a good king, Nicholas II would have made an admirable monarch." George F. Kennan writes that Nicholas had many of the qualities that would have fitted him excellently for the position of a constitutional monarch and practically none of those that were needed for the exercise of that absolute power to which he stubbornly clung." "Breakdown of the Tsarist Autocracy," in Pipes, ed., *Revolutionary Russia*, p. 15.

18. *Tsarstvovanie Imperatora Nikolaia II* [The Reign of Emperor Nicholas II], Vol. II (Munich, 1949), pp. 127-28.

19. T.S. Eliot, "Burnt Norton," *Collected Poems, 1909-1962* (Harcourt, Brace & World, 1963), p. 175.

20. Mendel, "On Interpreting the Fate of Imperial Russia," pp. 38-39; Katkov, *Russia 1917*, where his theory of a wartime conspiracy is summarized in Chapter 16.

21. The author's father, S.F. Oldenburg, was an internationally renowned Indologist, founder of the *Bibliotheca buddhica* (1897-1962), executive secretary of the Imperial/USSR Academy of Sciences (1904-29), and director of its Institute of Oriental Studies from 1930 until his death in 1934. In 1917 S.F. Oldenburg briefly held the post of Minister of Education in the Provisional Government. His son, S.S. Oldenburg, remained in Russia until 1925, when he emigrated with his wife and three children to France where he earned a livelihood principally as a journalist. His daughter Zoé Oldenbourg, born in 1916 in Petrograd, is a successful novelist and biographer of Catherine the Great.

22. The historical idea of power as consensus is analyzed in Hannah Arendt, *On Violence* (Harcourt, Brace & World, 1970); see especially pp. 35-44.

23. Ibid., pp. 48-49.

24. I.F. Gindin, "Problemy istorii fevralskoi revoliutsii i ee sotsialno-ekonomicheskikh predposylok" [Problems in the History of the February Revolution and its Social-Economic Preconditions], *Istorii SSSR*, 1967, No. 4, 30-49, which summarizes a four-day conference of Soviet academicians on the fiftieth anniversary of the revolution of February-March 1917.

Forty minutes of shooting well-intentioned petitioners on Bloody Sunday 1905 seemed to do more to alienate Russians from their tsar than forty years of radical propaganda. Although the matter hardly is settled, Russia's experience indicates that revolutionaries contribute little to their own success except to prepare themselves, however inadequately, for an opportunity that might arise.

25. Memoirs of imperial society under the last tsar, for example, describe a bizarre milieu of religious mysticism and occultism. Seances provided regular fare in the social diet. Palmists, astrologers, mediums, and phrenologists joined Russia's traditional seers and holy men without any apparent increment in the ranks of the unemployed. Western Europe was experiencing much the same phenomenon, and Russia may

have been closer to Europe in its appreciation of mystics than in its concern for constitutionalists. The question is of some interest, since the withdrawal of people from the affairs of the world may have some relation to the deterioration of the bonds of community, common purpose, and political power.

26. "Problems of Industrialization" in Stavrou, ed., *Russia under the Last Tsar*, p. 152. In *The Global City*, pp. 260-61, Von Laue explains that the "emissaries and agents" of the industrialized western metropolis "are laced into the affairs of state and society nearly everywhere. Yet they still remain outsiders, with little insight into the depths of local thought and action and with little power over them. They are confronted with problems they cannot solve . . . . They cannot make the surrounding fabric of social and political cooperation within the entire polity stand up to the new load. They cannot recreate elsewhere the social and political stability on which they have built their own achievement."

CHAPTER ONE

1. The age of reform, which dominated the reign of Alexander II, produced four basic pieces of liberal legislation: the abolition of serfdom, the principal reform, embodied in a series of statutes between 1861 and 1866; the judicial reform of 1864; and the municipal and military reforms of 1870 and 1874. To these should be added the three statutes on education of 1863-64.

The second major event of Alexander II's reign was the "War for the Liberation of the Slavs." The war marked the high tide of the Panslav movement in Russia, although Panslav influence on official policy was sometimes exaggerated. At the Congress of Berlin in 1878 the European powers compelled Russia to surrender part of the gains won on the battlefield in 1877-78 and confirmed in the Treaty of San Stefano. Virulent Russian nationalism supplanted Panslavism in the reign of Alexander III, expressing itself domestically in a notorious policy of russification and abroad in a generally cautious foreign policy. "The Slavs must now serve Russia and not we them," Alexander III declared in 1885. The standard history of this phase of the Eastern Question is B.H. Sumner, *Russia and the Balkans, 1970-1880* (Oxford University Press, 1937; reprint, Archon Books, 1962).

2. V.O. Kliuchevsky was Russia's greatest historian or, depending on one's preference, its second greatest behind his teacher, Sergei M. Soloviev. Born in 1841 the son of a poor village priest in the depressed province of Penza, Kliuchevsky too seemed destined for the priesthood. In 1865, however, he enrolled in the Faculty of History and Philology at Moscow University and from there forged steadily to the top of his profession. As Soloviev's ablest student, Kliuchevsky in 1882 completed his doctorate and succeeded the master (who died in 1879) as Professor of Russian History at Moscow University. This position, which he held until his death in 1911, was the most prestigious and influential chair in history in Imperial Russia.

Soloviev was the founder of the "statist" or "institutional" interpretation of Russian history, which conceived the formation and development of the Russian polity as the work of its central state system. The statist interpretation developed from the position adopted by the "westerners" in their celebrated debates with the Slavophiles in the 1840s and 1850s (see Note 3, below). In that view Peter the Great's use of the central state apparatus to "westernize" Russia represented a major development in the transformation of Russia from backward orientalism to modern European statehood. Without directly attacking the statist interpretation of his preceptor, Kliuchevsky shifted the focal point of national historical development from the top to the bottom, from the nation-building, centralizing exploits of monarchs to the persistent but less dramatic contributions of the peasantry and lesser classes.

Kliuchevsky's reinterpretation established him as one of the founders of the modern study of economic and social history. His *Course in Russian History*, the course of lectures he delivered at Moscow University, is a masterpiece of Russian prose and a monument of historical scholarship and artistry. His enormous popularity and influence reflected also the populist emphasis of his work and its affinity to the main intellectual current of his day. Although all Russian intellectuals of the late nineteenth century were to one degree or another his disciples, several of the original Russian Marxist economists and historians first discovered economic history through his lectures and writings. Modern Soviet historiography still commends Kliuchevsky for having been "the only Russian bourgeois historian to seek a fundamental theoretical explanation of the economic, social, and cultural . . . development of Russia" and for his efforts "to define the sociological laws underlying national and social development." (Quoting V.A. Aleksandrov in the *Sovetskaia Istoricheskaia Entsiklopediia* [Soviet Historical Encyclopedia], Vol. 7 (Moscow, 1965), pp. 434-35.)

The bent of Kliuchevsky's investigations is reflected in the titles of two of his most important works: *Boiarskaia Duma drevnei Rusi* [The Boyar Duma of Ancient Russia], 3rd ed. (Moscow, 1902), which is the revised version of his doctoral dissertation of 1882; and *Istoriia soslovii v Rossii* [History of Social Classes in Russia], 3rd ed. (Petrograd, 1918; reprint, Academic International Press, 1970). His fundamental work is the *Kurs russkoi istorii* [Course in Russian History], 4 vols. (Moscow, 1904-10); reprinted, Moscow, 1937; and reprinted again in Kliuchevsky's *Sochineniia* [Collected Works], 8 vols. (Moscow, 1956-59). An early translation by C.J. Hogarth is quite unsatisfactory: *History of Russia*, 5 vols. (Dutton, 1911-31), but it continues to be reprinted (Russell and Russell, 1960). Liliana Archibald's translation of two parts of the *Kurs* provides the treatment it merits: *Peter the Great* (Random House; Vintage Books, 1958) and *The Rise of the Romanovs* (St. Martin's Press, 1971). Soloviev's monumental study, a vast compendium of information and source material, remains unsurpassed in many respects: Sergei M. Soloviev, *Istoriia Rossii s drevneishikh vremen* [History of Russia from the Most Ancient Times], 23 vols., 3rd ed. (St. Petersburg, 1900). A reprint is in progress (Moscow, 1959-1965), and an American translation is being published by Academic International Press.

3. "Intelligents" referred to a member of the intelligentsia, that large segment of Russia's educated elite critical to some degree of existing conditions. The term "intelligentsia" implied opposition, often radicalism, but never intelligence or education *per se* (which was assumed). Thus, Dostoevsky was an *intelligents* before he became a conservative mystic.

"Westerner" or "westernizer" denoted an admirer of western achievements and institutions. Westerners generally held that Western Europe formed a model that Russia could, should, or would follow. Westerners of the late nineteenth century variously esteemed and hoped to transplant capitalism, industrialization, socialism, the British constitution, or almost any symbol of western "progress." The contrary, Slavophile position emphasized the uniqueness of Russian history and institutions and rejected the notion that Russia should emulate anything western. Whereas Slavophilism generally implied social and political conservatism, many Slavophiles actively supported reform and constitutionalism based on Russian traditions and institutions. Therefore, while a Slavophile could be a member of the intelligentsia, a westerner invariably was.

4. C.P. Pobedonostsev (1827-1907), the son of an obscure lecturer in rhetoric and Russian literature at Moscow University, became in his time the most influential man in Russia. Trained in jurisprudence, Pobedonostsev became Professor of Civil Law at Moscow University in 1859. In 1865 Alexander II summoned him to Petersburg to tutor his eldest sons in the law. From then on he was never away from the center of power. In 1882 the tsar named him to the State Council and in 1880 appointed him director-general of the holy synod, a post he held until his retirement during the Revolution of 1905. He was the chief advisor to Alexander III, and his influence extended only slightly diminished into the reign of Nicholas II, whose education he also had supervised.

A man of great erudition and narrow horizons, Pobedonostsev propounded a Hobbesian concept of society which expressed itself in political ultra-conservatism, intolerant nationalism, and religious bigotry. He believed that Russian greatness and prosperity flowed from the spiritual union between the tsar and his people. A tenacious zealot of autocracy, Pobedonostsev saw as Russia's greatest enemies the corrupt and self-seeking bureaucrats, who interposed themselves between tsar and people, and the champions of western rationalism and constitutionalism, who would "poison the entire organism." Even the staunchly conservative Alexander III felt occasionally uncomfortable with Pobedonostsev's extremism—"One could freeze to death, just listening to him all the time," he once remarked.

Oldenburg discusses Pobedonostsev's philosophy and influence on Nicholas II in Chapter II. A recent biography is Robert F. Byrnes, *Pobedonostsev: His Life and Thought* (Indiana University Press, 1968).

5. The Panama scandal, which rocked France in 1892-93, followed the collapse of the Panama Company in 1889 through fraud, corruption, and mismanagement. Trials and parliamentary inquiries in 1892 revealed that several newspapers and numerous deputies and senators had been bribed to publicize and condone the company's activities. Several officers

and directors of the firm, including its president, Ferdinand de Lesseps (builder of the Suez Canal), were convicted in 1893. A higher court, however, set aside these judgments, fines, and prison terms because of the expiration of the statute of limitations. This apparent injustice, the investment losses of thousands of small and large investors, and the government's attempt to cover up the whole affair shook the Third Republic to its foundations.

Pope Leo XIII's encyclical *Rerum novarum* committed the Roman Catholic Church to support the trend toward democratization and endorsed the *ralliement* to the republic which French monarchists and clericals bitterly opposed. The document recognized the popular demand for social reform and, by Christianizing modern industrial society, hoped to restore the faithful and not-so-faithful to the practice of religion.

6. Tanlongo, the manager of the Bank of Rome, had covered his embezzlement of bank funds with "loans" to various members of parliament and two previous cabinets. When the bank collapsed, Giolitti attempted to appoint Tanlongo to the senate. The senate refused to confirm him, however, and an investigation led to the resignation of Giolitti and the arrest of Tanlongo and several associates. Tanlongo went to jail and was never heard of again. Giolitti went abroad for a spell but returned to head three cabinets between 1903 and 1914. This confirmed that politics is a more rewarding profession than business.

7. The Penjdeh incident of March 1885 followed a period of Central Asian expansion that alarmed the British. Gladstone requested war credits, and war seemed imminent. Neither side had the capacity to fight a major war in Afghanistan, and the Russians had no desire to fight at all. Bismarck persuaded Italy, Austria, and France to join him in stiffening the Turks against British demands to open the Dardanelles and Bosphorus to the Royal Navy. This succeeded. In May 1885 a preliminary agreement, formalized in September 1885, established conditions for arbitration of the frontier and ended the crisis.

8. Leroy-Beaulieu, *L'Empire des tsars* (Paris, 1890), a translation of which appeared in the United States in 1898 as *The Empire of the Tsars and the Russians*. The author and the book were influential in swinging French opinion toward an alliance with Russia. Wallace's *Russia* (London, 1877), was based on extensive first-hand observations in the seventies.

9. The Fundamental State Laws *(Osnovnie gosudarstvennie zakony)* formed part of the Code of Laws of the Russian Empire promulgated by Nicholas I in 1833; the first eighty-one articles concentrated primarily on the supreme autocratic power inherent in the person of the tsar.

In the present translation the titles "tsar," "autocrat," and "emperor" are used interchangeably. Each term defined the office and was part of the formal title inherited by Nicholas II. But they held for him a special and personally meaningful historic significance. "Tsar" (from the Roman-Byzantine *caesar*) originally implied suzerainty. The Grand Princes Ivan III (1462-1505) and Vasily III (1505-33) occasionally used it to signify their independence from the Tatar khans. At his coronation in 1547 Ivan IV (1547-84) formally assumed the title "Tsar of All the Russias." The term "autocrat" *(samoderzhavets)*, first adopted by Ivan

III, signified independence from any foreign power, but his grandson Ivan IV interpreted it to mean unlimited and arbitrary power over his subjects. It was this interpretation that caused such particular difficulty for Nicholas II. The title "Emperor" *(imperator)* signified the establishment of the Russian Empire in 1721 by Peter the Great (1689-1725).

For further details see the *Dictionary of Russian Historical Terms from the Eleventh Century to 1917,* comp. Sergei G. Pushkarev, eds. George Vernadsky and Ralph T. Fisher, Jr. (Yale University Press, 1970), pp. 31, 119, 160.

10. The Table of Ranks, established by Peter the Great in 1722, created a fourteen-step hierarchy of offices and ranks in the civil and military services.

11. The two capitals were St. Petersburg, the capital of the empire, and Moscow, the former capital of the grand princes and tsars. A governor-general administered each city. The chief administrator of each province *(guberniia)* was a governor *(or nachalnik gubernii).* See below, note 23.

12. The Muscovite bureaus *(prikazy)* were a complex, generally uncoordinated melange of departments, offices, and agencies usually having specific though extensive administrative jurisdictions.

13. Peter the Great reorganized the old Moscow *prikazy* into several governmental departments or colleges with a president over each. An ecclesiastical college *(dukhovnaia kollegiia)* replaced the patriarch as supreme authority in the church. A director-general *(ober-prokuror)* presided and supervised this council, subsequently known as the holy governing synod *(sviateishii pravitelstvuiuschii sinod).* At the beginning of the nineteenth century Alexander I reorganized the government into ministries, but the collegiate character of the church administration was preserved.

14. Leontiev was a major conservative philosopher, essayist, writer and critic of the later nineteenth century. He was an individualistic thinker who exalted autocracy and condemned western rationalism, industrialism, and constitutionalism. He served from 1863 to 1873 in the Russian consular service in Constantinople and the Balkans, and this personal experience confirmed his belief in the supremacy of Greek Orthodox culture ("Byzantinism"). Although both Russian Panslavists and Slavophiles claimed Leontiev, he belonged to neither. His convictions embraced a conception of Russia's special destiny, but he held nationalism to be a false god and his inspiration grew out of Byzantine rather than Slavic antiquity. Leontiev's basic philosophy was outlined in a collection of essays, *Vostok, Rossiia i Slavianstvo* [The East, Russia, and Slavdom], 2 vols. (Moscow, 1885-86). In 1887 he retired to a monastery and became a monk on the eve of his death. A brief but distinguished study in English is Nicholas Berdiaev, *Leontiev* (1940; reprint, Academic International Press, 1968).

15. M.N. Katkov (1818-87) circulated among the highest levels of the imperial court and bureaucracy, and he was by far the most influential journalist of his time. Educated at the Universities of Moscow and Berlin, Katkov traveled in radical circles during the 1840s. Having decided upon a career in journalism, he edited the *Moskovskie vedomosti* from 1850

to 1855 and then became editor and publisher of the journal *Russkii vestnik* (The Russian Herald) in 1856. Both the newspaper and the journal expressed liberal opinion at the time, but, revolted by the radicalism of the 1860s and the Polish insurrection of 1863, Katkov became increasingly conservative and ultimately a rabid reactionary. Although he continued to publish *Russkii vestnik*, he resumed the editorship of *Moskovskie vedomosti* in 1863 and devoted most of his energies to that enterprise until his death. An extreme nationalist, Katkov espoused Panslavism in the 1860s and 1870s and subsequently endorsed wholeheartedly the russification policies of the 1880s. The frustrated anti-Germanism of Panslavism led Katkov, like many other former Panslavists, to form close ties with French nationalist circles, and Katkov became an ardent advocate of a Franco-Russian alliance.

A noted and influential journalist and belletrist, Prince V.P. Meshchersky (1839-1914) edited and published the daily *Grazhdanin* from 1882 until his death. Meshchersky was part of the inner circle around Alexander III, and he continued to exert over his successor an unexplainable but detrimental influence. "How highly he values Meshchersky!" wrote the tsar's mother of Nicholas in 1911. Prince Meshchersky was a major spokesman at court for the reactionary interests of the aristocracy. Both Alexander III and Nicholas II regarded the *Grazhdanin* as an authentic expression of Russian opinion, although its chief contributors were a narrow circle of the lesser clergy and a coterie of witless socialities. The memoirs of Meshchersky are valuable but neither so complete, candid, or revealing as to be indispensable: V.P. Meshchersky, *Moi vospominaniia* [My Memoirs] (St. Petersburg, 1912).

16. Empress Maria Feodorovna (1847-1928) was born Princess Sophie Frederika Dagmar of Denmark, second daughter of King Christian IX. For reasons of state she was betrothed to the eldest son of Tsar Alexander II, but the heir, Tsarevich Nicholas, died from tuberculosis before the marriage took place. On his deathbed Nicholas bequeathed to his brother Alexander both his crown and his fiancée. Princess Dagmar and the future Alexander III were married a year later in 1866. Despite the unusual circumstances that united them, the imperial couple lived a somewhat austere but serene life together—the petite empress, strikingly gay and vivacious, in contrast to the dour and imposing emperor who tolerated frivolity only as an official obligation. They produced five children, Nicholas (1868), George (1871), Xenia (1875), Michael (1878), and Olga (1882).

As Dowager Empress, Maria Feodorovna reluctantly and not entirely with good grace yielded her position of social pre-eminence to her daughter-in-law, the empress. Their relations were correct but never cordial. "My daughter-in-law does not like me," she told Count V.N. Kokovtsov. "She thinks that I am jealous of her power. She does not perceive that my one aspiration is to see my son happy." (*The Memoirs of Count Kokovtsov: Out of My Past*, ed. H.H. Fisher, Stanford University Press, 1935, p. 470.) During the first half of Nicholas's reign, Maria Feodorovna exerted some influence on policy. Either because of respect for her late husband's judgment or appreciation of Witte's abilities, she became the finance minister's staunchest supporter in the imperial family.

17. Skobelev, a popular war hero and Panslavist, denounced Germany before an enthusiastic audience in Paris in 1882: a war with the Teutonic enemies of the Slavs was inevitable and imminent, he said, and implied that he would be glad to lead it. Instead, he died a few weeks later in a brothel. His speech, however, created prolonged international tension.

18. S. Yu. Witte (1849-1915), the son of a colonial administrator, was born in Tiflis, Georgia, and raised in the Caucasus. At seventeen he entered the Novorossiisk University at Odessa, where he eventually settled, and upon graduating embarked on a career in railway administration. Uncommonly energetic and capable, Witte by 1886 had become the executive director of the Southwestern Railway Company whose network covered the western Ukraine and Poland from the Black Sea to the Baltic with links to Germany and the Austrian Empire. In 1889 Minister of Finance Ivan A. Vyshnegradsky brought Witte into his ministry to organize a railway department. In February 1892 Alexander III named Witte to head the ministry of communications and charged him with the construction of the Great Siberian Railway. In August 1892 he succeeded Vyshnegradsky as minister of finance and rapidly transformed it into the engine of Russian development.

Witte's near fanatic devotion to autocracy emerged in his economic policy which he predicated in part on the uniqueness of Russian conditions. He was never imprisoned by dogmatism, however, but remained a resourceful, creative, and dynamic statesman—a *praktik*, which in contemporary Russian meant exactly what one would expect. "What perhaps endeared autocracy most to Witte—at least in the reign of Alexander III—was the fact that under its firm protection a man could do a good job. Witte was an autocrat in his own right. Autocracy both as a symbol of government and as a concomitant of the industrial opportunities of the day favored men of his type. What he wanted was a secure position from which to direct the affairs entrusted to him. Under Alexander III, the last Romanov who made his will felt throughout the government, he could do his job with the efficiency that came from the possession of a delegated share of absolute power." When the autocracy of Nicholas II proved incapable of exerting this forceful control and direction, it was Witte himself who in 1905 reluctantly recommended and created the constitutional regime that irrevocably recharted the course of Russian history.

In his own day Witte was hated by the conservative aristocracy and distrusted by the liberal intelligentsia. Soviet historiography reserves all credit for Russian industrialization to Lenin and his successors. Consequently Witte and his achievements form a difficult historical problem, but the Witte era has been examined with great skill by Theodore H. Von Laue in *Sergei Witte and the Industrialization of Russia* (Columbia University Press, 1963). Chapter II of this work provided the substance of this note, and the quotation appears on page 68. Witte himself left a valuable and quite indiscreet memoir: S. Yu. Witte, *Vospominaniia* [Reminiscences], 3 vols., ed. A.L. Sidorov (Moscow, 1960); abridged English translation of the original 1921 edition: *The Memoirs of Count Witte*, ed. A Yarmolinsky (Doubleday, 1923).

19. Austria took advantage of Russia's peril in the Crimean War to blackmail the Russians into withdrawing from Wallachia and Moldavia and ceding southern Bessarabia. Austria's "malevolent neutrality" forced Russia to deploy a sizeable force on its southwestern frontier, troops which might have been put to better use elsewhere.

20. The district of Izmailia with an area of 8,128 square versts [3,541 square miles] and a population of about 125,000. (Oldenburg's note)

21. Oldenburg's characterization of the status of the alliance in 1892 is somewhat imprecise. In August 1891 Russia and France agreed to consult if either country was menaced by aggression. In August 1892 the Deputy Chief of the French General Staff, General Raoul Boisdeffre, arrived in Petersburg with the draft of a military convention to give force to the earlier agreement. The Russians still had misgivings and would agree to military cooperation "in principle" only. The Russian famine and the Panama scandal postponed further progress. Finally, in December 1894 and January 1895 the two governments exchanged notes which ratified the military convention and forged an effective alliance. The agreement was directed specifically against the Triple Alliance. The conditions and terms can be found in the text of the agreement reproduced in Appendix A. In the interest of secrecy (at the insistence of the tsar for reasons explained by Oldenburg) no treaty *per se* was concluded, although the convention itself was in every respect a treaty. The French constitution required the chamber of deputies to ratify all treaties. Defining the document as a military convention (an executive agreement) thus avoided parliamentary scrutiny, debate, and above all, publicity.

22. The Straits Convention of 1841 obligated the sultan, unless at war himself, to close the Dardanelles and Bosphorus to all foreign warships. The great powers subsequently reaffirmed this principle bilaterally or in concert at various times.

23. No zemstvos were authorized in the twelve western provinces where non-Russian landowners predominated, in the sparsely settled provinces of Arkhangel and Astrakhan, or in the Don Military Region and Orenburg Province which had their own cossack institutions. (Oldenburg's note)

The province (*guberniia*) was the major administrative unit of the Russian Empire; there were seventy-eight provinces at the end of the nineteenth century. The basic sub-division of a province was a district (*uezd*). The relatively smaller provinces of European Russia averaged six to eight districts and in 1900 the entire empire contained 504 of them. Administrative units tended to be larger in the outlying areas of Siberia, Central Asia, and the Caucasus. There the equivalents of the province and district were the *oblast* and *okrug*. There were twenty-one *oblasts* in 1900.

The term "zemstvo" is an acronym from the official designation, *zemskoe uchrezhdenie* (rural establishment or institution). Each zemstvo included an assembly and executive board. At the district level qualified voters elected the assembly. The district marshal of the nobility presided over the assembly which in turn elected an executive board and its chairman to three-year terms. Members of the district zemstvo assembly elected representatives to the provincial assembly, chaired by the provincial marshal of the nobility. The provincial assembly elected its executive board and chairman, and the provincial governor supervised the entire institution. The original regulations of 1864 afforded the zemstvos considerable independence within their assigned sphere of activity, but the legislation also permitted the government to control that activity. The government of Alexander III felt such a need but found the original regulations inadequate. New statutes in 1890 simultaneously increased the representation of the nobility in the zemstvos and the control of the provincial governors over these institutions.

24. By the end of the decade the nobility constituted about 57 percent of the national zemstvo membership, whereas around 1870 they made up about 47 percent of the representatives. Peasant representation during the same period declined from 40 percent to 30 percent. Townsmen and rural landowners provided the remainder, which remained basically stable at 12-13 percent.

25. The municipal regulations of 1870 introduced self-government into 700 settlements identified as *gorod* or city. At the time only five of the empire's cities had populations over 100,000 (Petersburg, Moscow, Warsaw, Odessa, and Kishinev), and only eleven had at least 50,000 inhabitants. Russia's urban population, estimated at eight million or 10 percent of the total in 1870, grew to over twenty million or 18 percent, by 1914. City government followed the pattern of the zemstvos. Municipal electors, divided into three groups according to the amount of taxes they paid, elected the municipal duma. The municipal statutes reflected somewhat more clearly than the original zemstvo regulations the principle that the more substantial taxpayers should have a proportionately greater voice in the expenditure of tax revenues. Thus from the beginning, oligarchic control prevailed in the cities. For added stability the provincial governor exercised supervision similar to his jurisdiction over the zemstvos. Following the zemstvo pattern, new municipal statutes in 1892 also curtailed the initiative of urban governments.

26. Several terms were used to describe the post-emancipation village community or commune. The ancient term *mir*, used by Oldenburg, was so thoroughly pervaded with complex cultural concepts that it became indefinable. Better was the term *obshchina* (commune) as the institution charged since the late seventeenth century with the periodic redistribution of land among peasant households. Best was the official emancipation term *selskoe obshchestvo*, village community or commune, which also retained the repartitional function of the obshchina. The village community, through its elected assembly and officials, maintained order in the village, regulated the use of communal land—over 80 percent of peasant land was held in common—and until 1903 was held collectively responsible for the payment of taxes. Every ten households elected one representative to a volost assembly. The volost was a peasant administrative unit comprising several villages. The volost assembly elected an executive board and a chief *(starshina)* and also a volost court, which disciplined members of the volost and handled litigation involving sums to 100 rubles. The volost chief, subordinate to the district authorities, was the point of contact between the peasantry and the central

government. Although peasants served in district and even provincial zemstvos, the volost was the highest level of government reserved exclusively to the peasantry. The volost chief and board rather quickly became bureaucratic extensions of the district administration. In 1889 the government created the office of *zemskii nachalnik* (superintendent of peasantry, or land captain) with direct and strict powers over all village and volost institutions. Frequently the new superintendent was the old landlord. This measure struck directly at the spirit of the emancipation which had sought to develop peasant self-government as a step toward national regeneration.

Two standard and readily available works on the peasantry and peasant institutions are Geroid Tanquary Robinson, *Rural Russia under the Old Regime: A History of the Landlord-Peasant World and a Prologue to the Peasant Revolution of 1917*, 3rd ed. (Macmillan, 1957; University of California paper-bound edition, 1969); and Jerome Blum, *Lord and Peasant in Russia from the Ninth to the Nineteenth Century* (Princeton University Press, 1961; Grosset & Dunlap, Universal Library, 1966). See also Pushkarev, *Dictionary of Russian Historical Terms*.

27. The Russian nobility was not a closed caste. Hereditary enoblement was available to anyone who attained the eighth rank in the Table of Ranks—collegiate assessor in the civil service, captain [company commander], or *rotmistr* [*Rittmeister* (Ger.)—captain, cavalry squadron commander] in the army. (Oldenburg's note)

A decree of 28 May 1890 raised the requirement for hereditary noble status to the rank of actual state councillor (fourth rank) for the civil service and to colonel (sixth rank) for the army.

28. The organization included S. Stepniak [Sergei M. Kravchinsky, a noted populist revolutionary], Nicholas V. Chaikovsky [a founder of a revolutionary circle in the 1870s], and Leonid E. Shishko. (Oldenburg's note)

The terrorist organization, "People's Will," is discussed later in this chapter in the section on "Revolutionary Movements of the 1870s and 1880s."

29. Herzen (1812-70), the father of Russian socialism, was the most important Russian radical of the 1850s and early 1860s. He believed and advocated that the peasant commune could form the nucleus of a future social order but only if western socialist theory infused and guided Russian radicalism. Although he approved the technological advantages of western capitalism, Herzen hoped that Russia might pass directly from peasant communalism to socialism, thus avoiding the grosser evils of capitalism and especially rule by the bourgeoisie, whom Herzen detested. Herzen, Nicholas A. Dobroliubov (1836-61), and Nicholas G. Chernyshevsky (1828-89) laid the ideological foundation of late nineteenth century Russian radicalism.

An exile from Russia after 1847, Herzen finally settled in London in 1852. There, with his life-long friend and collaborator, Nicholas P. Ogarev (1813-77), he published a successful review, *Poliarnaia zvezda* (The Polar Star, 1855-62) and the biweekly *Kolokol* (The Bell, 1857-67) which for a time was the most influential journal in Russia. Herzen welcomed the reformer Alexander II, but after the terms of the serf emancipation of 1861 became known, he denounced the reform as a betrayal. Herzen's influence began to decline with his support for the Polish revolt of 1863. Moreover, despite his fiery rhetoric, Herzen was a humane spirit who had turned against violent revolutionary action after the failure of the revolutions of 1848. He had little in common with the younger more violent radicals who were moving to the fore of the Russian revolutionary movement. In 1865 Herzen moved to Geneva to be in closer touch with the revolutionary emigres but, disillusioned by what he found, he moved again, to Paris, where in 1870 he died almost unnoticed by the movement he had inspired.

30. The "Regulation on Measures for the Defense of Governmental Order and Public Safety" of 14 August 1881 provided two levels of security measures, "reinforced security" and "extraordinary security." Applied to cities, districts, or provinces, the degree of security depended on the government's estimate of the local revolutionary threat. This regulation allowed the government to circumvent the judicial system in matters of "internal security" and thus to avoid courts and juries that sometimes tended to be too understanding toward radicals and terrorists. These "temporary" measures remained in effect until the fall of the monarchy.

31. In the provinces with zemstvos, generally in European Russia, students made up about 3 percent of the population. The number was higher (about 6 percent) only in the three Baltic provinces, sharply lower (1.7 percent) in the Caucasus, and miniscule (0.3 percent) in the newly conquered territories of Central Asia. (Oldenburg's note)

About 80 percent of the Russian population was illiterate in 1900, a rate comparable to that of the Balkan and Iberian countries. About half of the Hungarians and Italians were illiterate, but only about a third of the Austrians. Illiteracy had been reduced to about 5 percent in England and France and to no more than 15-20 percent in the rest of Western Europe. Eleven percent of the United States population was illiterate in 1900.

32. The author apparently meant Legras's *Au pays russe* (Paris, 1895), about half of which was devoted to the famine in rural Russia.

33. The "wanderers" were members of an organization formally known as the Society of Circulating Exhibitions.

34. The original text, vol. I, pp. 28-29, has been rearranged slightly to form this paragraph.

35. In 1883 only 500 desiatin were in cotton in Central Asia as compared with 220,000 desiatin in 1895. (Oldenburg's note)

36. The pale was that area in which Jews were forced to reside. Alexander III reduced the size of the pale, prohibited Jews from buying or renting rural property, and established quotas in secondary schools for Jewish children. The municipal regulation of 1892 deprived Jews of the right to participate in the government of the cities to which they were restricted.

Malorossiia referred to Little Russia or the Ukraine; Novorossiia was New Russia, the area north of the Black Sea, seized from the Ottoman Empire in the reign of Catherine II.

37. Gogol brilliantly attacked and exposed the evils and abuses of serfdom and the bureaucracy (especially in *Dead Souls* and *The Inspector General)*, but his *Correspondence with Friends* was sharply critical of the peasantry. Belinsky chastised him for his "betrayal" in his famous "Letter to Gogol" in 1855.

38. The aristocratic officers' revolt of December 1825 intended to replace the autocracy with some form of constitutional government.

39. Sentenced to death in 1849 for participation in the Petrashevsky circle, an imperial ukaz commuted the penalty as Dostoevsky and his comrades stood before a firing squad. He subsequently served four years at hard labor in "the house of the dead" at Omsk, followed by five years as a private in a Siberian regiment. The experience ruined his health.

40. A.K. Tolstoy, a distant cousin of Leo N. Tolstoy, was one of the most versatile Russian authors of the nineteenth century. The allusion to his acceptance in both camps recalled, on the one hand, his lifelong friendship with Alexander II and his serious epics and verse on national historical themes, and on the other, his satires and parodies of Russia in humorous poetry, epigrams, and proverbs. Much of the latter was published under the pseudonym Kozma Prutkov, a fictitious treasury clerk invented by Tolstoy and his cousins, the Zhemchuznikov brothers.

41. "Nihilism" originated in the campaign for "the destruction of ethics" of Dmitry I. Pisarev, Nicholas A. Dobroliubov, and Nicholas G. Chernyshevsky. It exalted reason, science, materialism, and atheism and alleged to believe in nothing (Lat., *nihil*) or at least nothing cherished by Russian conservatives—faith, Orthodoxy, tradition, and morality.

42. Razin and Pugachev each led great peasant rebellions in 1667-71 and in 1773-75. An ataman was a cossack military chief.

"V narod!"—"To the People!" was the mission urged on Russian students of the sixties by Alexander Herzen. When the government closed St. Petersburg University in 1861, Herzen addressed the student from exile in London through his influential journal *Kolokol* (The Bell): "Where will you go, O youth to whom the gates of learning are closed? To the People! To the People! That is your place, you exiles from learning." The idea was to spread over the countryside to proselytize, agitate, alert, and arouse the peasantry to the need to liberate themselves. From the Russian *narod* came the terms *narodnichestvo*—populism, and *narodnik*—populist. Until the Russian Marxist alternative emerged in the 1890s, "populist" was a generic term for Russian radicals and revolutionaries. Although narodniks espoused a variety of programs and differed on tactics, they stood on common ground philosophically in materialism and atheism, ethically in utilitarianism, epistemologically in the biological sciences, and politically in the advocacy of a socialist order based on the peasant commune. Narodnichestvo therefore principally described Russia's agrarian socialist movement of the second half of the nineteenth century.

43. *Narodnaia volia*, The People's Will, grew out of the narodniks' frustration at the failure of the people to respond to their revolutionary appeals. Narodnaia volia and an illegal periodical by the same name were founded in 1879. Since "the people" had failed to rise up and

topple the government by mass insurrection from below, The People's Will dedicated itself to destroying the government from the top by terror and assassination.

The basic study of narodnichestvo from Herzen to the assassination of Alexander II is Franco Venturi, *Roots of Revolution: A History of the Populist and Socialist Movements in Nineteenth Century Russia,* trans. Francis Haskell (Alfred A. Knopf, 1960). A popular account of great merit is Avrahm Yarmolinsky, *Road to Revolution: A Century of Russian Radicalism* (Macmillan; Collier Books, 1962).

44. The decree required all four of the empire's women's universities to be closed by 1889. Only the institution in St. Petersburg survived, but the others re-opened after 1900 and women's higher education expanded vigorously after 1905.

45. The Nobles' Land Bank was established in 1885 to provide loans to support landownership by the nobility. On the zemskii nachalnik see above, Note 26.

CHAPTER TWO

1. The "Asiatic fanatic" was a Japanese policeman who with his sword, and perhaps taking Kipling too literally, attempted to separate the east side of the future emperor from the west. The wound itself proved superficial, but it left a scar on his forehead and etched on his heart a hatred for the Japanese. At the time, however, he dismissed the incident with characteristic good grace. Prince Esper E. Ukhtomsky, wealthy editor of the *Peterburzhskie vedomosti* [St. Petersburg Gazette], wrote a semi-official chronicle of this tour of 1890-91. Ukhtomsky, who accompanied Nicholas, was a student of Buddhism and oriental art and a champion of Russia's "mission" in Asia. An English translation is Prince Ookhtomsky, *Travels in the East of His Majesty, Tsar Nicholas II of Russia,* 2 vols., trans. Richard Goodlet (London, 1896).

2. Nicholas's preparation for the throne was probably not as thorough in any respect as the author suggests, but the particular virtue of Oldenburg's history is its favorable characterization of the last tsar. The verdict of History, though generally negative, is not yet final. The unexpected death of Alexander III, stressed by the author, undoubtedly contributed to Nicholas's doom. It brought him prematurely to the throne for which he was formally and emotionally unprepared. Alexander was a large, powerful man in generally good health. He shared with members of his government the belief that the first decade of his reign had been preparation for the real programs that would provide the definitive character of his monarchy. If Witte's evidence is trustworthy, Alexander saw no important role in this for Nicholas, whose judgment he considered "truly childish." Alexander dominated the life of the imperial family. Although their relationships did not lack affection, all the children regarded their father with awe. Nicholas was not only unprepared to follow his father, but he was also quite clearly incapable of emulating him. As his sister Olga complained, "It was all my father's fault. I know how he disliked the mere idea of state matters encroaching

on our family life, but after all, Nicky was his heir." Subsequently the constant comparisons drawn by his mother and the endless harangues of his uncles stressed Nicholas's own sense of inadequacy for "the awful job I have never wanted." He understandably sought the solace and refuge of his own intimate family.

The often quoted conversation, recorded by his brother-in-law Grand Duke Alexander, on the day of his father's death, was hauntingly sincere and prophetic: "What am I going to do? What is going to happen to me, to you, to Xenia, to Alix, to mother, to all of Russia? I am not prepared to be a Tsar. I never wanted to become one. I know nothing of the business of ruling. I have no idea of even how to talk to the ministers."—Alexander, Grand Duke of Russia, *Once a Grand Duke* (Doubleday, 1932), pp. 168-69.

3. "Hesse" was Hesse-Darmstadt, a grand duchy northeast of the juncture of the rivers Main and Rhine. Given the state of Russia's foreign relations (above, Chapter I), the emperor and empress understandably preferred a union with someone other than a German princess, let alone a German raised at the English court. Alexander III loathed Queen Victoria (the feeling was mutual), and he had despised William II since they were children. Beyond that the imperial couple seem to have had no personal objection to Alice, although she had been brought to the imperial court for inspection, found wanting, and sent home. Young Nicholas's "other love," the gay, petite, and talented ballerina, Mathilde Kschessinska, was obviously even less acceptable, but for a time she made Nicholas's "struggle" for the hand of Alice more endurable. His parents' decision to send him on an extended tour of the east was intended in part to cool the Kschessinska affair, even though ballerinas were traditionally fair game for grand dukes—and vice versa. In the end (1921) Mathilde got hers, Nicholas's cousin, Grand Duke Andrei Vladimirovich. As for Nicholas, he had no other serious affair, and his deportment after his marriage was impeccable.

The fascinating memoirs of Mathilde Kschessinska (Princess Krassinska-Romanovska) have appeared as *Dancing in Petersburg*, trans. Arnold Haskell (Doubleday, 1961).

4. *Moskovskii sbornik* (Moscow, 1896), p. 27. The title recalls a famous slavophile journal of the 1840s. Oldenburg's page references for the subsequent quotations are incomplete, but the text indicates pp. 47-49, 70, 117, 121, and 123. The original English edition is: K.P. Pobyedonostseff, *Reflections of a Russian Statesman*, trans. R.C. Long (London, 1898); a recent reprint is: Konstantin P. Pobedonostsev, *Reflections of a Russian Statesman* (The University of Michigan Press, Ann Arbor Paperbacks, 1965). We have preferred our own translation to the somewhat dated and freer Long translation; the comparable passages in the University of Michigan edition appear on pp. 27-28, 34, 44, 49, 53-54, 67, 77-78, 80-81, 115, and 117-121.

5. Letter to S.Yu. Witte, 24 March 1905. (Oldenburg's note)

6. Not to be confused with [Alexander V. Krivoshein] the minister of agriculture during the second half of the reign. (Oldenburg's note)

7. General Vladimir I. Gurko, who was quite familiar with the circumstances of Krivoshein's dismissal, furnished the following information with his comments on the manuscript of this book: Having assumed his post as minister, Krivoshein appointed his brother-in-law, A.P. Strukov, to manage his wife's estate since he himself had no time for it. Without Krivoshein's knowledge, Strukov bid for a contract to supply sleeping cars to the Bologoe-Sedlets Railway then under construction. Its route crossed the Krivoshein estate. The rejected competitors, whose bids were more costly to the treasury, gave a distorted version to some liberal journals. Krivoshein learned all about it in the newspapers. (Oldenburg's note)

8. The manifesto on the death of Alexander II, drafted by Pobedonostsev for Alexander III, affirmed the new tsar's "faith in the power and truth of the Autocracy which we have been called upon to uphold and preserve against all impairment and harm for the benefit of the people . . . ." For the critical significance of this document for the new reign and the last years of the monarchy, see Robert F. Byrnes, *Pobedonostsev: His Life and Thought* (Indiana University Press, 1968), pp. 153-61.

9. 30/18 January 1895. (Oldenburg's note)

10. *Russkoe bogatstvo*, February 1895. (Oldenburg's note)

11. Liquor monopoly operations began in the provinces of Perm, Ufa, Orenburg, and Samara and covered the entire empire by 1914. The state had regulated the sale of alcohol since the end of the sixteenth century. Although the new system produced mixed social benefits, the monopoly was a fiscal success, annually yielding about 500,000,000 rubles or one-fourth of the total state revenues. A substantial literature exists, but for a concise summary see Margaret Miller, *The Economic Development of Russia, 1905-1914, with Special Reference to Trade, Industry, and Finance*, 2nd edition (Frank Cass, 1967; reprint ed., Augustus M. Kelley, 1967), pp. 245-49.

12. An amazing 1,886 versts [1,250 miles] of railroad opened to traffic during the year. (Oldenburg's note)

13. Leskov, a talented craftsman, wrote several popular novels and stories in which honest conservative heroes triumphed over villainous Polish and Russian revolutionaries.

14. The ten censuses taken between 1718-19 and 1857-58 were incomplete (by design) and inaccurate (by default). Subject to constant review and correction, they were known as *revizii*—"revisions" or "reviews." Their purpose was to enumerate only rural and urban tax-payers, and therefore they excluded large categories of people—the nobility clergy, the army and civil service, etc. The census of 1897 was the first complete census of the Russian Empire. Even the tsar was included, giving as his occupation "owner of the Russian land."

15. The 1911 edition. Alas, the *Britannica's* interpretation of the past changes with the vicissitudes of the political climate, and the new edition no longer contains these lines. (Oldenburg's note)

CHAPTER THREE

1. The Imperial Free Economic Society of St. Petersburg was founded in 1765 in the reign of Catherine the Great. The adjective "Free" signified its independence of the government. During 154 years of existence, the society was an influential and generally progressive organization. The intellectual elite of the day usually comprised its membership. In the 1890s the society published several of the works by narodniks and Legal Marxists in their debate on the future of capitalism in Russia. The Free Economic Society was a stronghold of agrarian interests opposed to Witte's policy of industrialization and all of its ramifications, especially railroad expansion, protectionism, and the gold standard (all discussed below).

2. The fall of the Bourgeois cabinet was the result of the first direct intervention of Russia into French domestic affairs. According to the German ambassador to St. Petersburg, Prince Hugo Radolin, Russian displeasure with the radical Bourgeois government was conveyed personally to France by the French ambassador, Count Gustav Montebello, in early April 1896. The government fell on the 23rd.

During the 1890s and as late as the Russo-Japanese War and the Revolution of 1905, Russia was the leader and France played the role of suitor in the alliance. Hanotaux in particular was willing to go to any length to strengthen the bond between Paris and Petersburg. Hence the pleasure of the Russian government at his return as foreign minister. In 1896 the distinguished French career diplomat, Paul Cambon, was complaining that the director of French foreign policy was not actually Hanotaux but Baron Arthur P. Mohrenheim, the Russian ambassador. See Radolin to Berlin, 7 April 1896, *Die Grosse Politik der europäischen Kabinette, 1871-1914* (Berlin, 1922-27), Bd. XI, No. 2845; and Paul Cambon, *Correspondance, 1870-1924* (Paris, 1940), Vol. I, p. 411; Vol. II, pp. 138-39.

3. On 22 May/3 June 1896 Russia and China concluded the famous Li-Lobanov treaty. Oldenburg considers this important agreement in Chapter V.

4. By a tradition established in 1742 by Empress Elizabeth Russian sovereigns crowned themselves, thus signifying their autocratic power and the fact that their authority depended on no earthly institution.

5. This was apparently a quotation, though not indicated as such in the text, Volume I, pp. 62-63; a slight rearrangement in the order of the original text also has been made at this point.

6. *Novoe vremia,* 5 July 1896. (Oldenburg's note)

7. S.Yu. Witte, who dominated Russian economic affairs from 1892 to 1903, sought to modernize Russia through industrialization and in this way to promote both national power and agricultural prosperity. The basic dimensions of Witte's program were threefold: 1) The government embarked on a massive program of railroad construction in order to stimulate the development of the basic industrial sector of iron, steel, and coal production. By 1900 the state controlled over two-thirds of the Russian railway system, and government orders provided certain profits to the producers of basic metals and fuel. 2) To attract foreign

investment and entrepreneurs to compensate for Russia's deficiencies, Witte needed to provide a hospitable and secure investment climate. This involved putting state finances in order, restoring the government to solvency, and establishing a sound currency. Witte achieved this through the accumulation of a large gold reserve, which meant that Russia had to export more than it imported and save more than it spent. Witte therefore tried to establish and maintain a balanced state budget. He instituted high protective tariffs (to the disadvantage of farmers who consequently had to pay higher prices for foreign and domestic manufactured goods). Finally, he increased taxes, especially indirect taxes (notably the state liquor monopoly), in order to increase revenues. 3) The net effect and, indeed, the inevitable result of the Witte system was to suppress and stifle domestic demand and consumption in order to create savings to finance industrialization—in other words, to accept a reduced standard of living. Witte of course realized what the consequences of his program would be, but he was willing to defer general prosperity to the future in order to create its solid foundation in the present. (These were the days, before the repeal of the laws of economics, when everyone understood that it was impossible to make something from nothing and that someone had to pay for social benefits.) The Witte system produced an unprecedented industrial growth rate of eight percent per year during the 1890s. But it also placed the majority of the empire's population under great fiscal and economic pressure and thus contributed to the rise of discontent and revolution in Russia.

For a general examination of the Witte system see Theodore H. Von Laue, *Sergei Witte and the Industrialization of Russia* (Columbia University Press, 1963; Atheneum, 1969). A larger perspective on this era is Von Laue's *Why Lenin? Why Stalin? A Reappraisal of the Russian Revolution, 1900-1930* (J.B. Lippincott, 1964).

8. Olga Nikolaevna, first child of the emperor and empress, was born in November 1895.

9. The veiled statue of Strasbourg commemorated the loss of Alsace in 1870-71. The League of Patriots was an extreme nationalist organization founded in 1882 by Paul Déroulède. The League supported the Franco-Russian Alliance as a means to avenge the humiliation of France in the Franco-Prussian War and to recover the lost provinces.

10. Anna Yaroslavna, daughter of Yaroslav the Wise, Grand Prince of Kiev (1019-54) was the wife of Henry I (1031-60) of France, the grandson of Hugh Capet (987-96) who founded the first French dynasty.

11. As Oldenburg himself observed a few lines above, political perception is relative to one's own interests. The Méline government of 1896-98, characterized here as "moderate," marked the final flowering of conservative clericalism and economic protectionism in the prewar history of the Third Republic.

12. Meshchersky was one of the favorites of Alexander III and a powerful influence on Nicholas II. His paper, *Grazhdanin*, existed on state subsidies paid at the order of the tsar himself. In addition Meshchersky used his reactionary columns to blackmail ministers for funds and favors for himself and his disreputable clients. His private life was an endless scandal—he was a homosexual—and his influence is considered one of the

great tragedies of the later empire. For some details on his influence see P.A. Zaionchkovsky, *Rossiiskoe samoderzhavie v kontse XIX stoletiia (Politicheskaia reaktsiia 80-x—nachala 90-x godov)* [The Russian Autocracy at the End of the Nineteenth Century: Political Reaction in the 1880s and Early 1890s] (Moscow, 1970); and V.N. Kokovtsov, *Iz moego proshlago: Vospominaniia, 1903-1919* [Out of My Past: Memoirs, 1903-1919], 2 vols. (Paris, 1933) or its English translation, *The Memoirs of Count Kokovtsov: Out of My Past,* ed. H.H. Fisher (Stanford University Press, 1935). Kokovtsov claimed to have been one of Meshchersky's victims.

13. In October 1893 a Russian naval squadron visited the French port of Toulon and received a tumultuous reception. The first formal steps toward the conclusion of the Franco-Russian Alliance were taken the following December and January. See above Chapter I, Note 16.

14. The Russian student movement of the late nineteenth century is described in numerous memoirs and in a few Soviet studies. A survey based on these materials appears in Lewis S. Feuer, *The Conflict of Generations: The Character and Significance of Student Movements* (Basic Books, 1969), pp. 88-172.

CHAPTER FOUR

1. See above, Chapter II.

2. The census of 1897 proved to be the only general census of the population during the imperial period. See Russia, Tsentralnyi statisticheskii komitet, *Pervaia vseobshchaia perepis naseleniia Rossiiskoi Imperii, 1897 g.* [First General Census of the Population of the Russian Empire, 1897], ed. N.A. Troinitskii, 89 vols. in 24 (St. Petersburg, 1899-1905); or, *Obshchii svod po Imperii rezultatov razrabotki dannykh pervoi vseobshchei perepisi naseleniia* [General Summary for the Empire of the Results of the Tabulation of Data of the First General Census of the Population], 2 vols. (St. Petersburg, 1905).

3. Peter the Great in 1704 established the modern Russian decimal system of coinage in which the basic unit of account was the ruble of 100 kopecks. The empire's first coins were minted in gold, silver, and copper. The fluctuation of the ruble, mentioned by Oldenburg, described its changing value only in international exchange. One could always get 100 kopecks for a ruble in Moscow but seldom more than 75 in London. For Russians this was a bad thing. The depreciated value of the ruble reflected the international financial and commercial appraisal of the solvency of the Russian government, that is, its ability to redeem its paper *notes* (or obligations of indebtedness) for real *money.* (The value of a nation's currency is established in the marketplace and not, as sometimes alleged and even believed, in the decrees of governments or politicians.) In 1768 Catherine the Great, one of the last big spenders, began to replace gold and silver coins with paper notes *(assignatsia)* redeemable in copper. This folly culminated rather quickly in 1770 when the government issued, and then withdrew almost immediately, a giant copper ruble that weighed over two-and-a-quarter pounds. All

subsequent efforts to stabilize the currency failed, since the government continually spent more than it earned. On the eve of Witte's restructuring of Russia's finances, the empire's legal tender was the credit ruble banknote *(kreditnye bilety)*. Its value was guaranteed initially in 1843 by the revenues from state properties and then in the 1880s also by a metallic fund.

By that time all great powers and all powers who hoped to be great had adopted the gold standard. Gold had begun to replace silver as the medium of exchange in the late seventeenth century. The reason was that the expansion of the world's supply of gold made it relatively more attractive than silver in exchange. In 1717 Sir Isaac Newton, the Master of the Royal Mint, calculated and fixed the value of the pound sterling at about 4 pounds sterling per ounce of gold. The British Crown and subsequently the Bank of England promised to redeem or convert pounds to gold on demand. This promise, faithfully honored except in time of war, in effect established the gold standard. The convertible English pound served as the cornerstone of the international monetary system for 232 years, until 21 September 1931 when England closed the gold window of the Bank and retired to the twilight of its greatness. (Newton's monetary system had outlived his theory of universal gravitation. In contrast the monetary system created in 1944 at Bretton Woods and ultimately based on the national debt of the United States, held together for only twenty-five years.)

It was, at any rate, membership in this select club to which Russia aspired in the late nineteenth century. Adoption of the gold standard was vital to Witte's program of industrialization, for without a convertible currency Russia would have to continue to pay a premium for foreign loans and manufactures. Moreover, foreign investments would seek employment more readily in an environment of solvency and stability. Witte therefore struggled to replace the old credit note with a convertible ruble, that is, with genuine money or paper representing tangible value.

4. The new official rate, of course, affected only items in international trade and exchange. It did not alter the price of goods or services produced, marketed, and consumed entirely within the empire.

5. S.F. Sharapov (1865-1911), an inveterate opponent of Witte's economic policy, was a reactionary Slavophile who spoke for the interests of small Russian industrialists. From 1897 to 1899 he edited and published *Russkii trud* (Russian Labor), a Moscow weekly mainly devoted to assailing Witte and his program. Sharapov inveighed against the gold standard, protective tariffs, railroads, factory legislation, foreign investments, and Jews. In 1899 Witte finally supressed *Russkii trud*. From then until his death in 1911, however, Sharapov received a small government subsidy for his agricultural equipment factory. The source of the subsidy remains a mystery—either Witte himself or Sharapov's influential protectors close to the throne.

6. Witte sustained a favorable balance of payments with foreign loans. Late in 1896 he negotiated a 100,000,000 ruble gold loan from the Rothschilds. Von Laue, *Sergei Witte*, p. 142.

7. The one-third devaluation of the old ruble was quite modest. Following Count Egor F. Kankrin's devaluation of 1842, a reform rightfully

regarded as exemplary, the government exchanged 3 rubles 50 kopecks in notes for each metallic ruble [a devaluation of more than 70 percent]. In our own time the stabilization of the French franc in 1928 fixed the value of the new franc at only 20 percent of the old franc. (Oldenburg's note)

8. France, already on the gold standard, wanted to unload some of its excess silver on Russia. The French therefore urged Russia to adopt a bimetallic currency. Von Laue, *Sergei Witte*, pp. 142-43.

9. Soon after he was established in the capital, Witte's first wife died. After a time he met and fell in love with Matilda Ivanovna Lissanevich, a married woman who conducted a salon on the fringe of official society. Rumor had it that more than lofty conversation passed between Mme. Lissanevich and the young officers who attended her soirees. Witte in any event paid her husband a considerable sum for a divorce. His marriage, then, to a divorced Jewess with a shady past (and present, according to continuing gossip) created an insuperable social barrier and also weakened Witte's political position. Protocol prevented the appearance of Matilda Ivanovna at court and compelled the Wittes to seek society outside official circles. Witte offered his resignation to Alexander III, but in this instance the tsar preferred to bend his moral convictions in order to retain his valued minister. There was no tampering with morality in the reign of Nicholas II, however. If Alexandra was the epitomy of prudery, Nicholas was her archpriest, and together they elevated peccadillo to the rank of transgression. In such an atmosphere Witte was a marked man.

10. A.I. Chuprov and A.S. Posnikov, *Vliianie urozhaev i khlebnykh tsen na nekotoryia storony russkago narodnago khoziaistva* (St. Petersburg, 1897). Both authors were members of the faculty of Moscow University. Whenever possible, Witte liked to mobilize expert opinion in favor of his projects.

11. Struve and Tugan-Baranovsky both figured prominently as founders of "Legal Marxism," one of the revisionist Marxist schools that flared briefly in the late nineties in Russia. Influenced basically by Eduard Bernstein, the German revisionist, the Legal Marxists renounced revolutionary action in favor of gradual improvement and reform within the framework of a liberal constitutional regime, which became the immediate goal.

Peter Struve (1870-1944), one of the leading Legal Marxist theoreticians, edited two of the movements' journals in the 1890s, *Novoe slovo* (New Word) and *Nachalo* (The Beginning). In 1898 he drafted the manifesto of the newly formed Russian Social Democratic Workers Party, the original party of the Russian Marxists. From then on, however, Struve gradually moved to the right. From 1902 to 1905 he edited the liberal journal *Osvobozhdenie* (Liberation), became one of the leaders of the Union of Liberation, and finally in 1905 helped to found the liberal Constitutional Democratic ("Kadet") Party. Between 1906 and 1917, while Struve was on the faculty of St. Petersburg Polytechnic Institute, his conservative orientation continued to develop. He took no part in the revolutions of 1917, but during the Civil War (1918-21), he joined the anti-Bolshevik forces in southern Russia. As an emigre between the world wars, Struve taught at the Universities of Prague and Belgrade and was closely associated with the extreme right and the monarchist emigration. The author, who was also a member of those circles, always refers to Struve as a Marxist in quotes.

The career of Michael Tugan-Baranovsky (1865-1919) closely paralleled Struve's. He was one of the founders of Legal Marxism in Russia and active in the nineties in its propagation and polemics. In 1899 he was dismissed, as a "political unreliable," from his professorship in political economy at St. Petersburg University, a position he had held since 1895. He was readmitted to the faculty in 1905, however, and until the revolution taught in Petersburg and Moscow. Like Struve, Tugan-Baranovsky grew increasingly conservative, especially after the 1905 revolution. He joined the Kadet party in that year, stood unsuccessfully for election to the State Duma in 1912, and served during the Civil War as finance minister in the Ukrainian Central Rada (Council). He died in Odessa in 1919 while on his way to represent the Ukraine at the Paris Peace Conference.

12. The following example illustrates the intelligentsia's baseless and uncertain conception of rural conditions: *The Influence of Harvests and Grain Prices* included research on peasants' budgets by F.A. Shcherbina. His research, incidentally, utilized rather meager and obsolete data—an investigation of 283 peasant households (168 of them in Voronezh province) conducted about 1880. Shcherbina concluded that peasant income was between 52.47 and 58.51 rubles per person and between 420 and 500 rubles per year for a family of eight (the average size of the households studied). The latter is not very high, of course, but during the debates of the Free Economic Society, many speakers used 55 rubles as the average annual income of a peasant household. This surprised no one, even though in the very same session the bread alone consumed by a peasant family of eight was determined to be 150 *pud*s [5,417 pounds] a year! (Oldenburg's note)

13. The Third All-Russian Congress of Trade and Industry is discussed above, Chapter III.

14. Adam Mickiewicz (1798-1855), the great voice of Poland, was born in the village of Novogrodek in the province of Minsk. He was the equal if not the superior of the titans of Romanticism and generally is recognized as the greatest Slavic poet next to Pushkin. His first great epic, *Konrad Wallenrod* (1828), thinly disguised his hatred for the Russians. It earned him international renown and a term of exile in Russia. Released in 1832, Mickiewicz vowed never to return to Russia or to Poland as long as it remained under Russian domination, and he spent the remainder of his life in self-imposed exile, mainly in France. In 1847 he unsuccessfully sought the Pope's blessing to raise a Polish legion to free Austrian Poland. When the Crimean War broke out, he went to Turkey to assist in the formation of a Polish legion to join the struggle against the Russians. He was struck down by cholera and died in Constantinople in November 1855. Mickiewicz was buried in France at Montmorency, but in 1900 his remains were removed to Cracow and placed in the great cathedral beside the kings and luminaries of Poland.

15. Muraviev's appointment as foreign minister seemed to confirm Nicholas's determination to be his own foreign minister. M.N. Muraviev (1845-1900) entered the diplomatic service in 1864 and served as secretary to various embassies, including France (1879-84) and Germany (1884-93), until his most significant appointment as Minister to Copenhagen (1893-96). Copenhagen, a dynastic outpost of the imperial family, was scarcely in the vital stream of European affairs. The chief function of the Russian ambassador was to serve as local travel agent, master of ceremonies, and general lackey to visiting Russian dignitaries. For a favorable estimate of Muraviev as foreign minister, however, one should consult William L. Langer, *The Diplomacy of Imperialism*, 2 vols., 2nd ed. (Knopf, 1956), pp. 445-78.

16. In February 1897 the Greeks in Crete rebelled against the Turks and proclaimed the union of Crete with Greece. While the fighting proceeded in Crete, Greece began to mobilize on the Macedonian frontier. Serbia and Bulgaria were eager to join in a war against Turkey, but firm warnings from Russia supported by Austria dissuaded them from mobilizing. The Turks meanwhile struck and inflicted a series of decisive defeats on the Greeks, who were saved from annihilation by the intervention of the great powers. At the insistence of the powers the peace settlement in September 1897 denied the sultan the fruits of his victories and restricted Turkey to minor territorial gains and an indemnity. Crete remained under international occupation and control until November 1898, when the great powers placed the government of the island in the hands of Prince George of Greece.

The Austro-Russian agreement of 1897 contributed significantly to the speedy containment and liquidation of the Greco-Turkish war. The agreement, concluded just after the outbreak of the war, committed each country to maintain the status quo in the Near East and to cooperate against any effort by another power to disturb it. If partition of the Ottoman Empire became inevitable, Russia and Austria agreed that the existing Balkan states, with the addition of an independent Albania, should divide the area equitably. The two powers each recognized the "eminently European character" of the Straits question although Russia insisted, and Austria agreed, that under no circumstances could the Straits be closed to Russian merchant vessels.

Considering the long-standing rivalry of Russia and Austria in the Balkans, they reached their agreement in 1897 with little difficulty. Austria was eager for an agreement for fear of some aggressive Russian move and because of the obvious British intention to reduce their traditional commitments in the Ottoman Empire. England was Austria's traditional ally in the Balkans, but British policy under Lord Salisbury was to make Egypt rather than Turkey the bastion of imperial defense in the Near East. Russian ambitions in the area had received a series of checks since 1878, and the Russian government had concluded that for the time being no possibilities remained to be tapped. In contrast, the Far East seemed to hold limitless opportunity for economic and territorial expansion. Consequently the Austro-Russian pact of 1897 had far-reaching implications for Russian policy. That agreement in combination with the French alliance effectively secured Russia's western flank and freed St. Petersburg to concentrate almost exclusively on its "destiny in Asia."

17. Kronstadt, the island fortress in the Gulf of Finland about fifteen miles from Petersburg, was the base of the Baltic Fleet and until the late nineteenth century the commercial port of the capital. Originally fortified by Peter the Great in 1703, Kronstadt was refortified in stone during the reign of Nicholas I.

Peterhof or Petrodvorets (Peter's Palace), a summer residence of the tsars, overlooks the Gulf of Finland and Kronstadt from a sixty-foot bluff lavishly embellished with terraces and fountains. The core of the palace was commissioned by Peter and designed by Alexander Leblond (1679-1719), but its rococo splendor is mainly the work of Bartholomew Rastrelli (1700-71), chief architect of Peter's daughter Empress Elizabeth. Petrodvorets, originally intended to be the Russian Versailles (Leblond was the student of Andre Le Notre who designed the gardens at Versailles), was superseded by Tsarskoe Selo (The Tsar's Village), now Pushkin.

Tsarskoe Selo, about twelve miles south of Petersburg, combined a central palace and other structures with several private villas in an imperial park some eighteen miles in circumference. The architecture at Tsarskoe Selo reflected the more refined classical taste of Catherine the Great. The central structure, the Catherine Palace completed by Rastrelli in 1756, was the last major Russian building in the grand rococo style. Tsarskoe Selo was the principal residence of the imperial family, although Alexander III had preferred to immure himself and his family at Gatchina, a less pretentious and more secluded residence ten miles to the south.

Krasnoe Selo (Pretty Village or Fields), a suburb of the capital, was the headquarters and encampment of the imperial guards regiments and the scene of their annual summer reviews.

18. These far eastern developments are discussed in Chapter V. (Oldenburg's note)

19. The Black Sea Fleet, prohibited from use of the Straits by the Treaty of Paris [1856], could not be counted as part of Russia's high seas naval force. (Oldenburg's note)

20. From the published text, *Letters from the Kaiser to the Czar, Copied from Government Archives in Petrograd . . .* by Issac Don Levine (Frederick A. Stokes, 1920), p. 49. Among the kaiser's abundant defects was his poor command of English, the language in which he corresponded with the tsar. Professor Levine published the letters without alteration, thus retaining the faulty construction and numerous misspellings.

21. *Ibid.*, p. 53.

22. Kuropatkin became minister of war in 1898 at the age of fifty, thus fulfilling the promise of a brilliant earlier career. The son of a minor provincial official, Kuropatkin was born in 1848 in Kholmsk in the province of Pskov. He graduated at eighteen from the Pavlovsk Military School and was posted as a lieutenant to the First Turkestan Rifle Battalion. By the age of twenty his courage had won him promotion and the command of a company. He served in Turkestan and Central Asia from 1866 until 1877 with time out for further training at

the General Staff Academy. Kuropatkin owed his early success to bravery, charm, and General Skobelev on whose staff he served until 1883. In that year as a major general he joined the General Staff, serving in various capacities until 1890 when he was placed in command of the Trans-Caspian Region. On 1 January 1898 Kuropatkin became minister of war. When the Russo-Japanese War broke out, he took command of the Russian armies in Manchuria and subsequently (13 October 1904 to 3 March 1905) became commander-in-chief of Russian forces in the Far East. Relieved from supreme command after the fall of Mukden, he led the First Army until the end of the war. In the months immediately after the war he engaged in a running debate with Witte on the reasons for Russia's unpreparedness and poor performance. When persuasion failed to silence Witte, Kuropatkin challenged him to a duel, an honor that Witte declined.

Restored to active command in World War I, Kuropatkin led the armies of the Northern Front to a series of defeats in 1916, was once again relieved of command, and served until the end of the reign as Governor-General of Turkestan. Arrested after the February Revolution, Kuropatkin was eventually released by the Provisional Government. He retired to his native province of Pskov and was a school teacher in the village of Sheshurino until his death in 1925.

23. The first five volumes of Bloch's *Budushchaia voina* (The Future of War) were a massive compilation of statistical military and economic data. The final volume, a summary, argued that decisive military victory would be unattainable in a total war of the future. Instead, all combatants would fight to exhaustion and ruin. Either war or the failure to end the arms race would produce the same result—"convulsion in the social order." According to Barbara Tuchman, Bloch obtained an audience with the tsar. This was more than likely since Bloch was the railroad baron who had put together the Southwestern Railway Company which Witte had managed before he entered the government.

An English edition of the sixth volume is, Jan Bloch, *The Future of War in Its Technical, Economic, and Political Relations*, trans. R.C. Long (Garland Publishers, 1972). See also, Barbara Tuchman, *The Proud Tower: A Portrait of the World Before the War, 1890-1914* (Macmillan, 1966); pp. 276-77.

24. Grand Duke Alexis Alexandrovich (1850-1908) was the fourth son of Alexander II and as General Admiral nominally commanded the Russian Navy from 1882 to 1905, when the rank was abolished. He was only lukewarm toward the proposal, noting that a proportional force reduction would preserve Russia's numerical superiority over the armed forces of its neighbors. He warned, however, that similar proposals previously had met failure and that Russian prestige would suffer serious harm if the tsar's appeal failed—it would be interpreted as an admission of Russia's inability to sustain a modern armament program. Maria Feodorovna also advised against the circular and urged her son to proceed with the introduction of new weaponry. The basic documentary material on the preparation of the proposal is L. Taleshev, "K istorii pervoi Gaagskoi Konferentsii" [On the History of the First Hague Conference], *Krasnyi arkhiv* [The Red Archives], 50-51 (1932), 64-96; and

"Novie materialy o Gaagskoi Mirnoi Konferentsii, 1899" [New Material on the Hague Peace Conference, 1899], ibid., 54-55 (1932), 49-79. Oldenburg apparently made use of this material although no references are given in the text.

25. The ministers did not travel together: Kuropatkin was in Paris from 6 October to 13 October; Muraviev arrived on the 15th and left on the 24th. Witte was also in Paris at this time seeking to raise a new loan. All in all, Russia demonstrated little sympathy for the difficult position of its ally, beleaguered on the one hand by the British and on the other by the Dreyfusards.

26. During this period, Russia paid off 258,000,000 rubles in foreign loans while issuing new bonds in the sum of 158,000,000 rubles. (Oldenburg's note)

27. Chamberlain's speech came nearly two weeks after Delcassé had ordered Marchand to withdraw from Fashoda. Joseph Chamberlain, a bombastic spokesman for empire, criticized the French government's "policy of pin-pricks"—its ceaseless pressure and prodding at all points of contact between England and France. Marchand, he warned, must not only get out of Fashoda, but France must renounce all its outposts in the Bahr-el-Ghazal. "Fashoda is only a symbol: the great issue is control of the whole valley of the Nile." J.L. Garvin, *The Life of Joseph Chamberlain*, vol. 3: *Empire and World Policy, 1895-1900* (Macmillan, 1934), p. 233.

28. *Letters from the Kaiser to the Czar*, (9 November 1898), p. 63.

29. The *Entente cordiale* was the improved state of British-French relations growing out of a general solution of their colonial differences. The Anglo-French rapprochement was the foundation of Delcassé's policy. The agreements were initialled on 8 April 1904.

Napoleon III capitulated to the Prussians at Sedan on 2 September 1870.

30. Albert Geouffre de Lapradelle (1871-1955), a noted authority on international law, published more than three dozen major works on the subject. Oldenburg may have been quoting a pamphlet, *La question du désarmement et la seconde circulaire du tsar* (Paris, 1899), or *Les conférences de la paix de La Haye de 1899 et 1907*, 2 vols. (Paris, 1909), the latter an edited translation of an original American edition by James Brown Scott.

31. The Conference was divided into three Commissions to which the various articles of the agenda of the 30 December circular were referred: First Commission—limitation of armaments, articles 1-4; Second Commission—laws and customs of war, articles 5-7; Third Commission—peaceful settlement of international disputes, article 8. All deliberations of the Commissions were reported to the plenary session for adoption. The official proceedings of the First Hague Conference are, *Conférence Internationale de la Paix. La Haye, 18 Mai—29 juillet, 1899*, 4 parts in 1 vol. (The Hague, 1899).

32. Zhilinsky explained that Russian forces in Central Asia and the Amur Military District fell into that category. (Oldenburg's note)

33. *Conférence Internationale*, II, p. 34. Oldenburg's italics.

34. For example, Vice-Admiral Sir John Fisher, commander of the Royal Navy's Atlantic Fleet, wrote: "The supremacy of the British Navy is the best security for the peace of the world." (Quoted by Tuchman, *Proud Tower*, p. 302.

CHAPTER FIVE

1. This statement refers to the Russian Panslavists' dream of uniting all Slavic peoples under the aegis of Imperial Russia. Most of the West and South Slavs, of course, were subjects of the German, Austrian, or Ottoman Empires.

"Slavic" is a linguistic not a racial term. The Slavic linguistic group includes West Slavic (Polish, Czech, Slovak, and Wendish), South Slavic (Serbo-Croatian, Slovene, Bulgarian, Macedonian, and Old Church Slavonic), and East Slavic (Russian or Great Russian, Byelorussian, and Ukrainian). The Slavic languages are derivatives of an ancient Balto-Slavic tongue which forms a major subdivision of the Indo-European family of languages. The Baltic languages are Latvian, Lithuanian, and Old Prussian. Although the Russian alphabet is a Greek heritage, the Slavic and Hellenic languages are quite unrelated.

2. The Russo-Chinese Treaty of Nerchinsk (1689) had excluded Russia from the valley of the Amur River. Generally, this condition was observed until 1847, when Tsar Nicholas I appointed Nicholas N. Muraviev as Governor-General of Eastern Siberia. In 1849 Muraviev began to send expeditions and to establish outposts on Chinese territory along the lower reaches of the Amur River, and on Sakhalin Island. In 1855 (one year after Perry's visit) Muraviev's agents opened Japan to Russian commerce and won joint occupation of Sakhalin. China, meanwhile, wracked by rebellion and the depredations of Europeans and Americans, hoped to find at least one friend in Russia. Consequently, in 1858 Peking agreed to the Treaty of Aigun which ceded the left bank of the Amur to Russia. The right bank up to the juncture of the Amur and Ussuri rivers (where Khabarovsk was founded in 1860) remained under Chinese suzerainty. The territory between the rivers and the Pacific Ocean was placed under joint Russian-Chinese suzerainty. Then in 1860, as a result of further Anglo-French pressure in the south and the wily diplomacy of General Nicholas P. Ignatiev, China in the Treaty of Peking gave Russia absolute possession of the maritime region. In a decade Russia, exploiting China's weakness and without firing a shot, had annexed 350,000 square miles of Chinese territory and expanded to the northern frontier of Korea. At the southern tip of its new empire the Russians began to clear the virgin forest and to construct their window on the Pacific, Vladivostok—the Lord of the East.

The Pacific empire proved to be more than Russia at that time could digest. Russian colonists failed to adapt to the soil and climate of the Amur region, and the maritime provinces failed to become the anticipated granary of the Far East. Communications were poor: European Russia was a year away by the overland route and a month and a half by sea. Russia, moreover, lacked the merchant and naval forces to sustain colonization and development. In 1867 Russia sold Alaska to the United States thereby cutting administrative costs, forestalling its possible loss to England, and at the same time introducing an American counterweight to British seapower in the northern Pacific. By 1880 Russians only slightly outnumbered Chinese and Koreans in the Amur-Ussuri basin. Vladivostok was a village of less than two thousand inhabitants, even with (or because of) the tigers that still strolled in occasionally for a night on the town.

Between 1865 and 1881 several Russian generals turned loose in Central Asia won fame and glory while conquering and adding to the empire of the tsars a dominion about the size of Western Europe. The latest round of conquest began when General Michael G. Cherniaev conquered Tashkent. Although the government rewarded his audacity by recalling him, in the following year it annexed the Khanate of Kokand. In 1868 General Constantine P. Kaufman, Cherniaev's successor as the new Governor-General of Turkestan, forced the Emir of Bokhara to cede the ancient trading center of Samarkand. Three years later, Kaufman temporarily occupied the Ili Valley and the Chinese district of Kuldja. In 1873 he crossed the Kyzl-Kum Desert to seize Khiva, and in 1875 the Russian government formally annexed both Khiva and Bokhara.

Meanwhile, Russia also advanced eastward from the Caspian Sea into the Kara-Kum Desert. In a particularly brutal campaign in 1881 General Michael Skobelev conquered the oasis of Geok Tepe. Within three years the Russians had seized Merv and soon were at Kushka on the frontiers of Afghanistan. This precipitated the Anglo-Russian crisis mentioned in Chapter I. To protect India against the Russian advance the British had invaded and defeated Afghanistan in 1878-80. England used its victory to force the Afghanis to cede two frontier districts and to yield control of their foreign relations to London. The definitive settlement of the Russian-Afghanistan boundary came in 1895. London recognized Russia's annexation of the Pamir region, and St. Petersburg agreed to an Afghan corridor separating Russian Central Asia from British India.

For a general survey of these aspects of Russian expansion and foreign policy, see: Barbara Jelavich, *A Century of Russian Foreign Policy, 1814-1914* (J.B. Lippincott Co., 1964) and Ivo J. Lederer, ed., *Russian Foreign Policy: Essays in Historical Perspective* (Yale University Press, 1962). The earlier aspects and nineteenth-century Russian expansion into the Far East are well covered by Frank A. Golder, *Russian Expansion on the Pacific, 1641-1850* (Arthur H. Clark Co., 1914); George A. Lensen, *The Russian Push Toward Japan: Russo-Japanese Relations, 1697-1875* (Princeton University Press, 1959); Ken Shen Weigh, *Russo-Chinese Diplomacy, 1689-1924*, 2nd ed. (University Prints and Reprints, 1967 [1928]). One of the best brief summaries of Russian expansion in Central Asia is N.D. Harris, *Europe and the East* (Houghton-Mifflin, 1926). Among the newer monographs are: Seymour Becker, *Russia's Central Asian Protectorates: Bukhara and Khiva, 1865-1924* (Russian Research Center Studies, 54; Harvard University Press, 1968); Firuz Kazemzadeh, *Russia and Britain in Persia, 1864-1914* (Yale

University Press, 1964); and Richard A. Pierce, *Russian Central Asia, 1867-1917: A Study in Colonial Rule* (University of California Press, 1960).

3. About twenty million people died in the Taiping Rebellion, which was undoubtedly the greatest revolutionary movement of the nineteenth century. The goal of its leader, Hung Hsiu-chuan (1814-64), was to establish "a heavenly kingdom of great peace on earth"—*T'ai-p'ing t'ien-kuo*. Hung's program combined ancient Chinese traditions with basic Christian teachings in a reform movement that was at once reactionary and extraordinarily progressive. Embracing many cross currents, the Taipings were united in the common goal of ridding China of the "foreign" Manchu (or Ching) dynasty (1644-1912). In 1853 the Taipings captured Nanking, the former capital of the Ming dynasty (1368-1644). An expedition against Peking in 1853-55 failed, but until the movement was crushed in 1864 the Taipings held the lower Yangtze valley and the southeastern provinces of Anhwei, Chekiang, Kiangsi, and Fukien. However, through direct invasion or the uprisings that it inspired, the Taiping Rebellion touched sixteen of the eighteen provinces of China proper.

The revolt in Yunnan (the Panthay Rebellion) and the Tungan Rebellion were Muslim revolts against Chinese-Manchu authority. Muslims represented sizable, closely knit minorities in these regions, but they were ostracized socially and also discriminated against politically by the government. By the middle of the sixties China's western frontiers from north to south were ablaze with rebellion, and considerable amounts of territory were in the hands of the rebels. Only after crushing the Taiping Rebellion was the harassed central government able to turn effectively to the suppression of these extensive revolts.

Find a general survey of this tumultuous period in the text, notes, and bibliography of Immanuel C.Y. Hsü, *The Rise of Modern China* (Oxford University Press, 1970), pp. 275-313.

4. Introduced into the court as the young concubine of Emperor Hsien-feng, Tzu-hsi rapidly enhanced her standing by charm, talent, skill, and the production of a son who was designated heir apparent. When the emperor died in 1861, she became co-regent for the young Emperor Tung-Chih together with the Empress Tzu-an and three royal princes. Tzu-hsi soon liquidated the princely cohort. At age seventeen Emperor Tung-Chih married a young woman approved by Tzu-an. Tzu-hsi had another candidate and, as the story goes, prohibited her son from visiting his wife. Tung-Chih, however, refused the alternate services of his mother's choice, who had been installed as an imperial concubine. Forgetting that mother knows best, the unhappy young emperor took up with common prostitutes, caught a veneral disease, and died in 1875 at the age of nineteen. Tzu-hsi then placed on the throne her three-year-old nephew, Kuang-hsü (reigned 1875-1908), and with the death of Tzu-an in 1881 she became sole regent. The emperor and regent maintained proper but unfriendly relations and died within a day of each other in 1908.

Tzu-hsi, who once boasted that she was more powerful than Queen Victoria, faced a dilemma in exercising her great power. She recognized that China needed to modernize in order to resist the demands and depredations of the western powers. She feared, however, that western technology could not be separated from western institutions. Moreover, the empire's progressive leaders were practically all Chinese, while the Manchus were almost exclusively conservative or reactionary. To follow the progressive Chinese lead might have upset the traditional balance and undermined the Manchu position in China. Consequently she gave some encouragement to modernization but not enough to allow it to succeed. Li Hung-chang, for example, was commissioned to reorganize and rebuild the Chinese navy. The empress and her chief eunuch, however, used the money earmarked for ammunition to rebuild the Summer Palace, pillaged and destroyed during the European occupation of Peking in 1860. When Chinese ships finally went into action against the Japanese, only three shells were available for the main batteries, and some of them were filled with sawdust. At the end of the war one of the palace eunuchs dismissed the complaint, explaining that "The Japanese would have beaten us all the same. As it is, at least we have the Summer Palace." Tzu-hsi had no difficulty in choosing between the salvation of China and the preservation of her power and that of the Manchus: "I prefer to give China to the foreigners rather than to surrender it to my own slaves [Chinese]," she once said. The Manchus lost Tzu-hsi in 1908, and three years later they lost China.

See Dun J. Li, *The Ageless Chinese: A History,* 2nd ed. (Charles Scribner's Sons, 1971), pp. 411-14; Denis and Peggy Warner, *The Tide at Sunrise: A History of the Russo-Japanese War, 1904-1905* (Charterhouse, 1974), pp. 118-19.

5. Russian occupation of the Kuldja district seized by General Kaufman in 1871 (above, note 2) was confirmed by the Treaty of Livadia in 1879. Peking, however, repudiated both the treaty and the ambassador who signed it. New negotiations were opened, but by then the Russo-Turkish War had exposed Russia's military weakness. Consequently the Treaty of St. Petersburg (February 1881) considerably reduced the territorial award, although it provided a larger indemnity and greater commercial privileges than the Treaty of Livadia. The revision represented a singular Chinese victory over a European power, and it embittered Russo-Chinese relations for several years.

6. The next major step toward the revival of friendly relations with Peking was a loan to China and the formation of the Russo-Chinese Bank. The annual indemnity due to Japan exceeded Chinese revenues by more than 12 per cent. Peking had no choice but to meet this obligation by contracting a loan. Witte, therefore, arranged a 4 per cent loan of 400,000,000 gold francs through a Franco-Russian syndicate. The loan was secured by the Chinese customs revenues which, in turn, were guaranteed by the Russian government. (Having been plundered continuously by foreigners for more than half a century, China's finances were a shambles. In 1896 and again in 1898 China borrowed similar amounts at 5 and 4.5 per cent from an Anglo-German consortium.)

In return for the assistance of French financiers in raising the Chinese loan and in fulfillment of a promise to extend French financial operations in China, Witte next formed the Russo-Chinese Bank. Chartered under Russian law on 22 December 1895, the bank's eleven directors, elected by its stockholders, had to be approved by the ministry of finance. The first chairman of the board of directors was Prince E.E. Ukhtomsky. Although the Russian treasury invested heavily in the bank at first, it gradually reduced its commitments. The French held the majority of the stock, apparently no less than 60 per cent at any time. In 1910 the Russo-Chinese Bank merged with the French Banque du Nord to form the Russo-Asiatic Bank.

In addition to normal banking operations, the Russo-Chinese Bank was authorized to collect duties in China, coin money (with the approval of the Chinese government), pay loans contracted by the Chinese government, and to construct railroad and telegraph lines anywhere in China. Thus under the guise of protecting China, the Russo-Chinese Bank was an important instrument for asserting Russian domination over the Chinese government. For further details, see Weigh, *Russo-Chinese Diplomacy*, pp. 54-56.

7. The author understates the Russian promise to "support China," which was in fact a secret alliance against Japan. The text of the treaty is given in Appendix B. Although the chief negotiators were Count Witte and the extraordinary Li Hung-chang, the agreement was signed by Witte and the Russian foreign minister and is generally known as the Li-Lobanov Treaty.

At the personal request of the tsar, Li was sent as the official representative of China to the coronation of Nicholas II. The Russian government took the added precaution of sending Prince Ukhtomsky to meet Li as he passed through the Suez Canal and thus to make certain that he was not waylaid or beguiled by some other government. Li was well-disposed already toward Russia, although allegations, denied by Witte, still persist that he was well oiled with Russian bribes. (Witte provided a liberal bribe in connection with another matter.) Witte instead attempted to persuade Li that Russia firmly endorsed the principle of China's territorial integrity, but that to uphold it "we must be in a position, in case of emergency, to render China armed assistance . . . . Thus I argued that to uphold the territorial integrity of the Chinese Empire, it was necessary for us to have a railroad running along the shortest possible routes to Vladivostok across the northern part of Mongolia and Manchuria." The essence of the Li-Lobanov agreement was that in return for Russian protection China would allow the Russians to construct a railway from China across Manchuria to Vladivostok. This route eliminated about 350 miles of extremely difficult construction along the mountainous great bend of the Amur River.

With the conclusion of the alliance Witte and Li turned to negotiate the concession for what was to become the Chinese Eastern Railway. Since China would not grant the rights directly to the Russian government, it was given to the Russo-Chinese Bank. The Bank in turn ceded its concession to the Chinese Eastern Railway Company. Thus the railway was an enterprise of the bank which was an agency of the finance ministry. If the relationship seemed obscure, Prince Ukhtomsky, the chairman of the board of the bank, also served as chairman of the board of the Chinese Eastern Railway Company. The agreement provided that shareholders of the company had to be Russians or Chinese. The Chinese, however, were given no opportunity to participate in the company. On the day set for the sale of shares on the St. Petersburg Bourse, the sale opened at 1:00 and closed at 1:05. No one saw any shares then, nor did any private shareholder ever appear subsequently to vote his stock at an annual meeting.

Although the Chinese Eastern Railway was formed ostensibly for defensive and commercial ends, it paved the way for Russia's virtual domination of Manchuria. The railway corporation enjoyed extra-territorial rights over the railway corridor, including complete administrative and police authority. These provisions allowed Russia to introduce its troops into Manchuria, gave it de facto jurisdiction over a sizable portion of Chinese territory, and laid the foundation for the annexation of all of Manchuria. Li Hung-chang, smugly satisfied at his success in playing off one barbarian against another, confided to his diary that the Russian-Chinese alliance would give China twenty years of peace. His prediction fell short by just over eighteen years.

All accounts of the negotiation of the secret alliance and the railway concession follow Witte's version: *The Memoirs of Count Witte,* ed. Abraham Yarmolinsky (Doubleday, Page and Co., 1921), pp. 85-93 ff. For an account of the negotiations and the contract and statutes of the Chinese Eastern Railway Company, see Weigh, *Russo-Chinese Diplomacy,* pp. 56-73 and 333-48. Li's diary, cited by Hsü, *Rise of Modern China,* p. 416.

8. This agreement was concluded in Seoul on 2/14 May and ratified in Moscow on 28 May/9 June 1896. (Oldenburg's note)

9. The two missionaries were Jesuit priests. The German reaction was extraordinary in that the Jesuit Order was banned in Germany.

10. This was the British offer to which Nicholas referred in his letter to Emperor William [May 1898], above, Chapter IV. (Oldenburg's note)

11. Reprinted in *Vestnik evropy,* Number 3, 1898. (Oldenburg's note)

12. Japan voluntarily relinquished Weihaiwei to the British. Tokyo correctly surmised that this move would further the developing friendship with England. Weihaiwei, located on the tip of the Shantung Peninsula opposite Port Arthur, in effect gave the Royal Navy the possibility of strategic control over the naval route to Port Arthur. The occupation of Port Arthur made sense to the continental mentality of the tsar and his advisors. From a naval point of view, however, the Liaotung Peninsula was a cul-de-sac, although it was the Japanese and not the British who proved the point.

13. Although Chinese historians dispute the origins of the Boxers (see Hsü, *Rise of Modern China,* p. 465, n. 3), it was an anti-Manchu secret organization that in the 1890s devoted itself to ridding China of foreigners and their Chinese collaborators. They vowed to get "one dragon, two tigers, and three hundred lambs," meaning the Emperor Kuang-hsü (the dragon), Li Hung-chang and Prince Ch'ing (primarily responsible for China's foreign relations), and other officials who had anything to do with foreigners. The Boxer program of extermination excluded only eighteen reactionary court officials who supported the Boxers.

The Boxers were most active in the 1890s in Shantung province where they enjoyed the secret support of the governor. In October

1898, in the wake of the German seizure of Kiaochow and the European scramble for concessions, they began to attack Chinese Christians, and their violence soon spread into other provinces. As the government wavered in its attitude toward the Boxers, they became more daring and began to attack the railways and telegraph lines that symbolized the foreign enslavement of China. Finally, in May 1900, the Dowager Empress Tzu-hsi openly endorsed the Boxers and half of the regular government troops joined the movement.

14. Taku and the Taku forts on the Gulf of Chihli at the mouth of the Peiho River commanded access to Tientsin which was one of the treaty ports. Peking was approximately one hundred miles northeast of Tientsin, which was about thirty miles up-river from Taku.

15. Prince Tuan, an early supporter of the Boxers, became head of the Tsungli Yamen or foreign ministry in May. His appointment signalled the triumph of the reactionaries in the imperial court. Tuan forged a list of exorbitant demands from the foreign powers to goad the dowager into a declaration of war. Tzu-hsi fell into Tuan's trap, and on 21 June the Manchus declared war on Europe.

16. V.N. Lamsdorf (1841-1907) spent his entire career in the Russian foreign ministry. Having joined the ministry in 1866, he became director of its chancellery in 1880, and from 1885 to 1897 served as senior adviser to the foreign minister. He was deputy foreign minister from 1897 until 1900 under Lobanov-Rostovsky and Muraviev and then, until 1906, Minister of Foreign Affairs. Lamsdorf, in the words of the Soviet diplomatic historian, Feodor A. Rotshtein, was tied too closely to the past to inject anything new into Russian foreign policy. He did, however, associate himself with Witte and others who attempted to restrain Russia's headlong quest for supremacy in the Far East and who urged the tsar to find some basis for agreement with Japan. Although before long Lamsdorf like Witte lost any influence or control over Russia's Asian policy, he did serve that policy by seeking to cooperate with Germany and Austria in the Near East. The goal was to ensure that some untoward eruption of the Eastern Question would not embarrass Russia, already heavily engaged on the Pacific.

See F.A. Rotshtein, *Mezhdunarodnye otnosheniia v kontse XIX veka* [International Relations at the End of the Nineteenth Century] (Moscow, Leningrad, 1960), p. 19; A.A. Gromyko *et al.*, eds., *Diplomaticheskii slovar* [Diplomatic Dictionary] (Moscow, 1971), Vol. 2, pp. 166-67.

17. If they could have laid their hands on him, the Chinese might have indicted William as a war criminal on the basis of his speech: "You must know, my men, that you are about to meet a crafty, well-armed, cruel foe. Meet him and beat him. Give no quarter. Take no prisoners. Kill when he falls into your hands. Even as a thousand years ago the Huns under King Attila made such a name for themselves as still resounds in terror through legend and fable, so may the name of Germany resound through Chinese history a thousand years from now . . . ." Quoted by Warner and Warner, *Tide at Sunrise*, p. 128.

18. V.S. Soloviev [born 1853, the son of the distinguished historian, S.M. Soloviev] died on 31 July 1900. His poem, *The Dragon (To Siegfried)*, was written in July. (Oldenburg's note)

19. Li Hung-chang, close to death but still serving as the principal negotiator between China and the Europeans, consistently had maintained that Russian friendship was the best guarantee of China's survival. As the Russians occupied'the ancestral province, Li protested his disillusionment: "We have admitted you to the courtyard, now you wish to get to the rooms where we house our wives and small children." Quoted by B.A. Romanov, *Russia in Manchuria (1892-1906)*, trans. Susan Wilbur Jones (American Council of Learned Societies; E.W. Edwards, 1952), p. 205.

20. Final agreement on the size of the indemnity, based on the revenues of Chinese customs, was reached on 7 September 1901; European forces evacuated Tientsin and Shanghai in 1902. (Oldenburg's note)

The price of Russian friendship came high. The American commissioner originally proposed an indemnity of 40,000,000 pounds sterling, but the Germans demanded 63,000,000 and the Allies finally compromised on 67,500,000. Russia received the largest portion—29 percent of the total—while simultaneously pressing the Chinese government to cede all of Manchuria.

21. This is probably a reference in part to George Kennan, *Siberia and the Exile System*, 2 vols. (New York, 1891). In 1885 *The Century Magazine* commissioned Kennan, who already had traveled extensively in Russia, to make a study of the Siberian exile system. His report created a sensation in the west, and the unfavorable publicity forced the Russian government to correct some of the most pernicious abuses that he had exposed. Efforts of the Russian government to colonize Siberia and relieve the rural overpopulation of European Russia are described by Donald W. Treadgold, *The Great Siberian Migration: Government and Peasant in Resettlement from Emancipation to the First World War* (Princeton University Press, 1957).

22. Siberian exile could be imposed as a judicial and also as an administrative sentence, the latter most frequently by village communities for "vicious behavior." Between 1887 and 1899 some 100,000 people were banished to Siberia—52,000 by administrative process (and of these 47,000 by village assemblies) and 48,000 by court-imposed sentences. Flogging with birch rods, a penalty inflicted by village assemblies, was abolished along with the Siberian exile system. (Oldenburg's note)

CHAPTER SIX

1. Chekhov (1860-1904) was born and raised in Taganrog (on the Sea of Azov) and graduated from the Faculty of Medicine of Moscow University in 1884. He turned immediately to writing for a livelihood, contributing comic stories to popular Moscow magazines. Ignored at first by radical critics, his talent was recognized by two influential men of letters, the novelist Dmitry V. Grigorovich and Alexis S. Suvorin, editor of the conservative *Novoe vremia*, Russia's largest daily newspaper. Suvorin invited Chekov to contribute to his paper and even established a weekly literary supplement for him. Chekhov's reputation as a serious writer was established in 1886 with the publication of his

Particolored Stories and formal recognition followed in 1888 when he received the Pushkin Prize of the Academy of Sciences. The characteristic Chekhovian style developed, however, only after his entry into "big literature." His association with the conservative Suvorin ended in the late nineties when they disagreed over the Dreyfus Affair. By this time Chekhov was friendly with and sympathetic to the social ideas of the younger, radical writers headed by Maxim Gorky (see below, note 2).

Chekhov's reputation as Russia's greatest dramatist—he has been compared to Shakespeare—rests on four plays written and produced after 1896: *The Seagull* (1898), *Uncle Vanya* (1900), *The Three Sisters* (1901), and *The Cherry Orchard* (1904).

Chekhov's mood and style dominated the final period of Imperial Russian literature. He had many imitators but no peer. In pure literary craftsmanship—the lyrical quality and unparalleled concentration and economy of his prose, characteristic even of his earliest works—he set unattainable standards. The leitmotiv of his mature works, which so engaged his contemporaries, was the mutual lack of sympathy between people, the impossibility for one person to understand another. The essence of Chekhov's mature style was "the 'biography' of a mood developing under the trivial pinpricks of life, but owing in substance to a deep-lying, physiological or psychological cause." See D.S. Mirsky, *A History of Russian Literature,* revised edition, ed. Francis J. Whitfield (Alfred A. Knopf, 1966), pp. 353-67 (quoted, p. 359).

2. Maxim Gorky (Alexis Maksimovich Peshkov, 1868-1936) was born and soon orphaned, in Nizhni Novgorod, which the Soviet government renamed in his honor in 1932. He received no formal education and for more than a decade wandered about Russia eking out a living in the basement of society. The Russian adjective *gorkii* means bitter or wretched, and it was under this pseudonym that his first story appeared in 1892 in a local newspaper in Tiflis. For the next three years Gorky contributed stories to the provincial press and finally enjoyed enough success to make a living at writing. He entered the world of "big literature" in 1895 when V.G. Korolenko, editor of the populist *Russkoe bogatstvo,* published one of his stories (Chelkash). Thereafter Gorky had access to the influential Petersburg monthlies, and in 1898 his stories were collected and published in book form. Their success was overwhelming and unprecedented in Russian literary history. For the next decade the Russian public acclaimed him second only to Tolstoy.

Although his fame stemmed from his romantic treatment of poverty and oppression, around 1897 Gorky forsook romanticism for realism. His subsequent works depicted the filth, barbarity, and ignorance of Russian life in which a few isolated and enlightened individuals, having grasped the inner meaning of life, attempted to show the way to the ignorant and oppressed masses. This was the quality recognized after 1917 when the political and literary authorities of the USSR officially proclaimed Gorky the founder of "socialist realism" and the father of proletarian literature.

Gorky's association with Lenin and the Bolsheviks began around the end of the century. He contributed to the Marxist review *Zhizn* (Life), and in 1901 the government suppressed that journal for publishing his poem *The Song of the Petrel*, a transparent allegory about the approaching revolutionary storm. This led to his arrest and banishment to Nizhni and also to the annulment of his election to the Imperial Academy of Sciences. He was arrested again during the Revolution of 1905. Throughout the prerevolutionary period, Gorky actively supported the Bolsheviks with his pen and a considerable portion of his substantial literary income. As a result and despite the great financial success of his works, Gorky never personally enjoyed the wealth that his writing produced.

In 1906 he journeyed to the United States and received a triumphant welcome in New York. America's adoration quickly turned to rejection and scorn, however, when it was discovered that the woman travelling with him was not his wife. Mark Twain refused to attend a banquet in his honor, and the management of his hotel requested him to lodge elsewhere. Gorky vented his puzzlement and wrath at this treatment in a series of stories on America (*The City of the Yellow Devil*, 1906) and then migrated to Capri, where he lived until the outbreak of the World War.

In 1917 Gorky returned to Russia where he worked indefatigably to save Russian writers and intellectuals from starvation. In 1921 he left Russia again, settled temporarily in Germany, and then in 1924 moved to Sorrento. He returned to Russia in 1928 for the celebration of his sixtieth birthday and in the following year moved permanently to Moscow. Until his death in 1936, he devoted himself to literary work and became an ardent defender of Stalinism. In 1938 the Soviet regime attributed his death to a medical murder perpetrated by members of the "Trotskyite-Bukharin gang." See Mirsky, *History of Russian Literature*, pp. 374-86.

3. Two literary schools dominated Russian literature in the first decade of the twentieth century—the symbolists and the realists (who hung the label of "decadence" on Russian symbolism). The new realist school, associated mainly with Gorky's publishing house *Znanie* (Knowledge), was by far the more popular in its time. Earlier Russian realists had avoided the morally delicate and cruder aspects of life. Tolstoy, however, had broken these taboos in *The Death of Ivan Ilyich* (1886), which confronted the horrors of disease and death, and in *The Kreutzer Sonata* (1889), which examined the physical foundations of love. Tolstoy also directed the realists, particularly Leonid Andreiev (1871-1919) and Michael P. Artsybashev (1878-1927), to the metaphysical and moral problem story. The influence of Chekhov's realism was less substantive and more technical; the younger writers sought to emulate his narrative style and acquired from him their predilection for the short story. The realists were the intellectual heirs of the older intelligentsia, but they lacked their predecessors' ethical foundation and humanism. They pushed Tolstoy's negation of contemporary values to the extreme and wound up as apostles of an unredeeming nihilism. By 1910 the movement had spent itself and except for a few sensational works had produced little of lasting value.

The symbolists, on the other hand, largely overshadowed during this period, ultimately proved the more significant and durable. The symbolists were men of superior culture who led a renaissance recognized in retrospect as a golden age of poetry second only to the great age of Pushkin. Their unifying concept was the perception of the world as "a forest of symbols" (Baudelaire) in which everything acquired significance not only for itself but also as the reflection of something else. Hence to symbolists the logical value of words was secondary to their emotional value. Consequently, symbolist writing possessed an obscurity which the public misinterpreted as a sign of "decadence." Dostoevsky inspired the movement insofar as every symbolist was affected by his individualism and tragic conception of life. But, whereas scientific agnosticism led the realists to annihilation, death, and finality, the metaphysical foundations of symbolism led to mystical optimism and grace. The symbolists, moreover, were kindred spirits with the Slavophiles (whom the intelligentsia, incorrectly, universally identified as reactionaries), and for that reason they played a major role in the rediscovery and fresh reinterpretation of Russia's literary past.

Literary history is only slightly less treacherous than literary criticism, and this summary follows Mirsky, *History of Russian Literature*, pp. 374-484, especially pp. 374-76, 387, 394-404, and 430-33. Mirsky was not without his prejudices and preferences, and an American reader might wish also to consult the skillful interpretation of Marc L. Slonim, *The Epic of Russian Literature from Its Origins through Tolstoy* (Oxford University Press, 1949), and especially its sequel, *Modern Russian Literature from Chekov to the Present* (Oxford University Press, 1953).

4. In 1894 Bruissov published *Russian Symbolists*, a collection of poetry so different from the type of verse that Russians recognized or understood that it and others that followed were the butt of jokes for a decade. Whereas other symbolists like Hippius, Sologub, and Balmont found their way into the literary press, Bruissov was excluded until 1905. Everything he wrote until then met with indignation or ridicule. Still he persevered. By 1903 he was recognized as the head of the symbolist school, and by 1906 symbolism had triumphed. It was recognized as the whole of Russian poetry and Bruissov as Russia's premier poet. Mirsky described Bruissov as "perhaps the most widely informed man of his generation," and his energy and activities were prodigious. He took no part in politics, but after the Revolutions of 1917 he became a Communist and for a brief time headed the Soviet censorship. Mirsky, *History of Russian Literature*, pp. 434-38.

5. Serov made two copies of this portrait: one was mutilated during the Bolshevik assault on the Winter Palace; the other is in Moscow. (Oldenburg's note)

6. Traditionally the imperial theaters—the Maly Theater in Moscow and the Alexandrinsky Theater in St. Petersburg—dominated the theater in Russia. In the last two decades of the nineteenth century, however, the reactionary policies of the government restricted these companies to the performance of "safe," mediocre plays under poor direction. To end this waste of intellectual and artistic talent, several private progressive theatrical enterprises organized around the turn of the century. Foremost among them was the Moscow Art Theater formed by Stanislavsky (1863-1938) and Vladimir I. Nemirovich-Danchenko

(1858-1943). In its quest for an appropriate style and repertory the Moscow Art Theater went from naturalism through impressionism and symbolism to psychological realism. The directors and a talented company were particularly successful in performing the "mood plays" of Chekhov, Gorky, Ibsen, Turgenev, and Dostoevsky. Chekhov's *Seagull,* for example, was staged originally in 1896 at the State Theater of Petersburg but, badly understood by the actors and poorly performed, it was a disaster. In 1898, however, the Art Theater produced it with great insight and understanding and it was a smashing success. Thereafter Chekhov turned with renewed vigor to dramatic writing with Stanislavsky's cast in mind. The "Stanislavsky method" of theater art, developed over thirty years and definitively formulated only in the Soviet period, consisted essentially of the principle of psychological identification in which the actor strives to *become* the character he is portraying.

      Peter E. Yershov, "Nemirovich-Danchenko," "Stanislavsky," and "Theater," *McGraw-Hill Encyclopedia of Russia and the Soviet Union,* ed. Michael T. Florinsky (McGraw-Hill Book Company, 1961), pp. 384, 541, and 562-63; Mirsky, *History of Russian Literature,* pp. 355-56.

      7. At the time Oldenburg was writing these lines, Marshal Joseph Pilsudski (1867-1935) was the conservative dictator of Poland. As a youth, however, he had been one of the founders and leaders of the Polish Socialist Party (PPS). The socialist movement took root in Poland in the 1880s, and the PPS was founded in Paris in 1892 by a group of exiles. The PPS was always strongest in Russian Poland, but after the Revolution of 1905 it split into two factions. The PPS "Left" favored cooperation with the Russian socialist movement with the goal of broad autonomy within a Russian socialist republic. The "revolutionary fraction" of the PPS, led by Pilsudski, saw no virtue in cooperation with Russians of any persuasion and insisted on complete independence for Poland. In 1900 still another faction formed under the leadership of Rosa Luxembourg (1870?-1919) (best known as one of the founders of the German Communist Party). Known as the Social Democracy of the Kingdom of Poland and Lithuania (SDKPL), it held that the partition of Poland should be preserved and that Russian Poland should become an integrated part of a Russian socialist republic. The SDKLP reasoned that the Polish economy was too dependent on Russia, Germany, and Austria for an independent Polish state to become economically viable.

      With the creation of the Polish Republic at the end of World War I, a consolidation of the radical parties took place. The PPS Left and the SDKLP united to form the Communist Party of Poland. The other socialist factions combined into one united PPS. The PPS supported Pilsudski's coup d'état of 1926 but soon found itself in opposition to the regime. Nevertheless it survived official persecution and, together with the Polish Peasant Party, claimed a majority of popular support on the eve of World War II. The Polish Communist Party, on the other hand, fell victim to nationalism, factionalism, and the Stalinist purge of the thirties. It was dissolved in 1938 on orders from Moscow.

      8. Nine representatives, all minor figures in the socialist movement, attended the First Congress of the Russian Social Democratic Labor

Party (RSDLP): three delegates from the Bund, four delegates from the major centers of Marxism in Russia, and two representatives of an illegal socialist paper. The founders and prominent younger leaders of Russian Marxism were either hiding in the West or in exile in Siberia. Peter Struve wrote the party's manifesto but did not attend the meeting. Although the Minsk Congress proclaimed the formation of the RSDLP, nothing existed but its manifesto. It had no program, no rules, and indeed not even a central committee, since the founders of the party were arrested immediately and never replaced.

The Jewish Bund, illegally founded in Vilna in 1897, was a league of Russian, Polish, and Lithuanian Jewish workers and socialists. Its program was the abolition of discrimination against Jews, the transformation of the Russian Empire into a federation of autonomous national units, and national and cultural autonomy for Jews. The Bund withdrew from the RSDLP in 1903 but rejoined in 1906 and generally adopted the Menshevik position (see below, note 9). After the 1917 Revolution, the Bund split into two factions (April 1920). A majority accepted the Communist program and entered the party; they were liquidated during the Great Purge of the thirties. A minority formed a separate Social Democratic Bund; they were destroyed more quickly by the Red Terror of the twenties. A new Bund formed in independent Poland between the wars. In 1939 leaders and members of the Polish Bund fled to Russia to escape the Nazis; they were shot.

9. The real founding of the RSDLP took place in Brussels and London in 1903, whereupon the leadership of the party promptly split into two factions on the question of party membership. Lenin demanded that membership be restricted to professional revolutionaries who "personally participated in one of the organizations of the party." Against Lenin's concept of an elite revolutionary organization, Martov asserted the concept of a broadly based, mass party of revolutionaries and their sympathizers—persons who simply worked "under the control and guidance of one of the party organizations." Lenin lost on this issue by a vote of 28-23. Martov's majority, however, included the votes of seven delegates, mainly Bundists, who subsequently walked out when their program was rejected. Their departure gave Lenin a majority of two when the time came to elect the members of the party's central organs. By virtue of this victory Lenin claimed for himself and his faction the title Bolshevik (majority), while Martov naively accepted the alternative, Menshevik (minority). These labels became permanent even though Mensheviks held majorities within the party and in future congresses. Indeed, for the next few years Lenin was virtually isolated. The split mainly concerned the leadership: local leaders and the rank and file generally were unaware or uninterested in the niceties and nuances of organization and strategy that engaged the leaders.

10. The following are the dates for the replacement of the ministers: 1894—Ways and Communications; 1895—Foreign Affairs and Internal Affairs; 1896—Navy; 1897—Imperial Household; 1898—War and Public Education; 1899—State Comptroller. (Oldenburg's note)

11. Russia seized Finland and the Aland Islands from Sweden in 1808-1809. As part of the general reorganization of the territory,

Alexander I granted the Finns a constitution in 1809. Under this charter Finland enjoyed greater autonomy and liberties than any other nation of the Russian Empire, including Russians themselves. (Poland enjoyed similar liberties between 1815 and 1830.) As a Swedish province, Finland had possessed neither legislative nor executive institutions. The situation did not change immediately under Russian rule. The constitution of 1809 created only a consultative body, the diet, to which the various estates (nobility, clergy, burghers, and peasantry) elected deputies. An administrative council, appointed by the tsar and renamed the senate in 1816, stood at the head of the civil administration. Alexander I presided over the opening of the first diet at Borgo in March 1809. There he solemnly promised to obey "your constitution, your fundamental laws." In practice, despite the frequent reference to constitutions, this meant that the crown alone legislated for Finland. The Finns, however, were permitted to live under the traditional Swedish criminal and civil codes to which they were accustomed. The diet, dissolved in 1809, did not meet again until 1863. During that period, Finland prospered and its relations with Russia and the crown remained even and uneventful.

The status of Finland was redefined during the reform era of Alexander II. Responding to Finnish nationalism and pressure for more active participation in government, Alexander II reconvened the diet in 1863. It met regularly thereafter. A new statute, approved by the diet in 1867 and confirmed by the tsar in 1869, formally affirmed that the emperor could not alter the fundamental laws of Finland without the consent of the diet. This law in effect made the tsar a constitutional monarch in Finland. It recognized that the grand duchy was not a Russian province but a state linked to Russia personally through its grand duke who was also the Emperor of Russia. The governor-general of Finland was the emperor's representative but not the ruler of Finland. This relationship, vaguely established in 1809 and definitively acknowledged in 1869, served without difficulty as the basis of Russian-Finnish relations until late in the reign of Alexander III.

The special status of Finland was a great source of irritation to Alexander III, who had no use for any constitution. In 1890 he appointed a commission to examine the Finnish question, but most of the repressive measures conceived under Alexander III were not implemented until the reign of Nicholas II. Nicholas probably shared his father's attitude toward Finland. At any rate several of his advisers—Pobedonostsev, Kuropatkin, Goremykin, and probably Witte—decided in favor of the suppression of Finland's autonomy and its full incorporation into the Russian Empire.

For the constitutional history of Finland in the nineteenth century, see P. Shilovsky, *Akty otnosiashchiesia k politicheskomu polozheniiu Finliandii* [Documents relating to the Political Status of Finland] (St. Petersburg, 1903); J[oseph] R[obert] Fisher, *Finland and the Tsars, 1809-1899*, 2nd edition (London, 1901), and Eino Jutikkala with Kauko Pirinen, *A History of Finland*, trans. Paul Sjöblom (Frederick A. Praeger, 1962).

12. The dowager empress strenuously protested the tsar's appointment of Bobrikov, a rabid nationalist, and also the campaign against Finland. In a letter to Nicholas in October 1902 Maria Feodorovna reminded her son that he had promised repeatedly that he would change nothing in Finland and that he would restrain Bobrikov in his zeal. "And now just the opposite is happening! There, where things have always gone so well, where the people were perfectly happy and contented, now everything is broken up, everything is changed, disorder and hatred sown—all in the name of so-called Patriotism! ... All that is being done in Finland is based on lies and deceit and leads straight to revolution .... Do believe me and dismiss Bobrikov, that evil genius ...." *Secret Letters of the Last Tsar,* pp. 162-166.

13. The exact figures were as follows: In a total enrollment of 4,017 no tuition was paid by 1,957 students, and of these 874 also received stipends. Student assistance consumed 419,070 rubles, but this did not include the cost of maintaining the Lyopin Dormitory or "other amounts not subject to accounting." (From the report of a commission of professors of Moscow University on the causes of the student disorders of 1901.) (Oldenburg's note)

14. Poles seeking to free themselves from Russian rule had revolted against Russian authority in 1768, 1794, and 1830-1831. The revolt of 1863 was the last. It was instigated and led by the Polish nobility and clergy and suppressed in part with the help of the Polish peasantry. Muraviev, Governor of Vilna from March 1863 until April 1865, established a military dictatorship and unleashed a reign of terror against the Polish aristocracy and clergy. He won the support of the Polish peasantry by increasing their allotments and reducing their redemption payments. He then organized a peasant militia which preyed on the Polish landowners and clergy. Landlords and priests were arrested, convicted, and sentenced in mass. During his relatively brief tenure, he publicly executed 240 insurrectionists and imprisoned or deported hundreds more to Siberia. His regime ended when the Polish nobility petitioned Tsar Alexander II for clemency and mercy. Muraviev set the pattern for the governors of other Polish provinces. In the aftermath of the insurrection Poland lost the remnants of its autonomy, and Russian authorities embarked on an intensive campaign of russification designed to obliterate all traces of Polish and Roman Catholic influence in the western provinces.

15. Vasily V. Shulgin, then a conservative student at Kiev, recalled in his memoirs the means by which unanimity was achieved. Photographs depicting "police brutalities" were distributed, but even a slightly experienced eye could detect immediately that the photos had been made from sketches! (Oldenburg's note)

16. The first honorary academicians elected in January 1900 were: "C.R." [Grand Duke Constantine Konstantinovich (Romanov)], Count Leo Tolstoy, A.A. Potekhin, V.G. Korolenko, A.P. Chekov, Alexis M. Zhemchuznikov, Count A.A. Golenishchev-Kutuzov, V.S. Soloviev, and Anatoly F. Koni. Gorky was elected in 1902, but the Academy [at the suggestion of the government] annulled his election because he was

under investigation for circulating revolutionary propaganda. (Oldenburg's note) In protest the liberal Chekov and the veteran socialist Korolenko resigned from the Academy.

17. The ministries represented were: Public Education (N.P. Bogolepov), Internal Affairs (I.L. Goremykin), Agriculture and State Domains (A.S. Ermolov), Finance (S.Yu. Witte), War (A.N. Kuropatkin), and Justice (P.M. Butovsky, Director of the ministry). (Oldenburg's note)

18. It appears that Witte entrusted the actual writing of this memorandum to one of his closest associates, A.N. Gurev, a young economist who played a significant role earlier in carrying out the monetary reform. (Oldenburg's note)

The memorandum was published as *Samoderzhavie i zemstvo: Konfidentsialnaia zapiska Ministra Finansov, stats-sekretaria S.Yu. Witte (1899 g.)* [Autocracy and Zemstvo: A Confidential Memorandum of the Minister of Finance, State-Secretary S.Yu. Witte, 1899] (Stuttgart, 1899). A second edition (Stuttgart, 1903) contains an introduction by Peter Struve.

19. In 1878 at Kharkov a liberal zemstvo leader, Ivan I. Petrunkevich, denouncing both revolutionary terror and the government's illegal measures to suppress it, organized a movement to restore legality to Russia. Unsuccessful in persuading revolutionary leaders to suspend their terrorism and cooperate with the liberals, he concentrated his efforts on the zemstvos. In March 1879 he succeeded in convening about three dozen zemstvo constitutionalists in Moscow. The government, however, feared the development of a grass roots constitutional movement. It closed the Moscow Zemstvo Conference, prohibited further meetings of that kind, and banished Petrunkevich to the province of Kostroma. Only after the turn of the century did he become active again as a prominent leader of Russian liberalism.

Loris-Melikov, a hero of the Russo-Turkish War of 1877-1878, was summoned by Alexander II in 1880 to suppress terrorism and the revolutionary movement. Given virtual dictatorial powers first as Superintendent of the Supreme Executive Commission and then as Minister of Interior, Loris-Melikov nevertheless proposed that repression had to be supplemented with public participation in legislative affairs. With the tsar's approval he drafted a plan for constitutional reform that would have given local self-governing institutions an advisory role in the legislative process. The assassination of Alexander II suspended the promulgation of the Loris-Melikov "constitution," which the tsar had signed on the morning of his murder. Alexander III, following Pobedonostsev's advice, abandoned the plan, and Loris-Melikov was compelled to resign. Disgusted, he left Russia never to return, and he died in Paris in 1888.

Upon the accession of a tsar all Russian organizations customarily sent felicitous greetings. The failure of the Samara zemstvo to welcome Alexander III was a silent protest against his refusal to accept the principle of public participation in the formulation of public policy. Pobedonostsev had no confidence in the ability of anyone but government officials and experts to construct or give advice on policy. Thus he invariably opposed any plan to give popular representatives a voice in the government of Russia. For that reason he easily convinced Alexander III to squelch Ignatiev's "Slavophile project."

Count N.P. Ignatiev succeeded Loris-Melikov as Minister of Interior. Ignatiev was a many-sided figure, but to the extent that he was a Slavophile he became enamored of the idea of cementing the union of tsar and people through a national consultative assembly. In April 1882 he presented his plan to the emperor. Ignatiev proposed to summon a Zemskii Sobor (Assembly of the Land) in the ancient tradition—some three thousand representatives of the peasantry, bourgeoisie, and nobility. The Sobor was to convene in Moscow at the time of the tsar's coronation and give witness to the "unity of the tsar with his people." The sincerity of Ignatiev's motives has been questioned, but there was no question of the tsar's attitude, especially after he had heard Pobedonostsev's prophecy of destruction and doom.

20. The Dukhobors—"spirit fighters"—were a religious sect who preached the absolute equality of men. Their precepts compelled them to follow their consciences and this often brought them into conflict with the government. Although hounded by the authorities since the eighteenth century when the movement was founded, their persecution at the end of the nineteenth century was the result of their pacifism. The military reform of 1874 made each citizen personally responsible for military service. Previously the Dukhobors had been able to hire conscripts. By the late nineties their leaders had been imprisoned or exiled to Siberia. Religious policy, including the persecution of schismatics and sectarians, is covered effectively in John Shelton Curtiss, *Church and State in Russia: The Last Years of the Empire, 1900-1917* (Columbia University Press, 1940).

21. All of the assassins were Italian anarchists. Elizabeth, the wife of Emperor Franz Joseph, was stabbed to death in Geneva on 10 September 1898; Humbert was shot to death at Monza (near Milan) on 29 July 1900. Although Humbert was not much of a king, he looked like a king and he possessed great personal courage. "These are the risks of the job," he remarked in 1897, just having evaded an assassin's dagger. The "attempt" on the kaiser was somewhat more remote. He was on his well-publicized pilgrimmage to Jerusalem in October 1898 when police in Alexandria (Egypt) arrested an anarchist holding two bombs and a ticket for Haifa.

22. Bogolepov died on 2 March. Karpovich was arrested and sentenced to twenty years' imprisonment. He escaped in 1906, joined the Battle Organization (the terrorist arm of the Socialist Revolutionary Party), and became an associate of the notorious double-agent Evno Azef. In 1907 Karpovich was part of an unsuccessful attempt on the life of Nicholas II. When Azef was exposed, Karpovich fled abroad. He died in 1917 when a steamer returning him to Russia was torpedoed by a German submarine in the North Sea.

APPENDIX A

THE FRANCO-RUSSIAN MILITARY CONVENTION

OF 27 AUGUST 1891

Animated by a common desire to preserve the peace, and having no other aim than to prepare for the necessity of a defensive war thrust upon either of them by an attack of the forces of the Triple Alliance, France and Russia have agreed to the following:

1. If France is attacked by Germany, or by Italy supported by Germany, Russia will employ all its available forces against Germany.

If Russia is attacked by Germany, or by Austria supported by Germany, France will employ all its available forces against Germany.

2. If the forces of the Triple Alliance, or the forces of one of its members, should be mobilized, France and Russia, at the first indication of that event and without prior agreement, will mobilize their entire forces, immediately and simultaneously, and they will transport them as near as possible to their frontiers.

3. The forces available for employment against Germany will be for France, 1,300,000 men, and for Russia, from 700,000 to 800,000 men. These forces will initiate total action with all due speed to ensure that Germany will be compelled to fight simultaneously in the east and in the west.

4. The Staffs of the Armies of the two countries will plan constantly and in concert to prepare for and to facilitate the execution of the foregoing measures. In time of peace they will communicate to each other all information regarding the armies of the Triple Alliance which is or which may come into their possession. Methods of communicating in time of war will be studied and prepared in advance.

5. France and Russia will not conclude a separate peace.

6. This convention will have the same duration as the Triple Alliance.

7. All provisions set forth above will be kept absolutely secret.

[signed]   [signed]

Obruchev   Boisdeffre

Signing for Russia, General Nicholas N. Obruchev, Chief of the Imperial General Staff (1881-1898); for France, General Raoul F.C.M. Boisdeffre, Deputy Chief of the French General Staff (1890-1894); Chief of the General Staff, 1894-1899). Although the Convention is dated 1891, its formal ratification took place through an exchange of notes in December 1894 and January 1895; see above Chapter I, Note 16.

Source: France, Ministère des affaires étrangères, *Documents diplomatiques: L'Alliance Franco-Russe* (Paris, 1918), p. 92. Translation by the editor.

APPENDIX B

TREATY OF ALLIANCE BETWEEN

RUSSIA AND CHINA, MAY 1896

ARTICLE I. Every aggression directed by Japan, whether against Russian territory in Eastern Asia, or against the territory of China or that of Korea, shall be regarded as necessarily bringing about the immediate application of the present treaty. In this case the two High Contracting Parties engage to support each other reciprocally by all the land and sea forces of which they can dispose at that moment and to assist each other as much as possible for the victualling of their respective forces.

ARTICLE II. As soon as the two High Contracting Parties shall be engaged in common action no treaty of peace with the adverse party can be concluded by one of them without the assent of the other.

ARTICLE III. During the military operations all the ports of China shall, in case of necessity, be open to Russian warships, which shall find there on the part of the Chinese authorities all the assistance of which they may stand in need.

ARTICLE IV. In order to facilitate the access of the Russian land troops to the menaced points, and to insure their means of subsistence, the Chinese Government consents to the construction of a railway line across the Chinese provinces of the Amour [i.e., the Heilungkiang] and of Guirin (Kirin) in the direction of Vladivostok. The junction of this railway with the Russian railway shall not serve as a pretext for any encroachment on Chinese territory nor for any infringement of the rights of sovereignty of His Majesty the Emperor of China. The construction and exploitation of this railway shall be accorded to the Russo-Chinese Bank, and the clauses of the Contract which shall be concluded for this purpose shall be duly discussed between the Chinese Minister in St. Petersburg and the Russo-Chinese Bank.

ARTICLE V. It is understood that in time of war, as indicated in Article I, Russia shall have the free use of the railway mentioned in Article IV, for the transport and provisioning of her troops. In time of peace Russia shall have the same right for the transit of her troops and stores, with stoppages, which shall not be justified by any other motive than the needs of the transport service.

ARTICLE VI. The present treaty shall come into force on the day when the contract stipulated in Article IV, shall have been confirmed by His Majesty the Emperor of China. It shall have from then force and value for a period of fifteen years. Six months before the expiration of this term the two High Contracting Parties shall deliberate concerning the prolongation of this treaty.

Source: Carnegie Endowment for International Peace, Division of International Law, *Manchuria: Treaties and Agreements* (Washington, 1921), pp. 30-31. For the manner in which this secret agreement became public and its relation to the alleged "Cassini Convention" see ibid., pp. 28-32.

CONVERSION TABLE

Linear Measure
   1 *versta* (plur., *verst*) = 0.663 mile
   1 *arshin* = 28 inches

Land Area
   1 *desiatina* (plur., *desiatin*) = 2.7 acres
   1 *kvadratnaia versta* = 0.43957 square miles

Weight
   1 *pud* = 36.113 pounds
   1 *berkovets* (10 puds) = 361.13 pounds

Volume, Dry Measure
   1 *chetvert* = 6 bushels (approx.)

Volume, Liquid Measure
   1 *vedro* (plur., *vedra*) = 3.25 gallons
   1 *bochka* (40 *vedra*) = 131.5 gallons

Currency
   1 *rubl* (gold ruble, 1896-1914) = $ 0.50 (approx.)
      (The "Witte" or gold-standard ruble of 1896-97 was equal to two-thirds the value of the old silver ruble.)
   1 *kopeika* (kopeck) = 1/100th ruble